BASEBALL LOVE

George Bowering

Talonbooks
Vancouver

Copyright © 2006 George Bowering

Talonbooks
P.O. Box 2076, Vancouver, British Columbia, Canada V6B 3S3
www.talonbooks.com

Typeset in Adobe Caslon and printed and bound in Canada.

First Printing: 2006

The publisher gratefully acknowledges the financial support of the Canada
Council for the Arts; the Government of Canada through the Book
Publishing Industry Development Program; and the Province of British
Columbia through the British Columbia Arts Council for our publishing
activities.

Library and Archives Canada Cataloguing in Publication

Bowering, George, 1935–
    Baseball love / George Bowering.

ISBN 0-88922-529-X
    1. Baseball. 2. Bowering, George, 1935– —Travel—North America.
I. Title.

PS8503.O875Z464 2006   796.357'092   C2005-906206-1

ISBN-10: 0-88922-529-X
ISBN-13: 978-0-88922-529-9

This book is for my travelling companion and then some, Jean Baird.

Contents

1

Good to Me

God watches over drunks and third basemen.

—Leo Durocher

WHILE HELPING ME PACK MY STUFF, Jean found a zip-lock bag containing a pair of mangled aviator glasses, the gold frames twisted, one of the yellow plastic lenses in pieces—the zip-lock bag into which an ambulance attendant had dropped these defunct eyeglasses, as is the procedure, apparently, for his occupation.

There was a terrible odour in the emergency ward of the University of British Columbia Hospital. It was caused, we eventually found, by the dog manure attached to the soles and cleats of my turf shoes, the ones with the old dried blood from a former eye injury still on the tops of the toes. My wife Angela would take these shoes somewhere and put them under the hot water tap, but this would be the last time, she said. I knew my way around the emergency ward of the UBC Hospital. This was where I had looked at x-rays once before, after I had broken my wrist on the same ball diamond a year earlier.

For my previous eye injury I had gone from a diamond on Eighth Avenue to emergency at Vancouver General Hospital, the same place to which I had much earlier gone for my New Year's Day concussion from our game at Twelfth Avenue. I have been to emergency at St. Paul's Hospital and St. Vincent's Hospital as well, but not for accidents on the ball field.

Baseball has been very good to me.

I have glaucoma in both eyes, and pay a lot of money for eye drops. I also had cataracts in both eyes, so I had the lens in the right eye replaced by a piece of modern plastic. I've been on the shortlist for surgery on my left eye for two years—either that, or they have forgotten about me. I've had astigmatisms for most of my life, so I'm used to wearing specs on the ball diamond. One of the causes of glaucoma is injury to the eye.

I had one of my eyes demolished at second base and the other at third. You could blame the fact that I was in my fifties and early sixties on those occasions, so my reflexes were a little slow. But the first one you could also blame on the pebbles in the infield dirt at the park on Eighth, where the Write Sox played their home games.

This was in the Twilight League, which used to be made up of book and magazine writers and newspaper reporters. We weren't playing the Write Sox. We were playing Mark's team. This team kept changing its name, but we all called it Mark's team. I remember our opponents that day because Mark's team had this neat, quiet, handsome guy who always played in slacks. Now I can't remember his name, but it was one of those classy male names like Warren, or Wilson, or Spencer. He was a polite, generous man, and he could hit the ball like a demon. He hit a nasty low liner just to the left of the bag at second, and all I should have had to do was put my open glove down and let the ball find the pocket off a short hop.

Remember that we were playing fastball, not baseball. You are a lot closer to the source if you are an infielder in fastball, and things happen a lot faster, though you don't have as much territory to cover. The ball in question was coming at 115 miles an hour. It hit a pebble and went right over my glove and into my right eye.

No ambulance attendant would have been able to find all the pieces of those specs. They had been made of glass instead of plastic, and when that hard softball hit, tiny spears of glass went everywhere, including into the thin flesh around my right eye.

Fast. That's what you think. Cripes, that happened fast. Now there was blood on my white Adidas and all over someone's shirt balled up and held against my face as I was being helped into Brian Fawcett's car.

It's a funny feeling, walking into a hospital in clacking turf shoes. After a while a microsurgeon showed up in his Sunday golf shirt, and he and Angela and Fawcett and I discussed my very good luck in not getting glass right in the eyeball. I did get a small fracture in my occipital bone. I felt the usual pride.

Other bones I have broken while playing ball: nose, finger, toe, wrist. Bones I have broken while not playing ball: hand, vertebra, toe, rib.

I was fascinated by my Uncle Amos. He had broken just about everything. Once a truck ran over him from foot to shoulder, then back down.

Wearing a cast is wonderful—the envy, the stink. Scars are good, but x-rays are even better.

It's not hard to understand those young German nobles with their university sword fights.

"Just look at this angular scar under my eye, Fraulein."

"Ach, Erich, place your tired head on my ample bosom."

So after my first eye injury Fawcett said that's it. From now on I would be banned from the ball field until I got plastic lenses.

"But aren't they susceptible to scratching?"

"You need to acquire some perspective on the situation," said Angela, or perhaps she said something in which the word "asshole" was a noun or an adjective.

"Perspective? I can't see a thing without my glasses," I said.

But despite all the amusing banter and all the pride of injury, I had been afraid for my eyesight, and maybe even adjusting to a life of one-eyedness. I had kept the bloody shirt to my face, and not removed it until the medical staff said that they had to get in there to do some cleaning.

So for a few years I got to play with that blood on my shoes, and after a while the blood turned brown and faded. It was a badge.

Meanwhile, I grew older and my reflexes grew slower. But I did not become smarter.

One luminescent evening in the nineties we were playing the Secret Nine on the grassy diamond behind Magee High School in leafy Kerrisdale. I don't know what the members of the Secret Nine did for a living, but they didn't seem like journalists. They were a recent expansion team.

All the people on that team, even the two women, were young and athletic and more talented than smart. Except for their pitcher. We liked him. He was older and left-handed and in possession of an ancient, tiny baseball glove with no laces, such as that glove favoured by our own pitcher Jim. Steve, for that was his inevitable name, had a wicked curve, and the trouble with curveballs in fastball is that the pitchers don't seem to have to take much speed off them.

This lambent evening, though, I was playing third base. Now, my personal tragedy is that I have to be more knowledgeable than most people about things such as baseball and grammar. Most of the talented but otherwise ordinary third base players in the league would play behind the bag, as they do in baseball, probably out of a certain fear of line drives to the "hot corner."

So of course I would show them how it's done in fastball: crouch a few paces *inside* the bag (that is baseball talk meaning closer to the plate than the base is). This way, of course, you are ready for the bunt, or you persuade the batter not to bunt. But more important, if you are back of the bag you will likely pick up a grounder on the second bounce and be too late to nab the runner at second or the hitter at first.

Did I mention that these Secret Nine guys were young and athletic? Do you know anything about arithmetic? I was crouching about forty-eight feet (ball diamonds are not measured in metric) from home plate.

Jim fired an inside fastball at about 80 miles an hour, and the right-handed hitter swung his aluminum bat with such ferocity that the ball was probably propelled at about 110 miles an hour. For forty-eight feet.

I was wearing my beautiful gold-framed aviator glasses with yellow plastic lenses, really nice in the gloaming with an evening sun in the eyes of the third baseman and the left fielder.

I never saw it.

Cripes, that happened fast.

Oh no, not again.

It was my left eye now.

I don't remember any blood this time. There I was, a sixty-year-old man in my old authentic Cleveland Indians road pants from the double-knit days, a University of Guelph tee-shirt, lying on the ground beside a really ugly baseball cap in the lush dying light behind Magee High School.

One of the Secret Nine guys used his cell phone to call the ambulance. They must have asked him how old the victim was. He said that the victim was probably in his thirties, maybe late thirties. I heard Gill, my dear friend Gill, let out one of her famous snorts, then her famous laughter that comes out between her teeth. Then she corrected the young man. I don't know whether I was pleased or not pleased. I was preoccupied with the thought of opening my left eye to find out whether I could see. A part of me was adjusting to life with one eye. You don't see very many infielders with one eye.

Whenever someone gets injured on the ball field, his teammates have him lie on his back on the ground. When, as a kid, I got a line drive in the nuts while pitching at the Elks picnic at Okanagan Falls, though, Doc White tried to get me to lie on my front. I didn't want to do it then, but I did, and the doc was right.

But now the docs were young ambulance guys, so off I went again, on my back on a fracture board that felt like a two-by-four in the rear of the ambulance. What is that all about, I wondered. I didn't find out about fracture boards till my trip to the Welland Hospital on the Labour Day weekend of 2003.

At the UBC Hospital emergency place, where you always wait your turn and do not die while doing so, I lay on my back in clothes no sixty-year-old is supposed to be caught dead wearing. Gill had called Angela, so she was there yet again, and I had a look around me with my right eye, and a grey lack of environment with my other. The main topic of interest was not, as I said, my eye, but the smell. The whole emergency area smelled like dog manure.

"This is the last time I will ever do this for you," said Angela, as she removed my turf shoes. Imagine, you go to emergency in an ambulance, and for the whole trip you smell like manure. She took my shoes somewhere and washed them, sort of. It would actually be a year or so before the dog manure was gone from the cleats, but it would disappear long before the old blood spots did.

Baseball has been pretty good to me.

Yes, when I was at Air Cadet Camp in Abbotsford, BC, I was out playing catch with a brown baseball in the semi-dark of an August evening, fooling about, stepped in front of someone else's catch, or he in front of mine, and a baseball broke my nose. It wasn't the first time I'd had my nose broken, but this time I was at a government site. They would take me to Shaughnessy, the military hospital in Vancouver, to set my nose properly. I said no deal, because tomorrow was the day of the softball championship game.

It was us, BC, against Northern Ontario, and I don't know how it happened, but I was the catcher for the BC team. We had a star pitcher from Kamloops named Jones, and I called him Smitty in my catcher's chatter, or else his name was Smith, and I called him Jonesy. I mean I don't know how it happened, because I didn't usually make the team if it was representing something like a whole province, but there I was.

My father was a catcher, and my mother was a catcher when she was younger, so that must have meant something, but you can't rely on genes in baseball. For every Moises Alou there is a Pete Rose Jr. stuck in single-A.

But I'd been doing all right. I threw out two runners at second base in one inning in the game against Alberta, and let me tell you—up to that time I did not have many glorious baseball memories. And now we were in the championship game.

But when game time came around, I could not squat and receive Jonesy's pitches without blinking and even flinching, and my nose was too big for the mask. So for this game I played left field, something more puzzling than catcher. I remember making a grand running catch, but I can't remember whether we were champions or the runners-up to Northern Ontario.

A few years later I got my nose broken by a baseball again, this time off the bat. My first broken nose had come via a kick by Carol Wilkins, but that had nothing to do with baseball, so you won't be hearing that story now. My fourth broken nose was perpetrated by a fist. How mundane. Forget that one, too.

The predecessor to the Twilight League was the famous Kosmic League, to which I will devote a chapter of this book. The longest chapter, as a matter of fact. During the 1970s some of the all-stars and no-stars of the Kosmic League would commit a traditional New Year's Day ball game. A lot of people think that there is no weather in Vancouver during the winter, but they are wrong. This New Year's game would be played under whatever conditions prevailed—horizontal rain, wet snow, bitter cold and bad hangovers.

We prided ourselves on playing no matter what the weather, and some of us even desired to perform well despite winter arms and Christmas stomachs. I was, one New Year's day, fortunate to be involved, as shortstop, in a lovely brisk double play. The double play was completed when the ball landed in the glove of a young first baseman with more physical ability than awareness. He did not add well enough to know that the inning had ended with his putout, and started an around-the-horn with his powerful arm. The rest of us were walking off the muddy infield and toward the tub of warm red wine. Unfortunately, the young first baseman's throw was directed toward me, and as I was walking toward the third base dugout, it hit me on the temple.

I was knocked cold, and when I did come to, I knew what a concussion felt like at last. This time I was taken to the Vancouver General Hospital emergency, and that was not exactly embarrassing, but needed explanation, as the place was packed with people in bright skiing outfits, including those, like me, who were arranged on gurneys in the hallway. I was rather proud to be a softball injury instead of just another person with an expensive ski suit about to be cut open by a young medico.

Imagine! Your brain rattling around inside your cranium. If you are an accident-prone amateur athlete, you really do get familiar with your bones. Or, say, an amateur young lover—who breaks his hand by punching a concrete wall as hard as he can to impress his true love who sounds as if she's getting ready to let him go.

But I told that story in another book, which was only partly about baseball.

Get familiar with your bones, and grow to love them. What is it about male athletes, and probably female ones—they seem to have a kind of autoerotic fondness for their own bodies. It is a special kind of somatic narcissism. You see that in dressing rooms all the time.

You see a handsome guy with little in the way of clothing on, prodding some muscle, ruminative, a goony look of mild intensity on his face, this while he banters with a teammate or tennis opponent.

I run my palm and fingers over my knee right now, as I write on a house deck on the east side of Protection Island, taking time to check the boats and bird life. Once in the Kosmic League I was pitching, and took a line drive on it. It did not break my patella, darn it, but for the next week I had a yellow and blue bruise that went in tentacles to my ankle and up to my hip. Oh, I had a crush on my right knee that week, unable to play, but able to wear shorts and stretch out my legs in the Zephyrs dugout.

That knee hurts right now, thirty years later. That's something.

Kind of a homoerotic attachment to your own body. A logger or a mail-sorter can get injured and not do it. Coriolanus had it, showing his war wounds to the citizens of Rome, trying to get adored and elected. He was more an athlete than a politician. He loved his scars. I have a basketball scar under one of my eyebrows, courtesy of a guy named Dino Cicci from Hamilton, Ontario. The collision under the basket happened so long ago that I can't remember which eyebrow.

Have you seen bicycle racers in their Lycra outfits, stretching their long muscular legs before the day's race? Self-directed erotomania in the summer sun.

It was not that Coriolanus was *proud* of his war wounds. He *loved* them. When a ballplayer goes on the DL (disabled list), he has mixed feelings. Oh, not again, he says, thinking of his career; and hello again, familiar limp, pull up a chair.

In grade five, Mary-Ann Rutherford was not watching where she was going, and got hit in the head by a bat when she walked too close to the strike zone while a ball and a bat were also travelling through it. I have flinched every time I've thought about that in the past fifty-five years.

2

You Have to Have a Team

There's nothing in the world like the fatalism of the Red Sox fans, which has been bred into them for generations by that little green ballpark, and *the wall*, and by a team that keeps trying to win by hitting everything out of sight and just out-bombarding everyone else in the league. All this makes Boston fans a little crazy and I'm sorry for them.

—Bill Lee

When, in the early winter of 2004, the Boston Red Sox came within a pitch of being eliminated from the American League playoff, then won four straight games against the juggernaut New York Yankees, then swept the St. Louis Cardinals in the World Series, and were major league champions for the first time since 1918, they screwed everything up. I was actually cheering for the Cardinals in the fourth game. Now in the coming year, all the teenagers would be wearing Red Sox hats instead of Yankees hats with their Nike shoes. My irony had been stripped from me; no longer could I be a grim Bosox follower. And what about my baseball book? What about my perpetually-losing-against-all-odds Bosox as a running joke, or what my editor calls a leitmotif?

HAVING A FANTASY BALL TEAM in a national fantasy league is a lot of fun, even though you get frustrated a lot when your pitchers go on a season-long DL, or give up seven earned runs in the first inning. But there is one thing you cannot like about it. Having a fantasy team changes the way you read the box scores.

Instead of finding out how your favourite major league team did the night before, or how badly the Yankees did, you go looking for the individuals who make up your fantasy team. And you feel a little guilty because that makes you, in some way, a second-rate baseball fan. Not as bad as the people who get interested only when the playoffs begin, but nevertheless—

I'll give you an example. I have a fantasy team in a group called the Seaver League. We are owners of National League players only, and that makes us superior. My team is called the High Sox, another sign of superiority, and I am, as I write these words, in third place in my division. When I open the newspaper at the box scores I do like to see that the Red Sox have won, but I have no players that toil for the Red Sox. I check the Cardinals' box score to see how Pujols did last night, and I check the Phillies' box to see how Jimmy Rollins fared. Remembering that I had seen yesterday that Hideo Nomo was starting against the Mets, I scrutinize the numbers that follow his name in the Dodgers' box score.

I give the American League the most cursory of glances. This is all right in a sense, because the American League is only the American League, a place for Yankees and a lot of thin organizations such as Kansas City and the Tampa Bay Devil Rays. But one should at least give them more attention than I do. I see how Ichiro Suzuki and Frank Thomas went, and then go back and look at the National League stats again. Or at least at mine. If Milwaukee played San Diego, I don't bother much.

But all the time I feel as if I am doing something wrong.

A real baseball fan checks out *his team* in the box score. Everything about his team. Unearned runs. Sacrifice flies. Attendance. Everything.

And you have to have a team. I date my loss of interest in football from the moment I realized I didn't really have a team. I will root for Minnesota to defeat Chicago, but I won't watch the game. Just to be funny, I want the Saskatchewan Roughriders to beat whomever they are playing.

Between that paragraph and this one, I got a package in the mail from my high school chum Joe Makse. It contained a beautiful Gonzaga Bulldogs tee-shirt, two neat photographs from our class reunion a couple of weeks before, and a note in which he asks whether I have yet read *The Teammates* by David Halberstam. This last is a recollection of the wonderful Red Sox players of my youth: Ted Williams, Johnny Pesky, Dom DiMaggio and Bobby Doerr. Ah, I know about the book. I've seen bits in a magazine. I look forward to it as if it were Christmas, as if it were the 1948 Boston Red Sox. There were a couple of other wonderful teams of men in those days, the Cleveland Indians of Joe Gordon and Lou Boudreau et al. and the Brooklyn Dodgers of Carl Furillo and Jack Robinson et al. In 1948, the greatest year in human history, I was twelve years old, the perfect age for baseball on the radio and in *Sport* magazine, to which my parents bought me a subscription that year.

A lot of people have heard me say that 1948 was the greatest year in human history, and no one has ever contradicted me. No one has ever suggested a different year, though I would have listened to a reasonable defence of 1066 or 1867. Someone might suggest that I am fond of 1948 *because* I was twelve years old that year, and anyone would want to be twelve years old, wouldn't they?

But really. In baseball that year we had the loveable Cleveland Indians, led by their young playing manager Lou Boudreau, coming out of years of obscurity to fly past the Yankees and Red Sox and knock off the Boston Braves in a World Series we remember mainly for the fact that the great Bob Feller lost the only two World Series games he ever started. I can remember the lineup and pitching rotation of the 1948 Indians more than a half-century later.

It was a marvelous sports year all round. I was even interested in hockey back then, and a fan of the Toronto Maple Leafs, because that was the home team on *Hockey Night in Canada* on CBC Radio from Watrous, Saskatchewan. The Leafs won the Stanley Cup, knocking off the Detroit Red Wings four games to none in the final. This was sweet, decades before there were teams from Tennessee and Saudi Arabia in the NHL. In the 1948 Olympics, the Canadian team, the RCAF Flyers, tied for first place with Czechoslovakia, and won the gold medal on points differential.

Citation won the Kentucky Derby. What a wonderful horse! What a wonderful name!

Some sports fans would say that it was a bad year and a good year. Babe Ruth died, but Bobby Orr was born.

There was a lot of bad stuff in the news, but Harry Truman put an end to racial segregation in the U.S. military, while Bill Veeck did the same for the pitcher's mound in the World Series—as aged Satchell Page became the first African-American to climb one with serious intent.

There was a lot of good news in the book-writing world. Norman Mailer published *The Naked and the Dead*, and as soon as the drugstore paperback came out, I gobbled it up. The Kinsey Report was probably the most newsworthy book that year. Tennessee Williams's *A Streetcar Named Desire* won the Pulitzer Prize for drama. T. S. Eliot won the Nobel Prize. Ezra Pound's *Pisan Cantos* caused a few fistfights among the literati when it was given the Bollingen Prize by the U.S. Congress. It is, by majority consent, the greatest U.S. book of poetry in the twentieth century.

Christian Dior's "New Look" arrived in Europe in 1947 and swept the Americas in 1948. For the first time in my little life I saw that women's outer clothing could be interesting.

I have to admit that popular music was not enjoying a high spot. I can remember the words to most of the songs, but unfortunately the songs were things such as "Buttons and Bows" and "A Tree in the Meadow." The movies were another story, though. Most people say that the best film of 1948 was *The Red Shoes*, and maybe they are right. But this was the age of Humphrey Bogart and Lauren Bacall, wasn't it? In 1948 they did *Key Largo*. There was a movie that made a kid grow up fast. At the time my favourite 1948 movie was *Red River*. Sure, it had John Wayne in it. But it also had Montgomery Clift. He is the actor we paranormals had to settle for until Marlon Brando and James Dean came along. But here is a fact that a lot of people forget: in 1948 there were three new westerns starring Randolph Scott, and Randolph Scott is generally deemed to be the greatest actor that Hollywood ever produced.

In 1945 I was nine years old when the World Series came round on my Uncle Red's big radio that looked like a mahogany jukebox. My dog Caesar and Uncle Red's dog Beans were in his back yard killing each other, biting to the bone as they always did. They were both wire-haired terriers. Once in a while Beans was capable of getting over Uncle Red's seven-foot wooden back fence, which was bad news for everyone.

Inside, in the living room, I was becoming a fan of the Detroit Tigers. They were ruining the Cubs' dream, and I decided that I had to have a team. A year later, listening to the World Series during lunch break because school was on, I became instead a Boston Red Sox fan. There was a lot of tension involved in listening to weekday World Series games in Oliver, BC. At twelve noon they would be in the seventh inning. In those days even a World Series game would be over before three hours had gone by. You might, though, have to head back to school with one out in the ninth inning. I was in math class when the ignoble Bobby Thomson hit that "shot heard around the world," and wrought the final humiliation of the 1951 Dodgers, who had been ahead of the Giants by twelve and a half games on August 13, and were still six games up on September 14. If you think that I am going to recount that repulsive story, think again.

In 1948 I made a scrapbook out of newspaper stories regarding the six-team National Hockey League, and I still have that scrapbook. But that's only hockey. Now, Columbus and Tampa Bay have NHL teams. Maybe Omaha; I don't keep up. In 1946, when I was still an impressionable ten-year-old who had never seen an actual hockey game, I sent away for Toronto Maple Leaf stuff, adjustable rings, "autographed" photos and so on. Gus Bodnar. I told my dad that my stuff was "Officially Afflicted with the Toronto Maple Leafs." He thought, being a rare Montreal Canadiens fan, that that was a terrific joke. I hadn't meant it as a joke. I was trying to learn bigger words.

Across the street from the house in which I wrote this book live the Horvaths, John and Beryl. John played a couple of decades of professional hockey, mostly in the American Hockey League, and he is the brother of Bronco Horvath, one-third of the famous Uke line (with Johnny Bucyk and Vic Staziuk) of the Boston Bruins in the 1950s. It is a thrill to go to John's big basement, where he mainly lives, and look at all the memorabilia from my youth.

But it's still only hockey.

That my dad and I supported different teams was important. It made for a wonderful relationship between us, an understanding based on humour. If my team were to beat his team 10-1, he would say that the Dodgers had "edged" the Giants. If the score were 5-4 in his favour he would proclaim, while holding the newspaper at arm's length and peering at the line score over his rimless glasses, that the Giants had delivered a "thundering avalanche" of a victory.

I did a lot of things the way my dad did them. He was missing most of his right index finger, so I learned to type (hunt and peck) with my middle fingers, and to press the trigger of a .22 rifle with my right middle finger.

Whatever sport my dad was following—well, baseball and hockey—he had a favourite team and a second-favourite team. In the NHL his second-favourite team was the New York Rangers. In the National League it was the St. Louis Cardinals. In the American League he liked the Cleveland Indians and the St. Louis Browns, later the Baltimore Orioles.

So I decided that I would have a favourite team and a second-favourite team. In hockey I decided that the Boston Bruins would be my second-favourite team, even though they were my Uncle Gerry's favourite team. I think that I was probably trying for a kind of Boston consolation: I had the Red Sox in the American League, and in basketball I had the Celtics. I didn't have a team in football because Boston, unaccountably, did not have a professional football team.

Of course, in the National League, I had the Boston Braves, but they were kind of a boring team. When they moved to Milwaukee, I was not reluctant to switch my small-town western Canadian allegiance to the St. Louis Cardinals, even though they were also my dad's second-favourite team.

The Cardinals. Before I reached job age, I used to spend a couple of weeks every summer at my grandparents' place in Summerland. My grandfather had been a Baptist minister before he became a postmaster on a crutch and a cane, and my grandmother, Clara Bowering, was a good Christian woman, who went to church every Sunday, though my grandfather no longer did, which was to me a puzzle I always thought I would find the solution to in later years. I was a reading kid, as most baseball fans were, usually favouring westerns, but reading whatever drugstore paperbacks took baseball as their subject—*Bat Boy of the Giants* by Garth Garreau, for example. *My Greatest Day in Baseball*, for example.

My grandmother. Her favourite comic strip was *Little Orphan Annie*. She would read it aloud, and when a mobster said "yeah," she pronounced it "yea," as if expecting a "verily." This little old Christian woman—did she think that U.S. gangsters talked like the Bible?

Anyway, one time the book I was reading was *The Gashouse Gang*, by J. Roy Stockton, all about the 1934 Cardinals—Pepper Martin, Dizzy Dean, Frankie Frisch, Leo Durocher and Rip Collins. These guys got the name because their uniforms were always dirty from the all-out way they practised their art. My grandmother, though, took one look at the title and upbraided me, an innocent country kid with a yen for reading. I thought about it for a moment and realized that this lady would never understand anything I might say about Frankie Frisch's pennant race. My guess is that her yea-sayers were never recognized by her as suited men belonging to a gang that never came sliding into the Polo Grounds.

The Cardinals. At the moment I have three Cardinal pitchers on my fantasy team, and am dickering for a fourth. All the sportswriters say that the Cards would win it all this year if it weren't for their cruddy pitching. My friend Jack Cardoso lives in Buffalo, but he is a life-long (and that *is* long) Cardinals fan, who is so vehement and opinionated that he has been thrown out of the Cardinals' chatroom—the only reason he ever got online. He gives me pity but no solace for my strange recruiting habits.

Where was I?

Oh yes. You have to have a team.

It can become pretty funny. My friend Paul Naylor is a life-long Chicago Cubs follower. Well, a lot of people are, the kind of people, I guess, who like movie stars such as Donald O'Connor and June Allyson. Every year Paul decides that it is time to quit torturing himself. The Cubs have not won a pennant since 1945, and they won that for the same reason that the St. Louis Browns won one in 1944—World War II had called up a lot of phenoms and draft choices, and the leagues were a little unbalanced. The Cubs have not won a World Series since 1908. For a few days Paul might be seen without his Cubs shirt or wristbands. Then the Cubs will slip into first place in early May, and Paul will smile with reconciliation, though he knows about his team's copyright "June swoon." It takes a loveable irony to be a Cubs fan.

Or a Red Sox fan. You will remember that I have been a Red Sox fan since 1946. Before the preposterous October of 2004, the last time the Red Sox had won the World Series was in 1918—against the Chicago Cubs. Most of the time between 1946 and 2004, I thought that I'd like to see the Red Sox win it all before I died. Other times I wondered whether that would be a big disappointment, whether it would remove a certain sense of irony mixed with superiority that the Cubs fan still enjoys and the Red Sox fan used to enjoy. We all look down our noses at New York Yankees fans. Cheering for the Yankees is like cheering for General Motors, or the U.S. Air Force. Bimbos drinking the lightest Mexican beer available in bars called "clubs" wear pink or light blue Yankees hats.

It is a little sad that the entrepreneurs and advertisers have begun to notice the Cubs and Red Sox, though. Eternal failure is mixed with endearment, rather than a far more interesting existential irony, when hawkers try to market something like our foolish sentimentality back at us. It is no coincidence, one still senses, that the two stadiums that have escaped the rapacious team owners' wrecking ball are Wrigley in Chicago and Fenway in Boston. They are the two oldest parks in major league baseball, and the two smallest. They are among the few that have not had their names changed to that of a bank or an investment company. They are the two best-liked parks among baseball fans, and they are sites of envy. Now that the Sox have won it all, we aficionados are beginning to fear that the naming rights to the Boston park will be purchased by some insurance company.

"Have you ever been to Fenway?"

"Yep. Fenway in 1970. Wrigley in 2001. The bleachers."

"Ah, you lucky bastard. I'll be there one day."

I have also been a Dodgers fan all my sentient life—at first because most kids were Yankees fans. In a similar fashion, I also liked Gene Autrey while they liked Roy Rogers. When a plush new movie theatre opened in Oliver, I kept going to the movies at the Legion Hall, sitting on a bench. I claimed that the films were more serious there. I liked Batman, though most of the kids favoured Superman. But I have never been to Ebbets Field, though I did get to Chavez Ravine, finally.

I was the same way about autographs. Every once in a while, going through my stuff, I find the little photo album in which I pasted the baseball autographs I used to write away for. I would send my request care of the ballpark, whose address I got from some magazine. Now, ordinary kid fans, of the New York Yankees, say, would likely send away for autographs of their Yankee heroes—Joe DiMaggio, Johnny Lindell, Bobby Brown. But I never got an autograph from a Red Sock, and I think I got one Dodger, though now I can't recall whether it was Clem Labine or Carl Furillo.

No, I would just settle on some player, and he didn't have to be great any more than he had to be a Dodger. When the O'Brien twins were playing basketball at Seattle University, before they went on to be light-hitting infielders for the Pittsburgh Pirates, I got their autographs. But my favourite autograph was from Enos Slaughter. First, I got a little hand-written letter from him, explaining that the Cardinals were on the road, and that when they got back to St. Louis, he would send me an autographed photo—and he did!

I tried a few hockey players, too, but they always sent those photographs with the photographed autographs. In later years I wondered whether your average hockey player had trouble remembering how to write his name.

A couple of years ago my friend Jack Cardoso the Cards fan (hey, it's in his name! No wonder *Bo*wering is a *Bo*sox fan!) got to visit Enos Slaughter on his farm in South Carolina, and interview him for some history anthology. I wish I could have tailed along. I would have thanked Enos for the letter. And then maybe I would have asked him about his attitude toward Jackie Robinson. I think that I remember some bad public remarks made about him by Eddy Stanky and Enos Slaughter.

It was a wonderful time to be a kid baseball fan, the late forties and early fifties. My Dodgers were the first major league team in the twentieth century to have an African-American player, and my Red Sox were the last. When Larry Doby helped Jackie Robinson break the "color bar," I was tempted to switch my American League "affliction" from the Boston Red Sox to the glamorous Cleveland Indians. I don't know how much attention I paid to the irony back then—a Negro becomes an Indian.

And my only interview with a 1948 ballplayer was not with Enos Slaughter, or Peewee Reese. It was with Bob Feller. I have told that story elsewhere, how I told Bob that I thought that Phil Masi was out by "this much," holding my hands nine inches apart, and Feller, living in all time at once, said, "twice that."

I hated seeing him sitting at a table in the back of a sports store in Victoria, BC, and no one coming to get anything autographed. But I was nearly fifty years old. I wasn't collecting autographs anymore. I really felt for this USAmerican from rural Iowa, but in 1948 I wanted Johnny Pesky to hit a home run off him.

In 1948 and 1949 and 1950, I was immersed in baseball, and I felt myself becoming a USAmerican. Sure, we kids used to shout a derisive "Americaaaaaan!" at any automobile driving too fast along Highway 97.

But I was wrapped in U.S. "culture." Baseball made up a lot of that, along with western novels and west coast radio stations and DC Comics.

There was the odd Canadian in the majors then as now—Phil Marchildon, for example. But the National Pastime was my cult. I thought I was going to become a U.S. citizen when I grew up, starting with going to a U.S. university, and continuing with writing sports for a U.S. newspaper, like the *St. Louis Post-Dispatch*.

I knew that Jackie Robinson had been loved in Montreal, where he played for the Royals in 1946, but the majors were the majors, and in Oliver, BC, you had to have a team in the majors.

3

Fast Eddie's Van

I hate the minor leagues. I'd rather go out to lunch with my ex-wife's attorney than play in the minors.

—David S. Collins

BUT IN THE TWENTY-FIRST CENTURY the minor leagues are becoming more interesting to everyone. The main reason for that is marketing: the major league teams are marketing themselves out of business, and the minor league teams are marketing themselves in.

If you are like me and find it hard to resist acquiring baseball caps, you have quit buying major league caps. Especially now that there is such a thing as a cap for spring training—that hideous new thing with the pre-curled peak such as those you'd find in skateboard shops.

But then there are the minor leagues. What can you do? I mentioned to Jean in December that I wanted the gorgeous New Orleans Zephyrs cap for Christmas, ha ha, fat chance. Jean got onto the Internet, and on Christmas morning I unwrapped four different Z hats, including the new one, making me the only person in Canada to have it. Oh, my! We also have a poster that shows all the minor league caps in "organized baseball." There are ads in the back pages of the sports magazines and papers that tell you how easy it would be to get a Charleston Riverdogs cap in your size. Before the Zephyrs escapade I thought it was pretty bad that I had the Tacoma Rainiers home cap and the Tacoma Rainiers batting practice cap.

Here is the way I resist minor league caps. I have a rule that says you have to be able to see and understand the logo from the seats in the grandstand.

I wrote that last sentence so that I could mention that the place where you *sit* is called a *stand*. Later I will mention that a ball that comes off a bat and lands on the foul line is fair. Also, a pitch that you fail to strike with your bat? It is called a strike. There you are: three reasons to love baseball and praise your own ironic attendance.

Okay. A lot of the new minor league teams have cluttered logos that just look like ungraceful smears from any distance. Too much detail. An example would be the aforesaid Charleston Riverdogs. In fact, I believe that in recent years the owners of minor league teams, especially single-A teams, have chosen their goofy names so they can have stupid logos on their hats—some animal biting and breaking a baseball bat while being imperilled by large capital letters, for example.

So when it comes to purchasing minor league caps, I will look only at good classic readable ones. An example would be the Battle Creek Yankees, with their big *B* hooked by a big *C*. Another would be the Vancouver Canadians with their *V* or *C*. Sometimes what passes for political progress will result in cultural loss. When Syracuse had the Chiefs they had a clear profile of a handsome North American Aboriginal man. Now they are the Sky Chiefs, and have a messy *S* through which is flying a baseball bat becoming an airplane, and this idiotic image has big snarling teeth at its front end. In fact, I think we have come upon a rule here: any logo that features snarling teeth is going to be bad.

Usually the major league logos are good and clear, though recently some marketing moron had to have a tiger mincing around the *D* on the Detroit hat. A few years ago the Toronto team exhibited a maple leaf *and* a blue jay head *and* a baseball. The worst hockey logos have a hockey stick in them, and the worst baseball logos have a baseball or a bat in them. The one exception is the St. Louis Cardinals: two redbirds perched on a baseball bat. It has always been famous on the shirts. Now

29

some nimrod has put it on the special third cap, and all we see are desperate merchandisers poking their noses into our lovely baseball world.

All right. The major leagues have, generally, more taste. But it costs thirty dollars to sit in a remote seat in SkyDome or Pac Bell. Then a hotdog costs six dollars, and a USAmerican beer costs nine dollars, and those are U.S. dollars. Imagine: the strong dollar gets you the weak beer.

That's why people are getting interested in the minor leagues. A seat in a single-A park will cost you what a seat in Fenway used to cost in distant memory.

Which brings us to the baseball tour.

All baseball fans and wannabe baseball fans (*there's* a concept!) want to go on a baseball tour. The apogee of such ambition is the trip that takes you and your buddy to *every major league park* in one summer on the road. Well, that *used* to be the idea.

There is a tradition that Paul and Fast Eddie and I began a decade or so ago. We would get into one of our cars in Vancouver and head for a minor league game in the state of Washington. At first we would go to the delightful park in Bellingham, where the last twenty feet of the left field foul line go uphill, and there we would catch the "Baby M's," the Bellingham Mariners. I have two of their different hats. There, I once chatted with the highly positive mayor of Bellingham, and we all watched a game in which two of the competition's names were Elgin Bobo and Arquimedes Pozo. (These baseball names—that's another tradition I will tell you about if I have time.)

Since the Bellingham franchise folded, we have kept up our tradition by making trips to Everett or Tacoma. Between Everett and Tacoma is Seattle, is Safeco Field, home of the major league Mariners. But Paul and Fast Eddie and I go to see the Everett Aquasox (who, by the way, wear aqua caps and black socks) or the Tacoma Rainiers. (A few decades ago the Tacoma team was called the Tugs, and I wish I had *their* cap in my collection.) We've talked of attending games in Yakima or Eugene, but generally we go to Everett, partly because of the Tampico Restaurant.

Due to a lot of momentous circumstances, I finally got to do my ideal baseball tour with Jean Baird in July of 2003.

I had been hauling Jean to baseball games for a few years, and teaching her such things as the infield fly rule and how to keep a scorebook. She had not been a baseball fan before I showed her the light. Her daughter is as far from being an athlete as you can get. Her son plays soccer and basketball, and watches trash sports on television. Two years ago Jean and I met in Chicago, and looked at art and architecture for a while before sitting in the hot sticky bedlam of the Wrigley Field bleachers. We went on to games in Vancouver, Buffalo, Toronto, Syracuse and Montreal.

But July 2003 was to be a baseball glutton's barbecue for me. Here I was, a retiree in shorts and ball caps plunking myself down on unluxurious planks in the hot sun, cheering on the efforts of Latino-American infielders a half-century younger than I.

We had warmed up for the tour by taking in a few ball games here and there. You will recall that 2003 was the year that the Canadian Baseball League opened for business. When I found out about plans for the CBL a year or two earlier, I liked the idea because, after all, we Canadians invented the game, eh? But when I heard which cities were involved, I had to wonder how in hell they hoped to bring it off. Were there any baseball people involved in planning this league?

Victoria, Kelowna, Calgary and Saskatoon in the west. London, Niagara (Welland), Montreal and Trois-Rivières in the east. They would play on Thursdays through Sundays, and the players would be hired directly by the league. But the travel? I could not believe that they thought they could travel those distances by bus or pay for air, even with all the new regional Boeing 737 airlines. Well, you know by now that the CBL "suspended" operations halfway through its inaugural season, and later held a yard sale of its stuff.

I had been so excited, despite my pessimism. I'd lived in Victoria and Calgary, and I was raised in the Okanagan Valley, so I could have been a Kelowna fan. But I had also lived in London and Montreal, and in the summer of 2003 I was to move to Port Colborne, Ontario, a puddle-jump from Welland, where the Niagara Stars would play their home games. The Niagara Stars would be my home team.

In fact, I threw the Niagara Stars' first pitch in their first ever opening night game. Ferguson Jenkins, the only Canadian in the Baseball Hall of Fame, was supposed to throw out the first Welland pitch because he was the commissioner of the CBL, but their opener was rained out. Somehow, Jean had fixed it so that I was to throw out the first pitch at their second game, which became their opener. What luck! The reason I was allowed to do this was that I had been appointed Canada's first Parliamentary Poet Laureate, and I just happened to be a notorious baseball fan.

During the game the Stars would be giving out copies of my newest poetry book *Baseball* to lucky ticket holders. On top of that, I would be interviewed between innings by The Score, the sports TV network that I often watch for the baseball news.

I don't know how she pulled it off. Jean says to me, "What was better, getting the Order of Canada or throwing out the first pitch?"

I don't know why we say "throwing out" in this circumstance. That term was invented when U.S. presidents started tossing a ball from the stands to the home team catcher before important games such as season or World Series openers. In recent times we have had some hero or goof or businessman toss the ball from the mound to the catcher crouched behind home plate; or if the dignitary is particularly old or fat, he can toss it from somewhere between the mound and the plate. I once saw the famous baseball novelist throw the first pitch. He threw, as we used to say, like a girl, and bounced it, or really rolled it, to the catcher. How did I do? Ah, this was a dream come true, so I decided to play it for laughs, to be consistent with my usual behaviour, though I will admit that it was all going too fast as it always does during the highlights of your life. Squatting behind the plate was Rogelio Arias, a six-foot guy from Villa Duarte in the Dominican Republic. He waited. I shook him off. There was laughter from the stands, good. Now he flashed me the sign for a slider on the outside corner. I shook him off. He asked for the fastball. I delivered a forty-five miles an hour fastball low on the corner. Really low. But it did not bounce, and some right-handed hitter *might* have swung at it. This was great. Now we do the routine where Rogelio autographs the ball for me and we'll get our picture in next day's *Welland Tribune*.

This was May 31, 2003, my kid brother Jim's fifty-fourth birthday. The London Monarchs with their Japanese players beat the Stars 12-3, in front of 509 people on a night when it could have rained again. The next night we saw the Stars prevail 5-4, so June started well. Our home team had a third baseman named Legacy. Things were looking good.

But June was also the month in which a tough CEO woman with two kids was going to move into the big house that Angela and I had bought in 1973 and rebuilt over and over. There were countless rooms, and each one was full of stuff, as was the garage, as was the much-photographed garden. But it all had to go, too fast for regular thought. My daughter Thea and I and Gill Collins, the first baseman for two of my teams, were deciding what would go to auction, what would go to storage, and what would get thrown out. June went by too fast to be what it should have been, one of the saddest months of my life.

If the Vancouver Canadians had still been in the AAA Pacific Coast League, I wouldn't have had time to go to a game.

But then June was followed by July, and July would be one of the happiest months of my life, the setting for the Great Single-A Tour.

After we kissed the back door of the old house and left the yard for the last time, Thea and I went on a trip up Vancouver Island. We visited Angela's grave on the old Luoma farm on Quadra Island, stayed with

Angela's sister Joan, had lunch with Angela's girlhood friend Heather, and then headed south to Nanaimo and over to preposterously beautiful Protection Island, to crash at the home of Mike and Carol Matthews. The Matthewses don't have a television set, so there was no question of baseball whatsoever.

On July 4, Jean arrived in Vancouver on some ridiculous airline's kite, and we moved into the storied Sylvia Hotel for four nights. I had always wanted to stay at the Sylvia, but how could I do so if I lived in Vancouver? Visiting writers stay at the Sylvia, and once, while the poet David Bromige was staying there, we began a collaborative novel that begins and ends in the big, square, ivy-covered inn—four of us, Bromige, Mike Matthews and the Bowerings. It's a good novel, a funny nostalgic science fiction thriller.

Before the writers came the sports teams. Back in the fifties the visiting hockey, football and baseball teams used to stay at the Sylvia, the only hotel on scenic English Bay. Here we were, Jean and I, in the same hostelry that played host to the Sacramento Solons!

We were planning to nose my 2001 Volvo S60 eastward on the eighth, so I had alerted Paul and Fast Eddie that July 6 would be my last chance to make it to our annual junket, and so it came to pass. On that day still resonantly coloured by a warlike nation's celebrations of its founding, we assembled in Fast Eddie's van with all its cupholders.

Fast Eddie was wearing his Tacoma batting practice hat. I was wearing my Tacoma home game hat with Mount Rainier on it. Paul was wearing his orange Baltimore Orioles painter hat. Jean was wearing her Syracuse Sky Chiefs visor. Fast Eddie's youngest son Neale was wearing a baseball hat with, of course, one of those mysterious skateboard logos.

We were hoping beyond hope that it would be Bark in the Park Day at Everett Memorial Stadium. That's the day when they give away free dog food, and a few hundred dogs get to parade in the outfield after the sixth inning. This is when one hopes that only the catcher goes into a squat, eh?

I hear that they are going to have Pooch in the Park Day at SkyDome. I never thought that the dogs would go to the major leagues, or vice versa.

My favourite visiting team in the Northwest League is the Eugene Emeralds, in their grey uniforms with green pinstripes. I had seen them in Vancouver and Spokane. Now here they were in Everett. Tell the truth: how many times have you seen a game between two towns that start with *E*?

The Emeralds were particularly interesting this time because they had a familiar-looking guy playing first base. This was Fernando Valenzuela Jr., and he looked just like his dad, the Mexican phenom who came up with the Los Angeles Dodgers, oh, a few years ago. Fernandomania lasted all through the eighties, as the portly left-hander from a huge family in rural Mexico used his screwball to pitch a no-hitter a few years after winning the Cy Young Award and the Rookie of the Year Award in his first year up.

His kid looked so much like him that I loudly accused him of being Fernando Sr. making a comeback as a first baseman. The kid threw the ball crisply, even in practice—left-handed. You know he's a ballplayer, though he is short and kind of thick. His father was portly, but kept surprising people with his athleticism. In this game Fernando Jr. hit a line single to right, lined to the shortstop, walked, and was retired on a looping liner to left.

The Emeralds scored three in the top of the tenth, and won 5-2.

Now, these trips to Everett always entail two other stops. First, before the game, we go way out to the Everett Mall and investigate Half Price Books, a really big remainders place, from which we always emerge with plastic bags filled with books. This time I was terribly disappointed that someone had beaten me to the W shelf in popular fiction, and left a big gap where Donald E. Westlake should have been. But I did okay. Fast Eddie's kid Neale really scooped it. He bought a bunch of Gene Autrey videos, including an old serial in which Gene and his horse and buddies do battle with metallic robots twenty thousand feet below the surface of the Earth.

After the game, we drove—our mouths turned up at the corners, our nostrils flared—to Tampico. Jean had to be prepared. We had found this Mexican restaurant five years ago, we explained. All dietary restrictions are off. This is not a taco and quesadilla joint. It is a Mexican restaurant where you drink Bohemia or Modelo Negra, and face an enormous platter of absolutely *saporosa* stuff.

It always takes Jean an era to choose off a menu, but she got some chicken with a cream sauce of some sort, and ate her way through half of it. I got 65 percent of the way through my *chile verde*. Little Paul was the only one who cleared his dish. Jean's eyes were popping.

4

Growing up in Baseball

You're only young once, but you can be immature forever.
—Larry Andersen

WHEN I WAS DOING RESEARCH for my novel *Caprice*, I found out that baseball teams around Kamloops in 1889 would recruit players from across the line, find them good jobs and maybe even slip them a little gold or currency under the table. The more things change, I thought. When I was a kid in the Okanagan in the forties and fifties, our ball teams would look for USAmerican imports, too, and fix them up with good jobs, and, we heard, slip them some good strong Canadian dollars.

In Princeton, for example, they would get easy jobs at the brewery. Princeton Beer was the first beer I ever tasted. In Oliver, Princeton Beer was the kind everybody bought. Each bottle was wrapped in a kind of grey asbestos paper. Once in a while I get a taste that reminds me of Princeton Beer.

The Oliver Elks gave an infielder named Sibby a job at a gas station, plus whatever signing bonus was involved. A few years later a second Esso station opened in town, and it was called Sibby's Service. Sibby once claimed that his father down in Washington defeated cancer by eating 100 bananas a day. Later, in the air force, I knew a guy who ate 125 bananas in one day. I asked him whether he thought he might have cancer.

"Buhnana," he said. Over and over.

There was something gleaming about those imports from across the line. They seemed to have an ease in the world that we Canadians did not know. Well, it wasn't long since World War II had ended. I remember that rationing ended across the line before it did in Oliver. Across the line they could get bubble gum. If a Canadian kid looked carefully at his popsicle wrapper or comic book he could always discern the words "offer not valid in Canada."

But I never thought that baseball was a U.S. game. It was a birthright. And certainly it was normal. In the Okanagan sun, you got your baseball stuff out as soon as the ground got softer in, say, March, and you played the summer game till apple season was over in October.

The ballpark, with its big old grey grandstand made of obvious lumber, was the most important few acres in town. There was a sandy hill behind the grandstand. All along the south side, from back of the grandstand to past the left field foul pole, ran a huge wooden siphon that carried water from the east side of the valley to the irrigation ditch at the base of the hills on the west side. Out beyond right centre field was the Community Hall, with the scoreboard on its side. My friend Ronny Carter was the scoreboard boy. A lot of kids wished they could run along the gangway, putting up zeroes like that. Once in a while Cy Overton, the guy in the announcer's booth on the roof of the grandstand, would have to tell Ronny that there were actually two out, not just one.

"Two out, scoreboard," Cy Overton would announce so that you could hear it over the river and uptown, and Ronny would scramble.

My best pal Willy was not really a sports fan, much less an athlete, but we did just about everything together, serenading construction workers, developing pictures under his basement stairs, inventing clubs, building an airplane. Actually, we did partake in one athletic activity (besides the prodigious amount of swimming that any Okanagan kid does). We would save the little cardboard cylinder that one of the powders for darkroom chemicals came in, and using some badminton racquets, and the overhead power line as a net, engage in tennis games in the gloaming. Oh yes, and we invented a game called "economical ball," so titled because contestants sat in a circle of kitchen chairs and employed brooms in an attempt to roll a volleyball past one another.

Willy and I hung out at the baseball park, keeping track of the game and figuring ways to bring in some spending money while entertaining the crowd with our wit and musicality.

A popular way of getting rich was to retrieve foul balls and bring them back to the playing field for ten cents a shot. The trouble was that there might be thirty kids behind the stands, waiting for foul balls. You could acquire some pretty serious injuries back there, and I was rather disinclined to do all the running that such competition entailed. Once under the siphon I found a ball that must have been lying in the wet high grass for ten years. When I turned it in, they wouldn't give me my ten cents. So I told Willy that we were going to be hotdog vendors.

Between the huge siphon and the ball diamond was a long row of Lombardy poplars or cottonwoods or whatever they were, enormous pointy things, and sometime during the season, the white fluff would blow off in the wind from the hot south, and the sky would be full of cotton, white puffs, like snow in the middle of summer, drifting north, descending to cover Chevrolets, hiding the white baseball that sped at eighty-five miles an hour toward the plate.

Walking under this miracle that reminded us of something from the Old Testament, or just glistening in the still air of the Canadian desert, Willy and I were the hotdog vendors from Limbo. Back in 1949, they didn't have those thermal bags or coolers. We lugged pop crates and trays suspended from our necks. We worked the grey grandstand and the bleachers along the foul lines. We went from car to car. This was before they put up the professional-looking outfield fence with the advertisements for local businesses. There was a little lattice fence, and people would nose their cars up against it, sitting in their soft seats and taking in a game as if this were a drive-in theatre.

There was no air conditioning in the Okanagan Valley in 1949. All car windows were open. All car doors were ajar. Men did not wear shirts in the Okanagan, not after May and not before October.

"Ice-cold hotdogs," I would yell in my voice that was changing. "Get your ice-cold franks!"

"Red-hot soda pop," Willy would chime in. "Nice warming soft drinks right here!"

We never planned on doing this for very long. We were stocking up experiences for the movie we were going to make once we got our airplane aloft.

For Willy all this ballpark stuff was just more of our childhood buddy business. For me it was a lot more. Anything to do with baseball had that extra gleam, that magic—no, that is some hack's word—that *oh god this is so sweet* feeling that would not be there later, save in memory, that feeling that was also there when you got your Dick Tracy button with that *yellow* out of the Bran Flakes box, or the new Silvertip book by Max Brand at Frank's pool hall book rack, and if you can locate another nickel you'll have twenty-five cents, and kids under eighteen didn't have to pay sales tax.

Damn, I will never be able to describe the specialness of some experiences, and I can only hope that you have had something like that in your life and know what I mean, and you will be happy that I seem to have had it too, but there's no way we can find out for sure, though we have had the experience of catching another listener's eye when John Coltrane starts to wail.

Remember that pesky problem you had as a kid? What if your red is what I see as my blue, but of course we call it red because that is what someone told us it was when we first saw it?

Humour works that way, too. It can give you hope that you are not alone in this world with the horizons so far away. Else why write books?

Still, there are going to be things in your book that no one will get, no one ever.

My buddy Willy's kid brother Sandy recently told me to put Squeaky into my book. Squeaky was, I guess, the town drunk in Oliver. He looked and sounded like Gabby Hayes, and he never missed a ball game. At Christmas he went to church and fell asleep in the pew. While the choir was attempting a carol, Squeaky would wake up and sing, "Take Me Out to the Ball Game."

When I first got to Oliver, the Oliver Elks were in an international Okanagan league that included teams from south of the border— Omak, Tonasket, Chelan, Riverside, and teams from north of the border—Vernon, Kelowna, Penticton and Oliver.

I don't know why, but after a few years the U.S. teams were only around for exhibition games; they were replaced by teams from Trail, Summerland (the Macs, starring the three Kato brothers), Princeton and Kamloops. I think that the Princeton team dropped out when a big Ontario beer company bought the Princeton Brewery and closed it.

In a book called *A Magpie Life* I have told the story of how I took away my father's job as scorekeeper and newspaper reporter for Oliver baseball. I would love to find an original example of my reportage and insert it here, but I had to cut out the stories, measure them, and take them to the paper for my fifteen cents an inch.

I felt pretty important when at last I could tuck my scorebook under my arm and climb up through the trap door in the roof of the swaying grandstand, walk to the front of the roof, and stoop to enter the little tarpaper skybox there, where I would join Cy Overton, the public address announcer, and the visiting scorekeeper from the *Vernon News*, say.

I was as professional as all get-out, which is more than I can say about Cy Overton, a grown-up with thinning hair. Mr. Overton did not really comprehend the difference between a PA announcer and a play-by-play man. "Foul ball," he would say, and I would roll my teenage eyes.

Like my dad before me, I was inclined to assess an error rather than a base hit when a slow ground ball bounced off both the shortstop's ankles and rolled into shallow left field. There were a lot of times when Richie Snyder, the Oliver third baseman, got in my face about a dent to his batting average or an error I gave him for throwing the ball over the chicken wire behind first base. Richie was a bit of a whiner, but he was a pretty good ballplayer. I never liked him much. When I was a pinsetter he used to fire his five-pin bowling ball so hard that it didn't hit the wood till it was halfway down the lane. When he was coaching the junior team he told Ordie Jones that he had to quit either Boy Scouts or baseball. Ordie was a King's Scout and a terrific ballplayer. He quit the team.

Boy, you got a good view up there in that box on the roof. Whenever anyone made a hotdog run, you could feel the roof swaying, and as the afternoon wore on the hot Okanagan sun blasted its way in.

I was really glad when the outfield fence went up. It made my dicky little town (officially still a village then) seem a bit more like the professional leagues.

"What do you figure?" I asked my dad. "Is the Okanagan Mainline League sort of equivalent to Class B, or maybe Class C?"

"I think you have to learn a little more of the alphabet," he replied.

He always said stuff like that. He's my role model, though I have never been patient enough to match his subtlety.

You have to understand that the sun is blazing down about 99 percent of the daytime hours in the South Okanagan. When those cars were parked in the outfield, pointed toward home plate, the reflected sun glare off the windshields made hitting a challenge, especially when Vern Cousins or Eddie Stefan was pitching. Often you would hear Cy Overton announce, "Would the owner of the blue Mercury in right field please move his car or cover the windshield!"

When the fence went up and local businesses bought ads on it, I thought oh boy, real home runs. Not triples with an extra ninety feet of dead-out running, but real over-the-fence home runs, like those the Cleveland Indians hit. The Washington Senators. Well. Okay. There would be about one over-the-fence home run every ten games, and it would be hit by some big U.S. import playing for Trail.

Just more proof that I lived in a dicky little town that couldn't do things the way they did them in real places, especially across the line. The putting "greens" at the local golf course were made of rolled sand mixed with oil. There was no radio station. There was something amateurish about the high school cafeteria. It just didn't have the *confidence* of the ones we saw in U.S. movies or in *Archie* comics.

But all things considered, I figured that our baseball was as close to real as anything in Oliver. That is why I hated it when they changed the name of the team. Part of the problem was that one of the two Kamloops teams that had joined—and changed the loop's name to the Okanagan Mainline League—was also called the Elks. The name had been used by baseball teams in Kamloops since the 1880s.

So the players and managers and small-town businessmen—what did they decide to call the team? Did they name it after a fact of local life, such as the rattlers? Or coyotes? They could have anticipated the seventies and given the team an ABA-like name, such as the Oliver Sage.

No. Not a chance. They called it the Oliver Baseball Club. On the hats and shirts they stitched the letters *OBC*. I had to call them the OBCs in my articles in the *Chronicle*. I was embarrassed again.

I haven't said anything here about *playing* baseball when I was a kid.

I didn't, much.

I was afraid to try out. I had an inferiority complex, and I had developed a superiority complex to protect it.

It was the same way with basketball. Instead of trying out for the basketball team, I became official scorer and newspaper guy. One year there was a school volleyball team and I tried out for it and made it.

There was probably something to the fact that my father had been a baseball player and a basketball player, and got his name in the papers.

Certainly, the fact that he was a teacher at my high school had something to do with the fact that I tended to get C+ in my courses. I never got an A in a final report. Or so I like to remember it. Nowadays, when you get an A just for showing up, I would have had to play hooky. I never missed a day of school to play hooky.

So here I was, the kid who was famous for knowing everything about baseball, keeping track of the kids with natural talent who did beautiful things but didn't know who Tris Speaker was. I never had a decent glove, just some old flat thing with no pocket. I had my father's old, old spikes and my father's old, old skates, and they both hurt my feet. I had a big heavy baseball bat, which I kept in my various offices till the summer of 2003. I had a Bremerton Braves uniform, which I kept in a secret place in the basement, along with a copy of *Sunbathing for Health* magazine.

We didn't have Little League, yet. Didn't have Pony League, Babe Ruth League, Connie Mack League. Maybe if we had had Little League I might have tried out. Maybe I would have scrounged a decent glove somewhere. We didn't have much organized baseball. There was the Okanagan Mainline League, and there was the Juniors. I think the Juniors' age limit was sixteen. Maybe fifteen. Maybe seventeen. In there somewhere.

For a short time one season I played some Junior. For some reason my classmate Ron Carter was manager of the Oliver Juniors. Maybe he was just barely over the age limit. Anyway, he talked me into suiting up. I liked that part. I knew how to roll the socks inside the pants. My feet were killing me inside my father's old, old spikes. I could feel the metal spikes through the thin leather. I figured I was going to embarrass myself.

I can't remember what position I was playing, and therefore can't remember any fielding plays. I figured I would commit errors aplenty. But here is what happened my first time at bat in the late spring of some year at the beginning of the fifties.

I don't remember whom we were playing. We had the bases loaded. I was taller than a lot of the kids, having grown like a blackberry bush in the past year or so. People said that with my long legs I should be able to run like a deer. I could not figure out what long legs had to do with running fast. Once in a track meet near the community hall, I finished third in some dash, and got the red ribbon. John Lundy got the white ribbon. Ronnie Carter got the blue ribbon. We three were the only runners in the race.

The first time up in my Junior career I hit a single up the middle with the bases loaded. This can't be me, I thought.

The age limit must have been fifteen, because I was fifteen between grade ten and grade eleven. That's when I was going with Wendy, and one of the few memories I have of this Junior career was going to a road game in Penticton, where they had a beautiful fence—and lights. I remember two things there: I taught Wendy how to keep score in my scorebook, and I got her to rub my calves with wintergreen oil. I knew about wintergreen because my grandfather had moved in with us.

Early in the season I got traded to Naramata. They had a black cap with a simple white *N* on it, and I wish I still had that hat. Well, it was not really a trade. School was over, and cherry season was on, to be followed by apricot season, peach season, pear season, prune season and apple season. I spent the summers on the big orchard above Naramata, where my uncle Gerry was foreman for these rich people. (Fifty years later I would buy a Gertrude Stein first edition in my favourite bookstore in Penticton, and it would say inside the cover that it had belonged to someone in that rich family.)

So I played a bit for Naramata. But then the fruit season grew hectic, and there were road games I could not make it to because we were trying to keep up with the cherries, and then there were home games I could not make it to because we were picking on Sundays and after supper, and when we weren't picking we were thinning apples and propping apple trees.

It was a funny place, Naramata. It was ten miles north of Penticton, on the east side of Lake Okanagan opposite to the highway. Unusual religious groups set up camp there, and there were a lot of people fresh from England. Naramata was a tiny place at the bottom of the clay cliffs, and playing fields were at a premium. Sometimes we had to sit there in our black caps, or play useless catch, while the cricket players finished their incomprehensible game. We would razz them. Then they would stay after their game and razz us.

I am so glad that I had that team experience that one year. But generally I was too chicken to try out. Partly it was because I was afraid of the ball. Even before I broke my nose on one. That's why it was so amusing to come to bat that season against Ted Bowsfield.

In the late season of 1958, Ted Bowsfield would come up to the Boston Red Sox and defeat the World Series-bound New York Yankees three times. He and Bill Monbouquette were the two Red Sox *wunderkinder* on the mound that September. Bowsfield was injury-prone, but he lasted eight years in the American League, went 11-8 for the expansion Los Angeles Angels in 1961, and carried a no-hitter into the ninth inning for the Kansas City Athletics two years later.

The year I played for Oliver and Naramata in the Juniors, Ted Bowsfield was pitching for the Penticton team. He was bigger than anyone, and he had a pitching cage alongside his parents' house. He was, despite what *The Official Encyclopedia of Baseball* maintains, a left-hander, and therefore dangerous. We batters were clearly outclassed. We were like me in my first-year French class at Victoria College in 1953. Bowsfield threw a fastball that was plain invisible, and a big roundhouse curveball you could not afford to wait for.

I have to tell you, I was scared witless standing in the batter's box, even if I was a right-handed batter, and I was even more scared or maybe just relieved when I was sitting down on the dirt just outside the batter's box. Ted Bowsfield was wild. He walked and hit a lot of batters. He was wild *and* invisible, a combination a lot of us admired and dreaded. It *is* nice to remember playing a guy who made it to the majors. I just wished, at the time, that we were on the same team.

I don't know what Ted Bowsfield is doing now. He finished at 37-39, with an ERA of 4.35, over seven years with the Red Sox, Indians, Angels and Athletics. He was signed after that by the Phillies, but did not see action in the National League. In later years he was manager of the Kingdome in Seattle. That would be like having your own giant pinball machine.

Here's my favourite image from the old grandstand in Oliver.

Look at photos of stadium baseball crowds in the olden days. All the men are wearing fedoras. All the men at hockey games are wearing fedoras, which means that when a player scored a hat trick, valuable headgear came out of the stands onto the ice. These days you see a bunch of see-through plastic mesh ball caps.

Hundreds and thousands of men wearing fedoras, in black and white.

At a game in Oliver Park some Sunday in the very early fifties, a guy was sitting alone in his fedora, intent on a close game, let us say, between the OBCs and the Vernon Canadians. Behind him were sitting two teenaged girls consuming a giant bag of peanuts. Each time one of the girls cracked open a peanut she would deposit the light shell on the brim or the dented crown of the guy's fedora.

It was a work in progress. And it still is, because I don't remember seeing any outcome.

Someone recently told me that my memoirs often contain the phrase "I don't remember." It escapes me right now, who that was.

5

Welcome Home, George!

Baseball is like driving, it's the one who gets home safely that counts.

—Tommy Lasorda

"AHA, THE OPEN ROAD!" I always crow when starting out, especially if the traffic is snarled, but this time my love and I were heading east to her Ontario for a year, and the first stop would be Oliver, my home town, as they say, in the sagebrush valley at the end of cherry season.

I've driven the Hope-Princeton highway for half a century, gulp,

Here there is a two-week hiatus in my manuscript, while I broke the ball of my hip bone off while trying to stop a dog fight, and then spent some rueful time in the Welland Hospital, in a room with two old guys who barked in their sleep.

and every once in a while the drive is a little different. For example, once I drove it in my chopped and channelled 1947 Pontiac, with all my possessions aboard, and no front brakes or second gear. This I do not recommend. Now in July 2003 I was heading generally eastward, beginning my new life with Ms. Jean Baird, Ph.D., custodian of my heart and organizer of my poet's life. The first time she operated as the latter was during a memorable visit I made to Port Colborne, Ontario, when Ms. Baird was editing a glossy young adult arts magazine called

In 2 Print. She had organized a big weekend celebration of kids' writing and art, and asked whether I would come.

This is the way *In 2 Print* worked: young people did the writing, drawing and editing, and the work did not have to be fitted around any ads for pimple remover or menstruation supplies. Each issue would contain some work and/or advice from a well-known Canadian artist, such as Susan Musgrave, John Boyle, bill bissett or Charles Pachter.

Sure, I'll come, I said. I had no idea what I was coming to. There was a national competition among the young people to create a new cover for my YA novel *Parents from Space.* There was a portrait contest in which kids built their impressions of G. Bowering in various materials, such as plasticene, fruit, marshmallows and the like. There was a humungous cake in the shape of a baseball park. There was a theatrical performance of my poem about fudge at Granville Island. There was my favourite Canadian musical ensemble, the Nihilist Spasm Band, and Murray Favro let me play one of his electric guitars next to an amp turned up to 10. John Clement, band member and MD, told me that I would get most of my hearing back after four days. There were lots and lots of wonderful events, with lots and lots of young folks in attendance, some of them with video cameras. Most of the events took place at Roselawn, a terrific arts centre in an old mansion in a city block park.

Oh, I forgot to mention my transportation from Toronto to Port Colborne. One reason that I was able to make it to Port Colborne was that I had to perform at the Harbourfront Festival of "Authors" in Toronto anyway. So Ms. Baird just had to get me down to the so-called Niagara Peninsula. Well, Baird is Baird. She decided that I would fly from Toronto's little harbour airport to Welland's dinky little strip in one of those tiny planes, a Piper or something. Okay, I had been in little low-flying planes before, sometimes even taking pictures of the ground. But this one had the eccentric Canadian poet David McFadden in it! Sitting beside the pilot in the front seat! In reach of the controls! It would have been completely within McFadden's character, I thought, to say "What does this gizmo do?" and reach for some switch. In the back seat I leaned forward all the way to Welland, prepared to grab McFadden's arm. Some of you know David McFadden. You know what I mean.

On the way south, though, David grew somewhat morose, because from three thousand feet in the air, you couldn't really see much of the Niagara Escarpment—maybe a different shade of green on this autumn day. All his life David had been extolling the mighty Niagara Escarpment in his poetry and narratives. In his twenties he had lived in Hamilton and published a little poetry magazine called *Mountain*. Flying to Welland, I did not rag him about his dicky little ridge. I didn't want him to lose it and plunge us to a fiery death in such a featureless countryside.

So we landed on the grassy strip near Welland, and there was no tower, no jet planes parked anywhere. There might have been a shed or two, and near the strip was a little bench, and sitting on the bench were two women in colourful dresses. These were Jean and Jane, and a couple of years later David McFadden would publish a lengthy poem about them.

They were here to welcome us to the Niagara "Peninsula" and drive us from Welland to Port Colborne, a strange little town on Lake Erie. The problem was that neither of them was currently capable of driving Jane's Jeep because of the refreshments they had been enjoying on that bench beside the air strip at the Welland airport.

Well, I thought, if I survived a flip with Dave in a Piper Cub, I can survive a ride in a Jeep with him driving, even though he does not own a vehicle to practise with—as long as he is not distracted by a bunch of kids having a hot-rod race. Dave used to navigate while his brother drove rallies in the Hamilton-Wentworth area.

Now I will get to the reason for this story about my first visit to Port Colborne, Ontario.

I knew that Ms. Baird had somehow bamboozled the City of Port Colborne into declaring George Bowering Day. She had told me to log onto the Port Colborne website, where I did see their proclamation. But now here I was in a Jeep, driving around town, Jean doing her best to give McFadden directions—and everywhere we went we saw signs and banners announcing the occasion. My name was on banners on the Roselawn fence, at the Dairy Queen, on the hockey arena, and so on. The only place that had it spelled wrongly? The Port Colborne Public Library.

In 2002 Ryan Knighton and I co-authored a book called *Cars*. Here are my last words in that book:

> So, getting back to "Main Street." I am going to mention one of the great moments of my life. Willy and I had been away to UBC and who knows where else, but now we were back in town. Willy had his little red Morris Minor convertible, and I think it was a Sunday, because we were driving down "Main Street," and there was hardly anyone there. At least half of the parking places were empty. I was sitting up on the top of the back of my seat, turning in either direction, waving to a crowd that existed in my imagination. Willy was driving without looking either right or left, under a big banner that crossed above us and existed only in our imagination. There was one person visible in the doorway of some store, some guy who was younger than we. He waved back and shouted, "Welcome home, George!"

You guessed it. Jean Baird takes delight in making my fantasies come true—especially if I have been whining about how badly my country treats me. And the great thing is, she never says a thing about it, so it always feels so much more real. I suspect, for example, that she had a hand in getting me my job as Poet Laureate, and I'm almost positive she even got me into the Order of Canada. She probably had a hand or two in my most recent honorary degree as well. But there are some things in life that are just too good to ask too many questions about.

So here we were, coming to Oliver, BC, for the first stop in our cross-continent tour. In Oliver I would visit my mother and siblings, attend the fiftieth year reunion of my high school graduating class, and perform some poet laureate business. It happens that Oliver is now, according to highway signs and polo shirts and the town's coat of arms, the "Wine Capital of Canada." It so happens that I have complained in some interview about the fact that the British poet laureate gets a butt of sack or some such amount of wine, in recognition of the ancient relationship between Bacchus and poetry.

I am not going to tell you the whole story, because the events in Oliver in early July were only very marginally about baseball (I did wear my Tacoma Rainiers cap, for example). We had our hands and names set in concrete. There was a wine garden at the old community hall, where I signed books and for the first time signed wine bottles. During a sit-down dinner at the Tinhorn Creek winery south of town, I was presented with a barrel of Cabernet Franc, which was arranged in twenty-five cardboard cases, each containing twelve bottles of that delicious and powerful vintage, with my face and part of a handwritten poem about the Okanagan on the label. Another three hundred bottles would be sold at a steep price, to create a scholarship for some Southern Okanagan Secondary School student who, like me, did not necessarily attain high grades but did show interest in writing outside the cage.

There was also an auction of various items, to supplement the scholarship. One item was having one's name appear in Mr. Bowering's next book. The high bid came from Kenn Oldfield, proprietor of Tinhorn Creek. His name appears not in this book that you are reading, but in my collection of short stories, *Standing on Richards*.

And they gave us lots of trinkets. And they gave us a fistful of free tickets for inner-tubing down the Okanagan River. Lying on your back in the moving water in July, a retired gink with a sweetheart on the next inner-tube, and on the shore a mother and family, what an afternoon, and the "freedom of the Town of Oliver" to boot. And no clear idea of where the Volvo S60 would be parked a week from this day, save that it would be near a minor league baseball stadium. You lived this long for this. You have been officially retired from playing ball for eleven months, but you are happy. Jean catches a current and zips by you on her tube, leading the way.

But all right. To the point. As if!

I was not sitting atop the seat of Willy's goofy little convertible. I was driving down the main street of Oliver, also known as Highway 97, and I had a woman laughing her head off beside me. This was a woman who had been in e-mail touch with the Town of Oliver for a few months. She was now nearly peeing herself laughing at the signs.

Welcome Home George signs. There was one unfurled over the front entrance of the town hall. There was one at the pub, one at each motel, one at an air conditioning place. My favourite was the one at Freddie Fritz's enormous fruitstand:

> Welcome Home George
> —Fresh Apricots—

As my classmates arrived in town, two by two, they must have wondered why I was being singled out. I had been, after all, the class clown, with average grades and no athletic achievements.

"Oh, if only Willy were here to see this," one of us said.

"Keep this in perspective," I warned. "Up in Penticton and down in Oroville they don't have any idea that this is happening."

I drove over to the old baseball park. A few years ago some people were there making a little film about me, I guess, and the old silverwood grandstand had swayed with every step I took on it. Now it was gone altogether. Across the open area some young men were playing slo-pitch.

Aha, the open road!

Everyone loves to play disc jockey or tour guide. For this first day out of Oliver I had long anticipated showing Jean the environs of my childhood, the ground that looked the way our decent God intended what people call landscape to look.

First, Anarchist Mountain. This involves an awesome winding climb of Highway 3, up above the town of Osoyoos, where you can park and get out of your car and say goodbye to the Okanagan Valley, the most beautiful place on Earth. Maybe it is tied for first with the Dalmatian coast. Before your eyes stretches a valley carved by a glacier before the end of the last ice age. The mountains are brown, the vineyards and orchards are green, and the rest is a blue haze in the sunshine. You look south to Oroville, Washington, and north, lake by blue lake, to Oliver. From the southwest, among the mountains alongside the Cascade Highway in Washington, come the clouds of smoke from the first of the forest fires that will ravage two provinces and two states for the rest of the summer.

When I was a little boy I thought it was Annakiss Mountain; I didn't have a clue what that could mean, some foreign or Indian name.

In Greenwood I pulled off the highway at the baseball park, to have a look at the nearby house I had lived in from grade one to grade two, and at the hillside I burned down when I was five.

At Grand Forks we stopped for a terrific Doukhabour home-made bread lunch, before heading across the line. Every August, Grand Forks is home to the greatest baseball tournament in the world, and this year they had asked me to come and be the presiding baseball poet. Wonderful. Sixty years ago I was in love with the daughter of the Grand Forks forest warden. I'll do it next year for sure, I promised.

Then across the line we went. I drove the crappy unfinished road to Spokane, where we would have stopped to watch the single-A Indians if they had been at home, and Jean drove the fine smooth highway from Spokane south to Riggins, Idaho, where we stopped overnight in an old motor court—and here we were, on our way, the last pre-baseball night of our trip, the first night that would combine my nostalgia for the U.S. highway with the new spousal partnership of my life. Fairies winked in the darkening trees at the edge of the time zone. We ate way too much food at an outdoor steak shack, across the hour, into the dark, washing the road down with a local beer called Moose Drool.

On the porch of the office cabin at the motor court there were four gents in various pants and hats sipping beer and talking about life, fishing, mainly. They would be there in the morning too, having coffee and beer as we packed our bags and books and cooler into the Volvo, turned the air conditioning up good, as they put it down here, and followed the rivers to our first game.

I'd never been in Boise before. But I was brought up in sagebrush country—July heat isn't going to bother me. In the Okanagan we do have vineyards and orchards, green river towns and canyon breezes. It gets to be well over 40 degrees, or 105 degrees, as they say down here, but in the Okanagan you step under a tree. Here there aren't really any trees, or if there are, there aren't any breezes.

Slowly we are fashioning routines, or "traditions," as Willy and I like to call them. As Jean and I have seen our relationship growing more intimate and natural, we have delighted in recognizing differences we can kid each other about, and similarities we can embrace and look out at the world through.

Boy, I will never make a romance writer.

"I like to have routines in my daily life," I ventured a couple of weeks ago. "Routines help me get things done, get books written."

Even now while I am sitting in my wheelchair, I'm wondering: where did she put that shoebox I found in the basement? I plan to keep all our game tickets and team schedules in that shoebox.

"Me too," she said. "That's how I keep any order in this incredible, complicated life I seem to have found myself in."

"I'm looking forward to our daily routines this winter. As long as they include hoohaw."

"There will be hoohaw, but I can't guarantee that it will be routine," she warned.

We did have fun learning to organize our routine for a new baseball town. Jean is a lot more organized than I am, and I always thought that

I was pretty good. In every new state she would get us to the tourist bureau to track down motels and ballparks, city maps and special attractions. Is there a stilt-walking jamboree in North Dakota? Jean will find it.

So here is what we did. City map open on one or both of our laps, we would find our way to the baseball park. Often we would ask a local about it, and as likely as not, the local wasn't, as they say, sure. Having scouted the park, we then went looking for a place to spend the night (this routine would change at the eastern end of our tour). We did not know that Riggins, Idaho, would be our first and last site of any idiosyncratic colour, our last old cabin in the wild, or last non-chain accommodation. From now on it would be Comfort Inn or Red Roof or Holiday Inn Express at some highway exit cluster, where the eateries, too, would be signalled by tall poles with billboards on the top: Arbies, Red Robin, McDonalds. Not an apostrophe in sight.

Having credit-carded our way into the EconoLodge and moved my glaucoma eyedrops from the cooler into the little refrigerator, if there was one, we would head for downtown, for the museum, for the riverside walk we did every day. Sometimes we would have to drive all day, and get to the next town in time to grab a hotdog at the park. Sometimes we would get there at midday and have time to explore the cultural life of, say, Great Falls, Montana. The routine often made me thankful. If not for the routine, I might not have known what a great art museum they have in Toledo.

But in Boise it was just too damned hot and the air was just too damned still. Boise has an integrated downtown, a big hard-surface pedestrian walk-around. There are tall buildings with air conditioning, but these are not art galleries. We decided to forget downtown and all the money we had plugged into the parking garage slot, and drove out the strip to the motel for some air-conditioned reading, but the air conditioner in our room was not working, wouldn't you know it? Management sent up a couple of South Asian guys to fix it. Ah, these guys grew up in 140 degrees. It's only 107 degrees here. They will not be all that committed.

"How about them Hawks?" I asked, to see whether I was talking to local baseball fans.

They pretended to think that I had been addressing Jean.

"Okay," I said, addressing Jean, "while this place is getting cooled down, let's get a leisurely and early dinner at that fetching place we saw across the road from Campbell Memorial Stadium."

This was the Capala Restaurant. As Fast Eddie and Paul and I had demonstrated, all baseball trips are also Mexican food journeys. The Capala was a glorified burrito place with serapes on the wall, but out back, beside the sun-flattened parking lot, was a sculpture garden, metallic *mariachis* and *vaqueros* lonely in the heat blast.

Back we drove, full of Mexican food, through the heat mirages, along the strip to our motel.

"The air conditioner is perfect now," said the woman at the attenuated front desk.

Our room was stifling.

"We'll be back after the ball game," Jean said.

It was supposed to be down to 90 U.S. degrees by midnight.

"Aha, the open franchise strip!" I said.

At Campbell Memorial Stadium the tickets for seats in the sun were $5.75 U.S., and the tickets for seats in the shade, such as it was, were $7.75. We splurged and sat in the relative shadiness high up in row YY. We could see the shadows of our heads on the infield grass. In front of us on the field were a lot of college-age men cavorting in full baseball drag and 105 U.S. degrees. You would not have been able to get me to move fast in a Speedo.

"Thank the gods, such as Kenesaw Mountain Landis, that it is not 1948, otherwise the greatest year in human history," I said, holding my beautiful new Boise Hawks cap, size 7 7/8, in a plastic bag between my feet.

"Yeah, yeah," quoth my darling. "For what reason do you utter such thanks?"

I put on my favourite bodily expression. It is a combination of beloved professor and front porch yokel savant.

"In 1948, and for years on either side of that illustrious date, baseball players wore uniforms fashioned of wool flannel. Further, their shoes were of heavy leather, and their clothing was ample, twice as much cloth as necessary. Baseball duds always accord with street fashions. Just as Humphrey Bogart wore jackets with huge lapels and slacks with many pleats and wide knees, so Joe DiMaggio wore a Yankees uniform with commodious pantlegs and shirts."

The Boise Hawks are the Chicago Cubs' entry in the ancient Northwest League, a single-A short season loop designed for university ballplayers to show their stuff for minimum baseball wages through the three months of summer. The Hawks were the reigning NWL champions. This night their opposition was the Eugene Emeralds, in for a five-game series. As you know, I like the Eugene Emeralds. I have never seen their home uniform, but as I think I may have mentioned, I like their road uniform—grey with green pinstripes. I wonder whether any other professional team in North America wears green pinstripes.

But it's a Boise hat I have. Have I told you that it is one of my traditions that when I go somewhere for a baseball game, I buy a hat as worn by the local team? I mean I buy it if it is a fitted cap (actually Jean got a great hat in Welland, the most beautiful adjustable hat I have ever seen). I am a baseball cap snob. I will not buy a fan hat. I will not wear a Yankees hat. And I will not wear one of those new hats in alternative colours. I smirk when I see a young woman from Japan wearing a red Mariners cap. Did I mention that?

I have told you of my impatience with a lot of the recent minor league logos that are contrived to go with some of the cute new names. As I said, I want to be able to make out whatever is on the front of the cap from the seats, even from a seat in row YY. I hate to admit it, but the Tampa Yankees of the Florida State League have a nice readable hat. Given the far south location, the team nickname might be questionable, though. The New Orleans Zephyrs, formerly of Denver, have that wonderful seriffed *Z*. But no one who lives baseball could abide the mess on the front of the cap worn by an innocent Williamsport Crosscutter or a blameless infielder for the Erie SeaWolves.

The Boise hat is really nice. It has a blocky ornate white *B* with a thin red outline, on black. Have you noticed how many black caps there are now? How smart is that for the climate in Boise or Yakima? But then there is fashion, eh?

Jean has that beautiful red Niagara cap with its yellow and blue star. And she has that Syracuse Sky Chiefs visor. She figures that she has enough baseball caps for any rational person. But you ought to see the collection of team pins she has now.

She is also a mascot critic. We have a photo of her fallen into the fluffy arms of some orange creature in Buffalo. In Boise the mascot is Humphrey the Hawk. I don't like alliterative mascots. Alliteration is such easy, such amateur wit. No poet would stoop to alliteration. Jean doesn't care for Humphrey, either. She doesn't like mascots with beaks.

But I had a watery U.S. beer in my hand and a smile on my face. I was sitting in a minor league park with a lot of people in shorts. We had agreed to cheer for the home team. In Everett the visiting Emeralds had managed three runs in the top of the tenth to win 5-2. Tonight they got two in the top of the ninth to win 6-4.

Fernando Valenzuela Jr. went hitless.

The attendance was announced as 2,267.

When we got back to the motel we persuaded them to move us into a room in the smoking wing, where the air conditioning roared all night, and it was actually cold when I got up for my 3 A.M. pee.

6

Books and Ball

You take a team with twenty-five assholes and I'll show you
a pennant. I'll show you the New York Yankees.

—Bill Lee

I KEEP THINKING OF THAT TRADITIONAL TRIP Fast Eddie, Paul and I and
sometimes George Stanley and even his brother Gerald take to Everett.
As you know, we go for baseball, Mexican food and books. Maybe the
Mexican food is a particular quirk of our association, but baseball and
books have always gone together. Which is kind of funny, if you think
about it: I mean, when was the last time you heard of a professional
ballplayer reading a book? Oh, they *write* them from time to time. But
can you imagine Mickey Mantle or Pudge Rodriguez reading, say, a
novel by Philip Roth?

Just about every writer I know wants to play ball, and not that
abomination brought into Canada by the U.S. refugees during the war
on Vietnam, that puky thing called slo-pitch. But how many youngsters
in single-A development leagues read fiction or history during their air-
conditioned bus trips? None of them. How many have personal music
earphones jammed into the sides of their heads? All of them.

We old fart baseball fan intellectuals know that we could never
manage to live in the same house with ignorant, self-absorbed young
baseball players accustomed to a lifetime of social success; video-game

playing, TV-watching louts who would not be able to identify Connie Mack if he came up in conversation.

So, sure, my childhood baseball heroes were Ty Cobb and Ted Williams. But I know that I could never share the former's attitudes toward African-American people or Modernist poetry, or the carrying of firearms. As for the latter? He grew up in southern California and lived out his life in Florida. I rather expect that he did not vote against Barry Goldwater, and that he did not take William Burroughs's books with him on his fishing trips to New Brunswick or Key West.

Ty Cobb told reporters that he did not read even the papers or go to the movies, because he thought they would harm his eyes enough to affect his hitting. When I was a kid I was kind of impressed by such a sacrifice made to keep a batting average as close to perfect as possible. Later I thought that maybe the Georgia Peach was not really into sacrifice. He was a southerner, playing most of his career in Detroit, which was filling up with black southerners looking for jobs in the real world. I would not have liked listening to his racial table talk, I'm pretty sure.

We baseball intellectuals do like a certain kind of ballplayer, and forever mourn the fact that he doesn't show up often enough. This guy is often unpopular with his peers, or with ownership, or the bland press. He's called a "flake," or a "nut-case." He should be differentiated from a genuine bad actor. He doesn't beat up his wife or girlfriend, he doesn't carry a pistol in the glove compartment of his car, and he doesn't refer to himself in the third person by name.

A couple of decades ago, whenever I got a pack of baseball cards for some reason, it would always contain a likeness of John Kruk in a San Diego Padres outfit. He spent three years with San Diego, and then six with the Phillies. He finished with a lifetime batting average of .300 and an OPS of .843, both outstanding numbers between 1986 and 1995.

But that is not why we liked him. We liked him because he was a big sloppy guy with his hair spilling out of his hat and his shirt spilling out of his pants. Well, that would describe some guys we didn't like, too, especially in, say, a Yankees uniform. But once in an all-star game, John Kruk faced a Randy Johnson fastball with two batting helmets on, and bailed out on every pitch.

That isn't exactly true, but a lot of it is, and John Kruk inspires that kind of writing. Ask any intellectual baseball fan whom he likes more, Rickey Henderson or John Kruk. One time a reporter from the bland press espied John Kruk strolling through the clubhouse, shirt tail out, belly out too, and a hotdog in either hand.

"What kind of diet is that for an athlete?" she inquired.

Kruk pulled up and fixed her with a serious comic stare.

"I'm not an athlete, lady," he pronounced. "I'm a ballplayer."

John Kruk makes it into the flake hall of fame. When he was playing for San Diego, he almost made it into the baseball name hall of fame, because the Padres were owned by McDonald's® czar Ray Kroc.

I hope I get around to discussing the baseball name hall of fame.

But we are on the subject of flakes, though we are supposed to be on the subject of baseball literature. I think that all baseball intellectuals (aka snobs) will agree that one of the greatest flakes of all time had to be Jimmy Piersall. Piersall was not a big power hitter, but he lasted as an outfielder in the majors from 1950 to 1967, and had a lifetime batting average of .272. In the 1950s he was good enough to play in a Red Sox outfield with Ted Williams and Dom DiMaggio.

Remember that this was the time of Dwight D. Eisenhower and Pat Boone. But it was also the time of Marlon Brando and Jack Kerouac.

I was a teenager who kept hearing the word "mature," often in an interrogative sentence. I would hear it from my mother, my girlfriend and my teachers. The notion was never all that attractive to me.

It's not that I shared my peers' appreciation of the Bowery Boys—I was too much of a snob for those fellows. But I have to say that when I was sixteen years of age, I liked Jimmy Piersall as much as I liked Ted

Williams, and of course more than I liked Joe DiMaggio. In his book about hitting, Ted Williams said that no one ever played the outfielder better than Piersall did, but that greatness comes with hitting.

Later, when he was playing for Cleveland, Piersall put on his own version of the famous Williams shift. The Williams shift, which had been invented by Cleveland player-manager Lou Boudreau, had three infielders on the right side of second base, and the outfielders shifted way over to right. This is done a lot with certain power hitters nowadays, but it was controversial and astonishing when Boudreau did it. Piersall's version was not meant to protect against the pulled ball, but to irritate Williams and play havoc with his famous concentration at the plate. As Williams got set for the pitch, centre fielder Piersall ran like hell back and forth from centre to right-centre. Williams kept stepping out. The umpire threw Piersall out of the game. Piersall's manager Joe Gordon pointed out that his centre fielder had broken no rule. The umpire then threw Joe Gordon out of the game. It was Piersall's sixth ejection of the season. The umpires were laying for him.

The baseball establishment does not like any signs of intelligence or independence. They don't like players such as Jimmy Piersall. In the 1950s they called him a commie. If a player such as Mickey Mantle gets drunk and carries some woman's panties from rooftop to rooftop, that's okay, because it doesn't happen on the ball field. On the ball field Mick does everything by the book and never says anything original to a reporter.

After a third putout of an inning, Piersall might follow Dom DiMaggio off the field, imitating DiMaggio's peculiar duck-like walk. If he happened to be sitting out a game, he would lead the fans in a chant of "We want Piersall!" Once he told Satchel Paige that he was going to lay down a bunt. Then he laid down a bunt and beat it out. This was only the beginning of the Piersall problem for Satch, who was ahead by four runs at the time. Now on every pitch, Piersall mimicked Paige's famous extravagant wind-up, and let out a squeal every time the

Browns' pitcher released the ball. Pretty soon he was doing this off second base, then off third. Completely flummoxed, the great Satchel Paige gave up six runs in the inning and lost the game.

For that kind of thing, I thought, a guy should be in the running for a Most Valuable Player Award, but the baseball establishment thought that he should be disciplined.

Late in the 1952 season Piersall suffered a complete mental breakdown, and was hospitalized over the winter. When he returned in the spring of 1953, he was greeted by dimwitted catcalls from opposition players and spectators. In his first game of the season he went six for six and made a couple of great catches. Baseball, as they say, may not have liked him, but the Red Sox fans did. He was a clown with a golden glove.

Al Hirshberg, a Boston sports writer who wrote several books about the Red Sox, wrote Piersall's autobiography, *Fear Strikes Out*. This was a shocking event in baseball—Piersall and Hirshberg bared all, opening the doors that Baseball liked to keep closed. This was typical Piersall courage, the kind of honesty that would years later get him fired as a Chicago White Sox announcer because he pointed out a few mistakes made by White Sox management.

In 1956 Tab Hunter starred as Jimmy Piersall in a TV version of *Fear Strikes Out*. In 1957 Anthony Perkins starred in a Hollywood movie with the same title. I guess that U.S. filmmakers in the fifties figured that if they picked an effeminate man to look lost on a baseball field, they were getting the next best thing to a loony headed for a crash landing. Jim Piersall, who looked better than anyone on a ball field, did not like the movie, and who can blame him? Being a clown and having a breakdown does not mean forgetting how to throw a baseball.

Luckily, the book has been reprinted by the Bison Books imprint of the University of Nebraska Press. That is a wonderful press, by the way, especially if you are interested in the Native peoples of America. Piersall's honesty about his experiences and hospitalization and recovery is more important than his antics.

But the antics were important, at least to a fan who does not believe that rebellion means getting drunk and beating up your woman. Late in his career, when he was playing for the New York Mets, his manager Casey Stengel said that Piersall had a better glove than Joe DiMaggio's. But soon after Piersall ran backward around the bases to celebrate his hundredth career home run, the Mets' upstairs boys dealt him to the Angels.

Most baseball books are not like *Fear Strikes Out*. Most of them are no better than the scads of hockey books that are plunked onto the market every fall season, something to buy as a Christmas present for some male relative who is not really into reading much.

The most famous exception is Jim Bouton's *Ball Four*, purportedly a diary of the pitcher's 1969 season with the Seattle Pilots and the Houston Astros. When it was published in 1970, Baseball got really angry. The Yankees were angry because a lot of the book was about them. Parents were angry. Baseball reporters were angry. *Ball Four*, as far as we know, holds nothing back, and refuses to play along with the usual scenario, in which true-hearted young men from Oklahoma devote themselves to the grand old game, and despite all the odds become stars at Yankee Stadium or Wrigley Field.

Bouton names names, and for the first time heroes such as Whitey Ford and Billy Martin are shown to be ordinary men who can occasionally act like assholes. Fathers who thought they were keeping America alive by playing catch with their sons stole the book out of their sleeping sons' bedrooms and never brought them back.

Yet *Ball Four* became the most famous jock-written book going. It became a best-seller and led to a new genre of tell-all accounts, from baseball players, umpires, football players, boxers and so on. Its influence would reach into the popular press and change the nature of sport writing. Today we still do have puff pieces, and TV announcers are still hired by the ball team's executives; but fans, and not just the sophisticated ones, demand realism, humour and intelligence. There must be somebody out there reading Kelly Gruber's as-told-to biography, but most copies are in the twenty-five-cent bin.

Jim Bouton was portrayed by the baseball right wing as some sort of traitor. He had opened a door that was supposed to remain shut, and he had violated the sanctity of the clubhouse. That's what they said. The public was not supposed to know that their purported heroes got drunk and climbed fire escapes looking for nookie. This was as bad as finding out that Adlai Stevenson had lied to the United Nations, that Gary Powers's plane was indeed a spy plane, that the U.S. did so have something to do with the Bay of Pigs invasion. Criminy. Maybe the Lone Ranger did not always shoot the guns out of bad guys' hands.

Bouton's teammates had been suspicious of him. Here was a guy who spoke out against the U.S. war in Vietnam, for crying out loud. Here was a guy who talked about a players' union to stand up against the peculiar practices of the owners. Yes, they should have known. The guy used to read books on the plane and the bus, and at the hotel. Books.

There has been a lot of good baseball writing in the past thirty-odd years, by people such as Roger Angell and Roger Kahn. Baseball always has attracted good writers, as no other sport has, unless you count fishing or professional boxing a sport. *Ball Four* made an enormous impact for two reasons: it really did open the clubhouse door, and it was written by a literate ballplayer rather than a wannabe. Jim Bouton has gone on to write other books and to try out careers as movie actor, inventor, sportscaster and self-help guru. He also has an interactive Internet website, on which he carries on intelligent conversations with more thoughtful baseball enthusiasts.

Here is a recent "Question of the Week" on the website: "What are your thoughts about the idea of an openly gay man playing major league baseball?"

Jim Bouton's reply: "It will happen one day, but not as soon as it should. Unlike racial segregation, homosexuality is one social issue in which baseball is behind the rest of society. The first openly gay player will need to be as talented on the field, and as mentally tough off it, as Jackie Robinson. It will most likely be an established star who comes out toward the end of his career."

So there was a parade of revealing books, some little better than the old-fashioned as-told-to, some embarrassing because they were not leavened by wit. Most were easily forgettable, and most have been forgotten. Those strange people who collect sports memorabilia may be looking for them, but most city libraries threw them out years ago, along with the picture books of the Thompson Twins.

An exception was Bill "Spaceman" Lee, a left-handed pitcher who landed in Montreal in 1979 after a productive decade in Boston. Boston is, of course, a city full of high-performance tertiary educational institutions, and the centre field bleachers at Fenway Park are, at the beginning and end of summer, asprawl with wise-aleck young men and women from Harvard and MIT and Vassar and Tufts. In the fifties these double-domed horsehide fanciers were loud and witty supporters of Jim Piersall. In the seventies they took as their hero Bill "Spaceman" Lee.

At first people thought that Lee was just another left-handed pitcher, a breed that, according to the cozy baseball legend, is supposed to be harmlessly daffy. This just after the time of Sandy Koufax, the most earnest baseball player of his era, and its most honoured lefty chucker. Well, Koufax was a Jew. He wasn't allowed to be goofy, surrounded as he was by meaty blond men from Texas.

But Lee began to alarm the baseball establishment when he imported hippy-peacenik values into the ballpark and the dressing room. While his teammates were dining on steaks and lobster, Lee ate wheatgerm and practised Yoga. He read books, which was bad enough, but he openly read Chairman Mao and Jim Bouton. He opposed the military adventures of the U.S. government, and espoused the causes of the environmentalists and vegetarians and human rights organizations.

When reporters asked him what he ate for breakfast, he maintained that he sprinkled marijuana on his pancakes.

Bowie Kuhn, the feckless Commissioner of Baseball, could not let that go by. If Bill had said that he ate baby finches or some endangered species from central Asia, Baseball would have chuckled. But Kuhn, who had tried everything within his power to have *Ball Four* censored, fined the Spaceman $250, or a few minutes' wages. Now moms across the continent had to keep an eye on their sons' breakfast dishes.

You see, these troublemakers were supposed to let baseball alone, let it be a sanctuary from the fretful real world with its wars and industrial strife and unsatisfied minorities. But Bill Lee knew what ownership and management were about. He saw venery and stupidity among the club owners and their toady Kuhn. He knew that whenever there was a conflict between baseball tradition and a chance for some more dollars, the owners would be the first to abandon any sense of heritage. Here is the way he put his radical conservatism in his funny book *The Wrong Stuff* (a joke about the official NASA spacemen and the book written about them by Tory social critic Tom Wolfe): "I hated the D.H. and all the other new wrinkles that had been introduced in an attempt to corrupt the game. I wanted to go back to natural grass, pitchers who hit, Sunday doubleheaders, day games, and the nickel beer."

The owners had just begun their atrocities, of course. Now we have them leasing out naming rights for their stadiums to pet food or personal hygiene corporations who will fork out millions of dollars to get their ugly names on the new parks, where weak U.S. beer sells for nine dollars a plastic cup, and citizens have to throw their bottles of spring water into the garbage cans on the way into, say, Comerica Park.

The planet-polluting greed merchants with their Jumbotrons are winning the war, and the walled garden in the middle of the mill town has been replaced by huge structures as money-grubbing as any Disneyland or Rock and Roll Hall of Fame, where you can drop a week's wages to look at Jimi Hendrix's trousers.

They loved Bill Lee in Boston, or at least the college kids did. When he became an Expo they loved him in Montreal, because this was the town where Jackie Robinson first became a pro outside the Negro Leagues, because this was the town where a guy bought a grandstand seat for his duck. This was the team that would be targetted for closure by a later commissioner who saw how hard it was to control the irregular.

Bill Lee is the contradiction I like, the contradiction I tried to be, the contradiction I saw in the Kosmic League. He risked his career to fight for the planet against the polluters, but he remained a true competitor. He thrice won seventeen games for the Red Sox, and once won sixteen for the Expos. After his MLB years he played ball wherever he could find some team that needed a pitcher, in the independent professional leagues or on a sandlot in backwoods Vermont.

Whenever I stop and ask myself why I am interested in following the exploits of overpaid louts in boys' outfits, I remember that the game sometimes includes people such as Bill Lee.

7

Big Sky Baseball

For five years in the minor leagues, I wore the same
underwear and still hit .250.

—Dusty Baker

FORTY YEARS AGO I HAD A FRIEND who hitchhiked to Minnesota, snuck
into the Mayo Clinic, and got to within a couple of doors of Ernest
Hemingway's room before he got rousted. A week or so later
Hemingway put the business end of a shotgun into his mouth. For
years I cursed myself for not going to have a look at the town where he
did it. All my life I have done this: I cross half a continent to visit an
author, and wind up pacing back and forth in front of his or her house;
then I turn around and go home. I am the same way when buying a
pair of pants.

So for years and years I thought about going to the Sun Valley,
Idaho highway and visiting Modernism. Ezra Pound was born in
Hailey, Idaho, and just up the road in Ketchum, Ernest Hemingway is
buried. Very peculiar. How come a faraway rifle-and-truck state that
hardly anyone ever goes to managed to coast those literary bookends?

But I always thought, nah, I'm not likely ever to be in southern
Idaho. I go across northern Idaho, quickly. I once sat for the
mountaintop forest funeral of the wonderful U.S. fiction writer
Douglas Woolf outside of Wallace, up there east of Coeur d'Alene.

Ah, but Jean and I were now somewhere in southern Idaho. It would be a simple thing to take a little side-trip to the Valley of the Sun. The drive from Boise to Idaho Falls was short enough to make it easy. Here's where I started my pacing. From Boise to Idaho Falls you can take Interstate 84, passing through Pocatello, where the terrific U.S. poet Ed Dorn used to live. Or you can go straight over on Highway 20, which intersects with Highway 75, the road to Sun Valley.

"Ah," I said, "ah, it's out of our way. We don't have to go up there and double back, no."

A half-hour, probably.

Jean knew what was happening. Patiently, she talked me into a left turn. An old peace descended on me as we drove up that valley, a verdant strip in the hot dry highlands. There didn't seem to be any real Rockies down here in the U.S., just conical bumps in the flat brown landscape.

I get a newsletter produced in Hailey, Idaho and called *The Pounder*, so I knew what the house looks like. We went to the local info place and picked up a nice brochure, which guided us to the corner of Second and Pine. The white two-storey house in which Pound was born in 1885 was locked up, but we could peer into the windows. I was happy to see that the restoration I had read about was progressing well. The flowers in the garden were flowering, and Jean probably knew what to call them, and there were no crooked boards anywhere. Too bad we hadn't been here a couple of weeks earlier, for a nice celebration and conference starring the terrific U.S. poets Robert Creeley and Lawrence Ferlinghetti, as well as the great Canadian critic Hugh Kenner.

"But really," I said, "I am so happy to be seeing this, but this is a baseball trip. Ezra Pound threw the javelin, as you might expect, and played tennis all his life. There is no connection between Ezra Pound and baseball, unless it be made through me, and I am no egocentric, as anyone knows."

She looked at me out of the corners of her Irish-Scottish eyes as she will: "When you get home, check out *The Official Encyclopedia of Baseball*," she whispered. (Which I did. In 1903, the year in which Gertrude Stein claimed to have invented the twentieth century, there was a pitcher who appeared in one game for Cleveland and one game for Brooklyn, and wound up with a lifetime record of 0-0. He was born in Paterson, New Jersey, site of the great U.S. epic poem by William Carlos Williams, lifetime buddy of Ezra Pound, the other half of their great poetic twosome. The pitcher's name? William Charles Pounds). Jean Baird is an eerie baseball companion. She can make David McFadden, travel writer and prince of coincidence, look like a piker.

By the way, there is no player named Bowering in *The Official Encyclopedia of Baseball*. There is an Albert Baird who got into forty-eight games between 1917 and 1919, and batted .251. There is a Howard Baird who played for two teams in the National League from 1915 to 1920 and batted .234. And there was a guy named Bob Baird, who pitched for Washington in 1962 and 1963, and wound up 0-4 lifetime. No all-stars in that bunch.

Okay. We went up the road a few miles, and there we were in Ketchum. It is surrounded by hills with trees on them, and probably survivalists armed with thermo-nuclear sidearms in cabins among the trees. But Ketchum is a theme park for people who like to fly in to the airport down near Hailey, and head for the hills in their Abercrombie and Fitch Hemingway outfits, looking for some willing fish or mountain sheep to pit their sportsmanlike skills against. The town is all cute candle stores and places that purvey twelve-dollar hamburgers with creative names.

We ate something healthful and light brown at a fresh-air Yuppie place, then took a walk to the graveyard. It is on a slope next to the highway on the north end of town. At the top of the slope, under some tall trees of some sort, is the Hemingway compound.

Actually, I was impressed by the grave. It is a simple slab on the ground, about two metres by one. On it is the author's name and dates.

On the other side of a tree is Mary's grave with a similar slab. Nearby is John Hemingway's marker, and one waiting for Angela Hemingway, whoever that is, probably John's young wife.

There are coins all over Hemingway's grave, and Jean would like to find out why.

Ernest Hemingway wrote a little about baseball, but really, he was a boxing guy. Edson M. Hemingway, born half a decade before Ernest, made it to the major leagues as an infielder. In 1914 he got into four games for the St. Louis Browns and had no hits. In 1917 and 1918 he appeared for the Giants and Phillies, getting into forty more games and hitting .225. During this time, Ernest Hemingway was in Europe, working on the beginning of a somewhat longer career.

It hadn't seemed all that hot in Ketchum, tucked as the town is among what pass for mountains down in the States. But it was sure hot when we got to Idaho Falls for the Padres' game against the Casper Rockies. In fact, we were told more than once that the previous day had been the hottest July 17 on record.

"Dang, we missed it!" I lamented.

"You are going for your daily fitness walk alongside the river. You can get a good look at those biddy little falls."

Jean has lived the past decade and then some in the Niagara region.

On the way to Idaho Falls we had cut through the corner of Craters of the Moon National Monument. I didn't see anything that looked like craters—but we were impressed by the miles and miles of what looked like black bubbling lava frozen still. You get the impression, in this part of the world, that the landscape is out of human hands. Anything can happen, except for high rocky mountains. Towns are plunked anywhere that a little peaceful water flows.

At McDermott Field we plopped down in section CC, from where we could look right up the right field foul line. What an odd feeling. It's kind of a makeshift stadium compared to the one in Boise. We were in the Pioneer League now, where the players were clearly kids and the 2003 team schedule was printed in one colour.

The team schedule brought us the revolting news that July 18 would bring us a "Thunder Stixx giveaway presented by U.S. Cellular, KUPI, and Fox 31/Bettis Labs Night." I really hate Thunder Stixx. These are inflatable plastic tubes which, when slapped together, make an enormous noise, especially when there are 1,844 fans in attendance, half of whom are children, who just bang away all evening instead of waiting for a great play or a home team rally. In the third inning we moved from our home plate seats to some stands back of third base because we could see that there were hardly any kids there. We sat beside a married couple who were both on their cell phones most of the game. I couldn't tell whether they were patrons of U.S. Cellular.

Yes, the park was kind of dicky, but the foul poles were at 340 and 350 feet and the fences went deeper fast. I predicted that there would be no home runs this night. Young Brendan Kaye drove one over the centre field fence. And finally, we saw a home team victory, as the hapless Padres defeated the hapless Rockies 4-1.

The mascot was Diego the Padre. I thought he was okay, though maybe just a touch boring. Jean approved of him because he didn't have a beak. He had a fake tonsure, though.

Before we started this trip, I had announced that I would be happy to let Jean handle the itinerary, as she does every other schedule in my life, as long as it included a game in which the home team was the Missoula Osprey.

It would have been easy as pie to nip over to Missoula from Spokane, but this was a baseball trip, not an efficiency test. It is a good day's driving from Idaho Falls to Missoula, and even includes some westward driving, but it is all on the Interstate, and once you are in Montana, there is no speed limit. (Well, recently they installed one, but you can really zip in this high country.)

So it was a long Saturday drive, but we would be in Missoula in time for their game against the Great Falls White Sox. There would be time to take a little five-mile detour and look at Butte, Montana. I was sad that the Butte Copper Kings were no longer in the league, because my pal George "The Commissioner" Stanley had gone to a game there, and sometimes wore his beat-up Copper Kings cap at games in Vancouver.

Butte is just plain historical. You can see its century and a half on the side of the hill. The brave sullied remains of grand buildings tell you that the mines paid for the importation of anything that civilization had for sale in the last half of the nineteenth century. The city spills down the hillside, toward the Interstate, where the EconoLodge and Burger King sit. Every second building on this hillside is boarded up, and old wooden doors with fifty coats of paint are leaning on their hinges. It would be interesting to reside here for three months, reading the history of Butte, going inside buildings and looking at figured ceilings. I wanted to find a saloon and talk slowly with the locals, but we had to head west on the I-90.

As we nosed into the picturesque western valley with Missoula hugging the Clark Fork River, I was thinking of James Lee Burke, the great hard-nosed author of crime novels that take place in Cajun country and small-town Texas. More and more, the hills of western Montana are getting into his books. As we drove around town, looking for a non-chain motel, I peered through the windshield of every SUV, looking for James Lee Burke.

Besides motels and authors, we were looking for the ballpark. We asked waitresses, young truck guys on the street, college students with backpacks—they gave wildly differing guesses. Finally, Jean saw a sports bar on the side of a deserted downtown street. It had angle parking in front, so she did her patented U-turn and angled right in.

It turned out to be just the kind of USAmerican bar I like, a rackelly-backelly conglomeration of anything that might be thought to decorate a place, accidental decor, an old wooden floor with a trace of oil on it, some advertisements so old that the colours have faded to pastel and the products don't necessarily exist anymore. This one is a shrine to University of Montana sports, chiefly football. There are sports photos everywhere, and all the young men in the photos are white USAmericans. You can eat in this place too, and the menu consists of hamburgers cooked on a grill behind the bar.

We sat at the bar and ordered a couple of late afternoon beers. I'd noticed about four guys standing around with beers in their hands, shooting some sort of afternoon breeze. The kid behind the bar had a ball cap on frontward, so I started in on my usual baseball palaver, and got around to asking him where the mysterious ballpark might be.

It turned out that there was some controversy about that, something to do with "agreements." And if I had had the sense to read the Missoula Osprey 2003 game schedule I had snaffled two copies of off the bar, I would have seen that there were "stadium directions" inside, to Missoula Civic Stadium and to Lindborg-Cregg Field, which, as it would transpire, was the place to which we would want to go.

"Hey," I tossed off, "do you ever see James Lee Burke, the great American author around here?"

"More'n likely," said the kid in the cap, and I liked him because though he was a football fan, at least he had the decency and good sense to wear his cap with the bill in front. "But this guy here? He can probly tell you all you want to know, him being a book writer himself. On top of that, he claims to know everything there is to know about baseball."

Then we got into my second reason for preferring U.S. bars to Canadian bars. In Canadian bars it's difficult or even dangerous to get into a conversation with strangers. In U.S. bars people will generally talk to anyone. So Jean and I got into it with this middle-aged guy in western clothes, a beer in his hand and a good thick moustache, curved down at the ends. This was Bryan Di Salvatore, and we were going to find out that he had written a neat baseball book entitled *A Clever Base-*

Ballist: The Life and Times of John Montgomery Ward, about the famous nineteenth-century player who tried to unionize the players long before Curt Flood was even born. It was first published in the nineties by some big New York press, and has been re-released by Johns Hopkins University Press.

It's a lot of fun, shooting the breeze and talking baseball for an hour. The first two things that Bryan told me were: (1) there is no game tonight. It was played at 1:00 this afternoon.

"You dolt!" I commented to Jean. "You cost me a ball game, you and your lallygagging."

"Bubba, you light thinker," she advised, "we drove 350 miles today. We could never have made it to a one o'clock game."

And (2): the games are just about all played way out at Lindborg-Cregg Field.

So we yukked it up and had a couple of no-nonsense hamburgers, and I drank a glass of Moose Drool. Jean was having something that came in a small glass. Then she disappeared for a few minutes while we baseball writers griped about the Red Sox and stuff. When she returned, she was carrying a copy of my peculiar little poetry book entitled *Baseball*. It is shaped like a pennant and has a green cover made of thin artificial turf. Coach House Press published it in 1967, and Coach House Books did a new edition in the spring of 2003.

Jean got me to sign the book, and I presented it to Bryan. Then, just before we up and left the bar, she told him that I was the Parliamentary Poet Laureate of Canada. As we drove out to the western reaches of Missoula, I imagined Bryan Di Salvatore wondering, "What? What?"

We wanted to find our way to the ballpark before figuring out what to do till game time tomorrow. Thus we saw a lot of western Missoula, all the while congratulating each other for the skill with which we usually find those high lights that indicate the cultural centre of any burg. Last year in Syracuse we'd found the stadium in seven minutes off the Turnpike.

At 7 P.M. there was a luminous sign outside a bank that maintained that the current temperature was 103 U.S. degrees. And those kids played a nine-inning game starting at one in the afternoon?

We drove around and around, and eventually decided to take a street that looked like the first country road, and it conveyed our Volvo there, to the least prepossessing park we had seen yet. This was Lindborg-Cregg Field, and what it is is an American Legion park. American Legion is the level you get to some time after you've become too old for Little League. I am a baseball expert, but I could never figure out all those kid and youth baseball leagues. There's Little League, of course, and those kids are around twelve, I guess. But then there's Junior Little League, and Babe Ruth League, and Connie Mack League, and American Legion, and who knows what else? Maybe a Jimmy Piersall League for kids who don't automatically swallow all the guff.

When we finally found our way to the park there was a ball game just going into the final inning. It was an actual Western AA American Legion game, a bunch of older teenagers, I guess, and apparently the Missoula Mavericks had just finished a rally that put them ahead of the Lethbridge Elks 6-5. Well, we got in free, and who wants to go a day without baseball, and we had to root for the Canadian kids, so we joined the other twenty people in the "stadium" and watched while the ninth inning passed without incident. I may have been a little loudly patriotic in a comical way, but certainly not boorish, eh?

Next day in the *Missoulian* I would read that the Mavericks' pitcher, left-hander David Williams, had punctured his eardrum two days earlier when he jumped off a bridge into the Blackfoot River. Due to equilibrium problems, he had sat out yesterday's loss against Clackamas, Oregon.

Back in our non-chain motel, we found that the roaring air conditioner couldn't handle the far side of the room, where the bed was, so we moved the bed over, and lay there watching the Dodgers game on television. Things have changed in the mountains. The last time I was in this part of the world, television images were wobbly and few. Now, as we travelled eastward I would have to adjust to time zones. In Vancouver you get eastern night games at 4 P.M. In Ontario I'll have to get used to west coast games starting at 10 P.M.

These TV ball games were part of our routine, to go along with the occasional games we got on our car radio. In Oliver my brother Roger has both kinds of TV satellite dishes, so while we were there I could get just about any game I wanted to watch on his huge screen that takes up one whole wall of his living room. And him a hockey fan—what a waste!

We had a lot of neat routines on this trip. For example, we collected licence plates. By the time we were in Missoula, we had gathered thirty-five U.S. plates and eight Canadian ones. The only western plates we had not seen were the two Dakotas.

Jean made me go on a healthy walk with her every day, no matter the temperature or my degree of whining. (As I sit in my wheelchair while writing this, I long for those days.) In Missoula's heat we strolled beside the Clark Fork River until we came to a famous carrousel. The guy who had carved the vivid horses and set up the brass ring dispenser and all that had asked for as recompense only that his magnificent contraption, a bright, colourful nineteenth-century ghost at this joining of five salmon rivers, remain here all its life. I have seen the very fine carrousel at Port Dalhousie, Ontario, but this mountain one has it all beat for one thing—speed. I have never seen merry-go-round horses go round so fast! The horses are equipped with seat belts. We saw one little kid sitting in front of his dad, just *waiting* for this to be over so he could get his little feet on the grass again. It will be years before he leans out to grab a brass ring.

I have always liked to get the local newspaper. I don't like *USA Today* any more than I like CNN or the New York Yankees. I like to check the box scores over breakfast coffee. Jean hears me curse, or laugh maniacally, and knows how the Red Sox or Dodgers are doing. As for my weekly fantasy team results? That is why one travels with a laptop, in my case my trusty (well …) Mac iBook.

In this part of the world, rodeo is prominent in the sports pages. This includes high school rodeo. Really. But Missoula is also a university town, such as it is. It is also the service town for anti-government survivalists and time-travelling hippies back in those five river valleys that converge here. That means that among the muddy sports utes you will see the odd beat Volkswagen. But even with the University of Montana in town, there are very few African-American or Asian faces to be seen. I wondered when there would be any on the wall at the Missoula Club, or whatever our bar is called. When we finally got to watch the Missoula Osprey battle the Great Falls White Sox on Photo Night, we saw that lots of those Pioneer League players were black kids, mostly Latinos. There were no black people in the stands.

Well sure, those heavily armed survivalist people don't hole up alongside some secondary road in, say, Ohio.

So here we were, trying to find a shaded seat in a home-made ballpark, among the skimpiest crowd yet, announced as 1,254, a number that begged for a question mark. Jean had our scorebook, bought at a hockey stick store in Port Colborne, and she was valiantly learning to keep score. If a batted ball bounces off the pitcher and is scooped up by the third baseman for the ground-out, I will advise entering a 1-5-3. In recent years I have seen semi-amateurs marking F9 for a simple fly-out in right field. What horseshit. If it is a fair fly, mark 9. If it is caught foul, mark F9. If the right fielder nabs a hot line drive, you can mark it L9, in case you have to cover this game for the local paper in the morning, or you're looking at the scoresheet two and a half months later. For example, on July 20, the Great Falls centre fielder Nanita hit a line drive to Missoula third baseman Murillo for the first out in the ninth inning.

Yes, it was the dickiest crowd we had seen yet, except for the American Legion game, and it soon turned out that the little section of stands that we were in was pretty nearly full of Christians as you will find them in the western United States, with cute tee-shirts and shorts, including Polly, who was the grandma of many of them. She didn't really know what was happening, but she was having fun on this outing with her family and church on this blessedly hot day. I decided to cut down on my usual satirical or negative heckling.

Good thing, too. When the PA system played "YMCA," these Christians joined right in, trying to form all the letters with their arms, high-fiving one another when it was over. I was impressed. We tend to think that these back-country ultra-Protestant outfits are totally intolerant of the New Yorkish homosexual revolution, but here were all these inclusive fundamentalist folk, frolicking to the Gay Pride anthem! I was impressed, and vowed that from now on I would expect the best of my moral right brethren.

The game went eleven innings, and once again the home team prevailed, edging the White Sox 5-4 on a hit batsman, a passed ball, and an error by the Great Falls second baseman. Class A ball can be a lot like your Labour Day picnic softball game.

The further down you go in the minor leagues, the more between-innings promotions there are. I have never seen as many as we saw at Lindborg-Cregg, and were they ever inexpensive! We will never forget the costliest one, the famous Fish Toss. After the sixth inning, out came eight little kids, draped from neck to ankle in bright yellow slickers. On their heads, bright yellow sou'wester hats. I don't know whether the contest is judged according to how far your team throws the big trout, or how often you catch it cleanly. I understand the symbolism and local colour. Missoula is at the confluence of all those rivers, and the team is called the Osprey.

Polly said, "You should have been here last Sunday. There were chunks of fish all over the place."

81

Jean didn't care for the mascot, Ollie the Osprey, of course, he being a creature with a beak. Needless to say, she had no more regard for the between-inning promotion wherein kids competed to see who could best perform the Osprey Dance.

We did get to add a name to our collection of nifty baseball names—another routine that I might tell you about one of these times. This was the Missoula shortstop. I remember his name as Jason McStoots. Jean insists that it was Jason McScoots. I wish it were.

On the way back into town along Broadway we saw a North Dakota plate.

8

Readball

> I see great things in baseball. It's our game—the American
> game.... It will take our people out-of-doors, fill them with
> oxygen, give them a larger physical stoicism. Tend to relieve
> us from being a nervous, dyspeptic set. Repair these losses,
> and be a blessing to us.
>
> —Walt Whitman

EVEN AS A KID YOU KNEW that the baseball movies were terrible. You went to them—*Pride of the Yankees*, *The Monty Stratton Story*, etc.—but in your heart you knew they were terrible. It was not just that William Bendix did not look like Babe Ruth; you knew from all the submarine movies in which Bendix was a dumb but loveable NCO that he was not big enough, not big enough for myth, as you might call it later.

If Jackie Robinson played himself in his movie, you knew he was too old. In most of the movies a team from New York would have the letters *N* and *Y side by side* on their hats. Most of those Hollywood actors couldn't even throw the ball right. Ronald Reagan played a hall of fame pitcher in one movie, and they had to shoot it in reverse because he was left-handed and the hall of famer was not. As a kid you knew that the movies stunk because they were made by fat guys with cigars who had been born in Europe and didn't know anything about baseball. A little while ago I saw *Major League III: Back to the Minors*, and it was full of stupid mistakes any ten-year-old could have caught.

But there were books. Baseball works very well on radio and it works very well in books.

Since I grew up in the Interior of British Columbia, and then got stuck in the air force and at university on the west coast, I didn't see a major league baseball game till I was thirty-one years old. I saw Europe for the first time when I was thirty. What I am talking about here is fiction. In the Interior of British Columbia I read novels about Europe and was one of the many thousands of hinterland folk who maintained the collective fiction of major league baseball.

That's what it always was, a collective fiction. Where can one see more clearly the way the bargain of fiction works? What is it that is being settled there on the field inside the building where the automobile does not intrude? How many times has a kid been nonplussed by the fact that his mother couldn't care less that his team just lost the sixth game?

When I was a kid growing up in the Interior of British Columbia there was no television, so Mel Parnell and the guys at Fenway Park were fiction to me just the way that Perry Mason and Della Street were for my father.

So a kid like that—he would read everything he could get hold of, and it was amazing what he could get hold of in that little town in the sticks. He would read every word in the papers, collect all the magazines, and still have them squirreled away a half-century later. He would read every book there was, and it was, according to the logic above, all fiction.

My Greatest Day in Baseball was as necessary to the imagination as *The Red-Headed Outfield*. The advent of television and adulthood did a lot to change the economy of the imagination. Now that I'm grown up I know the difference between an as-told-to biography and a new novel about the grand old game.

Boys' baseball novels were a specific genre in the olden days. Clare Bee and Zane Grey produced plenty of them, aiming the syntax and plot-to-characterization ratio right at the juvenile head. The most prolific of the boys' baseball novelists was the redoubtable Lester Chadwick, who wrote long lists of such books. At the bottom of the list inside the back cover it always said "(*Other Volumes in Preparation*)." He penned one series about sports heroes in college, but his greatest success was the long, long series of novels about a wondrous and decent pitcher named Baseball Joe.

"It's a heap of money," agreed Joe, "and I do hate to pass it up. But I won't accept. I'm not an actor and I know it and they know it. I'd simply be capitalizing my popularity. I'd feel like a freak in a dime museum."

Baseball Joe understood the proper relationship between the acting business and the baseball business. If you enjoy sentiments such as his, check out *Baseball Joe in the World Series*, New York, Cupples & Leon, 1917.

But there are certain writers that will, though you encounter them in your normal adolescent pursuits, introduce you to adult versions of your dreams. For me those writers were Damon Runyan and Ring Lardner. Even in my purported adulthood, whenever I wrote a letter to Al Purdy, I would say at some point, "You know me, Al."

In 1916, when he was thirty-one, Ring Lardner published his first book of fiction, an epistolary novel or story-sequence entitled *You Know Me, Al: A Busher's Letters*. It was published by Bobbs-Merrill, a company that has always been more than hospitable to writers of serious baseball fiction. *You Know Me, Al* purports to be a series of letters by a rube who rides his great baseball talents into the major leagues.

Ring Lardner, unlike Lester Chadwick, was a great American satirist. Thus it was fortuitous that as a young baseball and book fan, I should fall upon his works, because it is a sense of humour that separates the baseball fan from the football fan or the hockey fan. The football or hockey fan is the slogan-chanting fellow who throws beer on you if you are sitting in front of him. The baseball fan has time during his three hours in the fresh air (if he is fortunate enough not to live where the anti-baseball developers rule) to look around and see whether there is anything funny going on.

At Jarry Park in Montreal, during the early days of the dismal but adorable Expos, there was a guy who, without introduction, played a fiddle on the roof of the Expo dugout. In the same section there was that guy who quite often bought a grandstand seat for his duck.

I think that Ring Lardner understood that kind of person. Anyone who has not read *You Know Me, Al* should get his or her hands on it, and its sequel *Treat 'em Rough: Letters from Jack the Kaiser Killer*. This one was published in 1918, and you can tell where baseball goes in this instance—over to that other setting for fiction.

But Ring Lardner was a sports journalist. Zane Grey wrote baseball novels and westerns. Neither, then, was quite inside the doors of the house of fiction, at least as it was renovated by Henry James. When I got to the University of British Columbia and began to pose as a serious young writer in the cafeteria, I was really taking a chance every time I showed up carrying *The Gas-House Gang* instead of *The Brothers Karamazov*.

Now, of course, baseball books have become chic. Hardly a day goes by that someone, a bookseller, a woman academic, the guy in the next booth at Helen's Grill, does not press a new baseball title on me. The field is so crowded that one no longer regrets leaving some new baseball book on the rack unopened. It has been many years since I bought Lamar Herrin's *The Rio Loja Ringmaster*. The edition I got has really small print. It is apparently a very hip novel set in the Mexican Baseball League. I may get round to it one of these years, as one says about a Joyce Carol Oates novel.

Serious USAmerican writers have for a long time included some baseball scenes in their books. William Carlos Williams, in his great novel *White Mule*, has a late chapter called "Fourth of July Doubleheader," in which his small-business protagonist goes to the

Polo Grounds to think about the most important decision of his career while watching a Giants game against the Cardinals. Jack Kerouac's novels are peppered with scenes in which his narrator reads the box scores in *The Sporting News* or describes his childhood home-made baseball league game.

We all (we baseball virgins) had home-made baseball leagues when we were kids. Kerouac's worked with playing cards. Mine used a handful of dice. The best-known such game appears in Robert Coover's *The Universal Baseball Association, Inc., J. Henry Waugh, Prop.* (1968), one of the first "literary" novels to observe baseball throughout its plot. Coover is one of the most interesting experimental writers in the U.S., and his baseball book is a radical questioning of the nature of creation. The league and its happenings (including decisions on which players will die this season) all occur in the mind of Coover's central character, an aging accountant whose name, J. H. Waugh, sounds a lot like Jehova.

Philip Roth writes in the strong tradition of USAmerican satire, and hence had to join his love of baseball to his vocation, the excoriation of USAmerican venalities. The result was *The Great American Novel* (1973), a book that was trashed by the USAmerican critics, who wanted Roth to continue telling the standard stories about growing up Jewish and sensitive in New Jersey. They complained that the novel depended for a lot of its humour on bad taste. That is true, thank goodness.

They also complained that it was too long. I hear the same kind of people saying that baseball games are too long. Roth probably knew that was coming. Good writers who write about baseball do not care what the stuffed shirts who have never been to the bleachers think about their baseball books.

Roth seized upon the American (to use this word in the way it is used in the U.S. for a moment) hunger for great traditions, and he knows that the writer of the great American novel would be treated like the next man to bat .400 in the great American game. In *The Great American Novel* he takes advantage of the American readiness to identify the myths of baseball with America itself, to poke his twisted satirical blade deep into the pious rah-rah clichés of baseball. In addition he writes a ninety-page account of a ball game against a team from the loony bin, the funniest baseball story I have ever read. One gets the impression that W. P. Kinsella liked it a lot, too.

Mark Harris published a number of weepy adult novels about baseball during this time, and then there was the beginning of the current deluge of literate baseball nonfiction, by the likes of Roger Kahn and Roger Angell. All this time one of the most famous baseball novels from the high-rent district was *The Natural* (1952), by Bernard Malamud. People who do not know much about baseball but who know that I am fond of it tell me that I must like *The Natural*. Well, I did not like it when the book was new, and I still did not like it when the movie came out, though I must say that Hollywood made it look more like baseball than they used to.

Here is why I did not like it: it seems to me that Professor Malamud had a look at baseball and decided that it could use some heavy symbolism, to make a literary epic from its homely details. Everyone knows the story by now—a guy named Roy Hobbes, too old for the game he likes, makes a baseball bat out of a lightning-blasted tree, and uses it to have one grand season in the bigs. Well, I still feel as if Professor Malamud were a carpetbagger. Baseball does not need myths brought over from the dictionary of mythology just to make it fit material for literature.

That gripe over, let me tell you about a baseball novel I love. It is *The Seventh Babe* (1979) by Jerome Charyn. Charyn, usually described as "zany," has published about a novel a year over the past forty years. I love him. I love the fact that he is always trying something new—New York cops, the FDR administration, Buffalo Bill, the concentration camps for Japanese-Americans during the war, and stuff you wouldn't imagine.

The Seventh Babe has a simple premise: Babe Ragland, the seventh player to get that nickname since Ruth's appearance, is a left-handed third baseman who joins the Boston Red Sox in 1923, and starts to fill the ballpark that has been emptied after Ruth was traded to the Yankees. Ragland, a kind of updating of Lardner's rube, messes around with a woman who belongs to management, and gets blacklisted from the majors. Ragland then lies about his race and becomes a regular with the Cincinnati Colored Giants, a team that travels in a convoy of Buicks and plays in cemeteries and other such parks.

Any fan of baseball (someone with a sense of humour, remember) and reader of hip fiction will love it. Not only is Charyn a daring inventor of plot; he is also a very funny and fast stylist. If your hypothetical literate baseball fan is like me, he will go to Charyn for his baseball book and stay for his table-tennis book, for his Pinocchio book, for his Vietnam book, etc.

The opposite to Charyn's wild inventing ought to be the documentary novel. But have a look at Joel Oppenheimer's *The Wrong Season* (Bobbs-Merrill, 1973) some time. Oppenheimer listened to New Yorkers say that 1972 would be the year that the dismal New York Mets came back to conquer the National League. He decided that the resurgence would be a fine subject for a novel, so he recorded his following of the hapless louts by radio, TV, and in person.

The book is filled with poems about baseball, portraits of the author/narrator's family, wise words about the conduct of life—and mainly terrific funny/sad writing about the observed failure of one's most useless love interests. The book reminded me of Turgenev's hunting stories, though some other fan might see no such connection. I can tell you that you can derive a great deal from the book without caring to remember what the 1972 final standings looked like.

But finally, I have to say that my favourite baseball fictions are written by Fielding Dawson, a contemporary and friend of Oppenheimer. Dawson did not write Baseball Joe stories. In his books about love and art and childhood, baseball is just *there* a lot of the time. For forty years I have not gone through a day without thinking of baseball. Dawson's books are like that.

A Great Day for a Ballgame (Bobbs-Merrill, 1973) is about a writer's love affair with an editor. *The Mandalay Dream* (Bobbs-Merrill, 1971) is about a man's re-encountering of his childhood. *The Greatest Story Ever Told* (Black Sparrow, 1973) is about a boy's teenage sexuality. In each of them, as in Dawson's other books, baseball is just what and where it sensibly should be. It is not a guilty pleasure for an intellectual, and it is not a ritualized event that needs the veneer of myth to make it worthwhile.

A great day for a ball game is a great day for just about anything.

Now that baseball and baseball fiction have become chic, everyone is giving it a try. The poets have been writing about baseball indefatigably for years and years, but what the poets do is seldom chic. So there will be lots of baseball books out there. Hell, there will even be lots of *Blue Jays* books.

If you have time for just one baseball novel in your busy reading life, you might want to try George Plimpton's *The Curious Case of Sidd Finch* (Collier-Macmillan, 1986). Plimpton was for a few decades the backer of a very important poetry magazine, and it would be hard to deny his interest in sports. *Sidd Finch*, though, was his first sports novel.

In the April 1, 1985 issue of *Sports Illustrated*, as a matter of fact, there was an article about a phenom named Sidd Finch, a simple country boy who had enormous bare feet, played the French horn, studied Buddhism (hence the two *d*s in his first name), and could throw a baseball accurately at 168 miles an hour. Given that Bob Feller and Nolan Ryan were clocked at about 100 miles an hour, you would have thought that no *Sports Illustrated* readers would be sucked in. No one I knew was, of course.

But apparently Plimpton's article (it was graced with photos that never quite showed the kid's face clearly) did con the gullible. Well, baseball is a democratic game, as they keep telling us. Unlike football and basketball and horseracing, it is played by people who look a little ordinary. It has been played at the major league level by a pitcher who had only three fingers, a pitcher with a wooden leg, an outfielder with a missing arm, chainsmoking first basemen, pot-bellied pitchers and diabetic shortstops.

Yes, it has always made room for characters who are a little bizarre, who are, as they say, the stuff of fiction. No-Neck Williams, Spaceman Lee and Larvell Sugar Bear Blanks all played in the American League in the 1970s. In a number of Walter Mitty books, George Plimpton tried to make himself a character from the book world who could step into the shoes (and shoulder pads) of the "real" sports universe. With his bird, Sidd Finch, he finally got the relationship between fiction and baseball right.

In all my so-called prolixity I have written only one baseball story, though I have committed a few baseball poems along the way. I have never given in to the temptation to start a baseball novel. But I do like to slip a baseball scene or at least a baseball reference into all my fictions. When I was writing *Caprice* I thought that I would forget about baseball for once. The novel was set, after all, in the rangeland of BC around 1889. Then, while I was doing the research, I read that a baseball game in Kamloops was delayed in the fifth inning on New Year's Day that year—because of an eclipse of the sun. What could I do?

9

Saddles and Stuff

I AM in shape. Round is a shape.
        —Montana bumper sticker

THESE LITTLE CITIES IN MONTANA show us the past in a way that older cities back east cannot do. When you drive into Butte, or Helena, you see the entire history of the city at once. At the same time, nature is right there, a treeless hillside only a couple of blocks from a big stone bank with pillars.

So it is in the ballpark. These little Pioneer League ballparks are ringed by mountains, not the huge, hard, pointy and frightful mountains of the Canadian Rockies, but nice little USAmerican mountains poking up out of the cowboy plains. It's pleasant to go to a night game in July and see the mountains beyond the fence turning into silhouettes. It'll be a different setting in Ohio and New York, where the stadium is surrounded by insurance company highrises.

It's a short drive from Missoula to Helena, so we arrived mid-day, parked the Volvo in a pay lot in the "Historic Center" of town, and got out of the air conditioning into the white blast of sun on stone at Last Gulch Lane. There were very few Montanans out—I think they were holed up in their dark and coolth, like the rangeland hares. We went for a look around some quaint real estate and browsed in the severely air-conditioned shops. Not that we were going to buy anything—we were restricting our purchases mainly to baseball souvenirs. Well, except for my shoes and striped underwear.

The last two times I'd been in this part of the world were 1955 and 1956, once in a Monarch with a bunch of people I will never remember, all of them in air force greatcoats while I shivered in a jacket, and once with my RCAF roommate Fred Bing, in his Meteor. Nothing seemed familiar. In fact, I didn't remember anything around there except for the close-up photo Fred took of me in my James Dean sunglasses, zooming down a hill, bordered by unfocused trees in the Idaho panhandle, me without a driver's licence or experience.

So Jean asked a young woman in a jewelry shop, what is it with this heat?

"It's usually about 85 degrees this time of year," she said.

"Oooh, that must be very enjoyable," I said.

There's nothing wrong with talking about the weather. Even the people who deride the practice do it.

"It's been over a hundred all month, and they say it's going to stay that way."

I saw a family of round people in shorts walk by on the Gulch, big Montana ice cream cones melting on their chins.

"I bet you're glad to be working in this icy air conditioning," I suggested.

"I can't believe people ever lived without it."

"I guess it was nice and cool down in the mines," I said.

"I never thought of that," she said, keeping an eye on Jean and the jewelry case but not being obvious about it.

By game time it was only about 95 degrees, and I began to hope that the next few days would dip below a hundred. Kindrick Field was more accomplished and sedate than the yards we had seen so far. There was actually a grandstand, and that was where we sat, among sedate adults who applauded a home run or a good fielding play by the visiting

Billings Mustangs as easily as they did for the Helena Brewers. There were very few between-inning promotions, and when it came to the seventh-inning stretch we got to hear a quiet instrumental recording of "Take Me Out to the Ball Game." The grown-ups were dressed better here too, but at the beginning of the night they still placed the palms of their hands over their left nipples while the national anthem was telling us about bombs and rockets.

Maybe they were more sedate because most of them were state civil servants, Helena being the capital of Montana.

With this in mind, I told Jean that I wished they had named the state "Handbasket."

As usual, she gave me a good whack.

It was a long, slow game, a kind of capital city game. Games must be like this in Victoria and Sacramento, I figured.

There had to be two team mascots, this being Lewis and Clark country. They were, of course, Lewis the Lion and Clark the Cougar. They had inexpensive little plastic faces, and I guess that isn't so bad. But I don't think much of alliteration, as you know; it displays such lack of ambition for the imagination. Jean said that she didn't mind them, these guys, because at least they didn't have beaks. They could have been Lewis the Loon and Clark the Coot, I suppose. I suppose that they went along with the capital city sedation, I mean sedateness.

The adults were soberly dressed, as I said, with very few super-patriot tee-shirts or hats with antlers on them. But the place was full of kids, and I didn't recognize my own childhood in any of them. The little ones were running back and forth laterally, expensive junk food in their fists, completely unaware, I was sure, of the score. The teenaged girls in shorts strolled back and forth or up and down the aisles in their make-up, faces totally unexpressive, certain that there is nothing as interesting in this world as a blank-eyed teenaged girl. Very occasionally they would leave off their ambulatory positioning of breast and hip, and they would speak.

"Oh my God," they would say.

"Whatever," they would say.

How different they were from a short woman a few years older than they. This is a person whose name escaped us during the PA introductions; she was dressed in black despite the heat, and served up our entertainment as a base umpire in this night's game.

In the year 2003 we were far past the date when there should have been female umpires in the major leagues. Baseball led the U.S. when it came to matters of race. As Jim Bouton said, baseball is lagging when it comes to sexuality. Two decades ago, when the Vancouver Canadians were in the AAA Pacific Coast League, we got to see the good work of Pam Postema, a female umpire who had made it to within one jump to the majors. Postema was not quite the first female ump in professional ball, but she was the longest-lasting, working for thirteen seasons, seven in AAA, the last four as a crew chief.

The Pioneer League was true to its name in 1999, when it hired five-foot-ten-inch Ria Cortesio as the sixth ever female umpire in organized baseball. By 2001, she was in the single-A Midwest League, and a year later in the single-A Florida State League. When Roger Clemens was sent to Tampa to pitch some rehab, she umpired his ninety-two pitches against Sarasota. Clemens thought she was "great," but Yankees owner George Steinbrenner was not so sure. When told that Cortesio had once umpired Clemens's sons in Little League, Steinbrenner expostulated, "Is that right? Well, that's good. I guess she'll go back there."

"Go back where you came from" is a suggestion often heard by newcomers that bigots don't want to welcome.

In 2003 Cortesio made it to the AA Southern League, and became the first female instructor in the famous Jim Evans Academy of Professional Umpiring. She must have done all right: in all three of her single-A leagues she had been selected to umpire in the playoffs.

It was in the heady days of the 1960s liberation movements that Bernice Gera decided to see whether she could break the gender barrier in baseball—not as a player (that day may never come), but as an umpire. She had lots of amateur experience, and knew the game as well as any of those fat guys behind the plate on television. So she applied to the National Association of Baseball Leagues.

The NABL guys met and said to one another, "Oh shit! What'll we say?"

No problem. They told Ms. Gera that she was too short, too light, and, uh, too old. She had been born in 1931.

But not only was Ms. Gera a woman; she was also a USAmerican. She decided to sue. In the late sixties we were treated to the sight of the baseball establishment spending a lot of legal fees to keep a woman from calling a foul ball. In October 1969, the case made it to the New York City Human Rights Division. No deal. In March 1971 Ms. Gera sued baseball, and in January 1972, the New York Court of Appeals ruled in her favour. She was assigned to the short season single-A New York-Pennsylvania League.

She got it as bad as Jackie Robinson, and finally, she did not have Robinson's advantages. Robinson had been a football player in university and a baseball player in the Negro Leagues. She got it from managers, from beer-guzzling fans and from her fellow umpires. She did not get it much from the fresh-faced players in the NY-Penn League. They were nineteen years old and she was forty-one.

On June 24, 1972, Gera umpired the first game of a doubleheader between Auburn and Geneva. It was a wild and acrimonious game. After several disputes, and pushed beyond her limit, she ejected the Auburn manager. There was hell to pay, yelling and threats, and ungentlemanly language. Before the second game, Gera resigned, and when she was asked what had finally made her quit after all the brave years of struggle, she said she felt betrayed by the other umpires. Instead of supporting her, they let it be known that they thought she was just taking a job away from a real umpire.

People who are part of a racial minority can tell you that they have heard that one.

Bernice Gera stayed in baseball. She went to work in the public relations office for the New York Mets. Irony abounds in the great game.

The female umpire on the bases in this game between Helena and Billings? Other than Ria Cortesio, she is the only woman on the job in all the leagues handled by the NABL. Her name is Shanna Kook, and she hails from Toronto, Ontario, a province in which there is a school for female umpires.

In the seventh inning of tonight's game she gave the old heave-ho to the Billings manager for using intemperate language while arguing about a call at second base. Jean led the staid grandstand dwellers in public acclaim for Ms. Kook's decision.

And the home team won again. Helena 6, Billings 1.

Shanna Kook was umpiring behind the plate the next night in Great Falls. This made sense, one realized, because umpire crews in the Pioneer League consist of two arbiters, as they used to say. She is neat to watch, if only for her way of signalling a called strike. Every ump works on his (or her) own style, especially for a called strike three. Shanna Kook has this nifty way of turning to one side, protective shoes together, arm reaching upward, emphasizing her shortness and spunk.

It's kind of enjoyable to drive between these little mountain cities, especially when you just have to make, say, 195 kilometres. We realized that we were just below Alberta, so this ought to be cow country. And then, sure enough, as if to exaggerate and USAmericanize my thought, there was a little rise of grassy land to our left, and on the nearby horizon and the nearer slope, a herd of Texas longhorns, first I had ever seen. One of many snapshots along the road. Lots more you are not going to hear about. Such is life.

As we were nearing Great Falls, I was thinking about being young and being old, and the distances, and the woman beside me, and how she doesn't mind hearing all this, except about being old. In other words, I was thinking about my first trips to and through Great Falls and how I couldn't remember anything but names of towns and numbers of highways, and the time we went into the ditch in Minnesota and got pulled out by a guy in a Kenworth truck, using his snow chains hooked end to end. The last time I saw Great Falls was from the window of a descending and climbing DC3 on my way to and back from a week as a visiting young poet in the Ruth Stephan Poetry Center at the University of Arizona in Tucson, which you had to get to via a number of flights in 1963, right after I'd started my first teaching job for the University of Alberta at Calgary.

Now, when we came over a little rise and looked down at Great Falls, it looked just like a little Calgary, a place of small trees and buildings poking up beside a river, all at once there, surrounded by cow grass. And the odd oil well.

The falls aren't all that great, partly because the Missouri River has been uglified and exploited by some brutal outdoor industry, but then the falls at Idaho Falls weren't all that much, either. I mean, Jean and I were headed toward our home in the Niagara region, eh? So I'm wondering: what if we had gone to Twin Falls, Idaho, and there were only one left?

We arrived in Great Falls at high noon, so we had time for all our routines. First, as usual, we gathered lots of print info at the tourist center, then took a drive and located American Legion Park, overlooking the Missouri River and the brutal industry on the other side. Then we drove to the opposite corner of town and splurged, slightly, on a pretty good hotel that featured an indoor swimming pool surrounded by vending machines.

Half the people we saw were pachyderms in shorts and tee-shirts. Thinking about this, we went for our brisk walk, in the 99-degree heat, along a pathway not far from the river on the edge of downtown. As usual, there were very few locals to be seen, as they were all somewhere feeling some icy indoor air. During this walk we had to keep our heads down because the whole park and its pathways were covered with Canada goose shit. I was too hot to be patriotic, and too busy playing my favourite role of cantankerous intellectual tourist, complaining about spelling mistakes in public signs and martinet women who force you to trudge around in the burning air rather than having a strawberry sundae in an air-conditioned ice cream emporium.

But during this afternoon we got plenty of cooled air as we visited the C. M. Russell western art museum, a place whose parking lot always has a bus or two in it, one gathered. It's a pretty good museum, not too big, not too diverse. If you are a fan of western painting and sculpture, and if you do not mind the corny titles the western artists laid on their images of guys on energetic horses, you should give it a gander.

There are also displays of saddles and stuff, including a dramatic display of sidearms and handguns. The notes to these latter explain that such and such a Colt's revolver brought "civilization" to the West. I think that people in the States believe this sort of thing.

The Great Falls White Sox were playing host, as they say, to the Helena Brewers, so that was kind of neat, seeing the latter in both their uniforms. American Legion Park is only a couple of years old, so it is pretty clean, has a grandstand and so on. There was a big crowd, 2,659 people, maybe because it was Meadow Gold Night, meaning that anyone bringing a package of Meadow Gold butter or some other dairy product would get in for one dollar. I don't know whether you were supposed to bring in a full package for a food bank, or just an empty package to prove a purchase.

Shanna Kook, our Canadian hero, didn't have to eject anyone from this game, and things were nice and tight till Helena scored two runs in the top of the ninth to prevail 6-5. We were sitting in the nice new grandstand, the tickets were only five dollars for people without butter, and the teenaged girls were as bare as they could get, never resting in their parade, their hair long and straight, their zombie faces perfect. They were thirteen or fourteen and they had pretty new titties, and don't you wish you did?

There was a tiny non-smoking section back of home plate, where middle-aged women with dyed blonde hair were enjoying cigarette after cigarette. And didn't I see guys drinking beer from bottles? This was Montana, and no state capital.

A blonde woman, probably, walked by, leading a toddler, and holding a baby and a bottle of Budweiser.

I saw a young guy with Down's Syndrome and remembered that I had seen at least one Down's Syndrome person at each game we had been to. That seems to me to be yet something more to say that's positive about minor league baseball. I'm coming to realize more and more that while you may be entertained and impressed at a major league game, you have *fun* at a single-A game, and so does everybody else.

And here comes my important point about all those little kids wandering around the stadium. Baseball, especially single-A baseball, is the only sport at which those little kids can do that. You can't imagine clusters of ten-year-olds wandering around the stands at a football game or a tennis match.

Promotions? The one I remember at American Legion Park is the water balloon toss. Enough said.

The mascot? This was a creature named Willy Winder. I think the family name was meant to rime with "cinder." He was wearing a White

Sox uniform and a stiff plastic face with red polka dots. Jean said that he was the worst she'd seen yet, even though he had a big red nose, not a beak.

The last image I took away from American Legion Park was of the 50/50 winner. In case you don't know what that is, it is a deal by which you buy a ticket for a buck, and then if your number is called you share the pot with a local youth baseball outfit. The guy who won this night was a white-haired white dude who had had several bottles of Budweiser. You will remember that the crowd was pretty good, so he was clutching four hundred U.S. dollars in his other hand, and fishing out several five-dollar bills for his two grandchildren. One of these was a Latino boy in a Mark McGwire shirt. The other was a little African-American girl with huge hair. They had greenbacks sticking out of their fists.

10

Middle-aged Ball

Our fielders have to catch a lot of balls, or at least deflect
them to someone who can.

—Dan Quisenberry

BY THE TIME I GOT TO MY THIRTIES, I thought I was kind of old,
considering. I mean considering playing ball. Throughout my twenties,
in Vancouver and Calgary and London, Ontario, I was never on a ball
team. My last ball team, I guess, had been the RCAF Macdonald
Rockets, for whom I had played a little second base when I was twenty
years old. The best I can remember after that was playing a game at the
Nihilist Party of Canada annual picnic in London, Ontario in 1967.
That was when I cracked a double, but Art Pratten, wind player for the
Nihilist Spasm Band, stuck out his foot and tripped me as I was
rounding first. Fair enough. At that picnic I was disqualified from the
James Reaney jumping up and down competition for just flexing my
knees rather than actually leaving the ground of Labatt Park.

I don't know when it was, exactly, that I decided enough time had
gone by since I was too unsure of myself to try out for teams when there
was no one around who would have any reason to doubt that I had
always been a pretty good ballplayer, lanky me.

But after a little while, maybe a year after arriving in Montreal, I got involved with some guys who played shinny in the winter, which in Montreal is of pretty long duration, and softball in the summer. The shinny we performed not on a frozen street, but in a real rink, with boards and lines and goals and everything. This was on the grounds of McGill University, halfway between the monumental gate and the impressive main building, whatever that was. The rink was half-sized, about a hundred feet long. We wore winter footwear instead of skates, and whacked a shaved tennis ball instead of a puck.

I have no hockey playing in my background. In the South Okanagan we had baseball in the summer and basketball in the winter. Football was too expensive, and hockey requires ice. During phys ed at school they tossed us a soccer ball and gave us an outline of the simple rules, and we kicked that ball around on the stony ground. Once I got sent off for just standing there and letting the ball hit me softly without offering to kick at it. Only when I eventually saw some photographs of soccer in an English magazine did I know that in some places the game is played on grass.

But I listened, as a kid, to the Toronto Maple Leafs on *Hockey Night in Canada* from the CBC station in Watrous, Saskatchewan. It was exciting to hear Foster Hewitt begin the broadcast in his Ontario accent, always near the end of the first period: "Hello, hockey fans from coast to coast, and listeners in the United States and Newfoundland." I read the hockey stories in the day-old Vancouver paper, i.e. the game results from the night before last. There was a modicum of hockey in *Sport* magazine, which I started getting in the mail in 1948, the greatest year in human civilization.

So in the McGill rink I was a left-winger with my own ideas of how to make the moves. I was pretty good at laying a pass right into the crease area so that my linemates could snap it in. But though our Sunday noontime games were decided by volleyball scoring—the first team to get to twenty-one goals wins, but you have to win by two goals—I would seldom get more than zero or one goal per game. I didn't have that finishing touch around the net, that killer instinct. I was a finesse player.

I should point out that we didn't have two or three lines per team, so my getting only one goal was a pretty serious matter of dividing twenty-one by five, eh?

After our games we would jump into our cars and head to the magazine store on Greene, for the *Sunday Times* and whatever else you might read for the rest of the Sabbath day so far from baseball season. I hated this part. It was winter and it was Montreal, so you had to wear a heavy sweater over a shirt, and at least part of the time a jacket over your sweater. After all that strenuous galoshing up and down the ice, you would be really sweating, and once you got inside the magazine store or the smoked meat deli, you could feel all that sweat and that sweater in a severely overheated room. I don't know about you, but I can't stand that. I am twitching and frowning right now.

Remember my list of baseball injuries? Well, I also got a really neat one while playing shinny at McGill. My pal Hanford Woods butt-ended me up against the boards, and I came away with a separated rib or two. I took no solace in the information that Gordie Howe, a man even older than I, was suffering a separated rib or two at the same time. For a few weeks, when you have a separated rib or two, you dread the onset of a cough or a sneeze. You try not to laugh. You therefore do not read press releases from the offices of the New York Rangers or the Social Credit party.

Hanford Woods wrote a terrific novella called *The Drubbing of Nesterenko*, about going to a Black Hawks game at the Forum. I think his dad was a dean of something at McGill. Hanford was the first guy I knew who had a collection of reggae records. He brought them from Jamaica by way of Bolinas. He had crazily bushy hair and always wore sweaters with sleeves that came way down past his hands. His favourite word was "amazing." It was a lot of fun going to the Canadiens games with Hanford and friends. He was also a key player on the York Street Tigers.

York Street is a very short street on the west side of Montreal, and Bob Holcombe, one of the Tigers, actually lived on it. The rest of us were scattered about town, from the student ghetto to the Town of Mount Royal. I lived in lower Westmount, a few doors up from Sherbrooke.

I can't remember how the York Street Tigers got started, my first ball team since I'd left the air force in 1957. Oh, a decade was a long time back then. Somehow I persuaded my friends, and some of them were good ballplayers indeed, that I'd always been a dandy shortstop, and so I became the regular shortstop of the York Street Tigers, Montreal, Quebec.

We played in a two-team league, the other team being made up of young guys who worked for Domtar. I never knew then what Domtar was, only that they had big factories and chimneys, and when I looked at the outside windowsills of my apartment I could see that they were piled an inch high with grimy black dust, and I would mutter "Domtar."

It turns out that Domtar is a huge pulp and paper conglomerate, U.S. in origin, and that is always getting into trouble for dumping crap into rivers.

They're all over the place. One of their sites was on what locals called the west end of the island, near Ste. Anne-de-Bellvue. There the company had built a nice softball diamond out back of the plant, and they had supplied their workers with plenty of top-notch softball equipment. All they needed was an opposing team, and Bob Holcombe got us together for that purpose.

So not only were we half of a two-team league, but Domtar was always the home team. There was no ballpark on York Street. Every Saturday morning we would pile into my maroon Bel Air and some other car, and zoom out the Métropolitaine highway to the end of the island and play a doubleheader, starting at 11 A.M. Then, before speeding homeward on the Métropolitaine, we would go to a bar in Ste. Anne-de-Bellvue, scarf down burgers, buy a few pitchers of *Cinquante* and watch what was left of the Game of the Week on television.

Gosh, that was fun. One of the people in my car was my old University of British Columbia buddy Mike Matthews. He and his young wife Carol lived in an apartment off Westmount Park, around the corner from us. As the summer progressed, Carol Matthews and my wife Angela would spend Saturday afternoon having tea at Carol's place, while their husbands were doing battle at Ste. Anne-de-Bellvue. When I returned Mike to his domicile late on Saturday afternoon, Carol and Angela would often be kind of drunk from the tea, but if we were lucky we would find some dinner the preparation of which had occurred before the tea's effect had progressed overfar.

It was around this time that I began my practice of handing out ballplayer nicknames, something I would excel at once the Kosmic League got going in the seventies. Well, actually, I had done a little of this while covering Oliver OBCs games for the *Chronicle*.

Mike Matthews, partly because of his initials, and partly because he was a third baseman who could not catch a foul pop-up, received the sobriquet "Magic Mitt." Even today, when I visit his waterfront kitchen on Protection Island, I occasionally call him that. Mike was a senior student at Sir George Williams University and a stevedore on the Montreal docks. Sometimes there would be unavoidable breakage as containers of steaks or vodka were being loaded or unloaded, and postgame dinners *chez* Matthews would turn out to be celebratory.

I was a teacher of sorts at Sir George Williams University, a rather undistinguished institution in downtown Montreal, and so was my friend Ed Pechter, who became "Easy Ed" when he patrolled left field out at Domtar Field. Ed was a pretty decent glove and an I've-seen-better hitter, who would accompany me on my first visit to Fenway Park and to McDonald's in Boston. At McDonald's I said, "This thing looks something like a hamburger, only skinnier, but it doesn't really taste like one. It'll never catch on."

I didn't trust Ed's taste in fast food. At Parc Jarry, where we watched the early Expos plough their trade, Ed would typically down five Shopsy's hotdogs, with no condiments—a bare wiener in a bare bun. I was confused: Ed Pechter was from Flushing or some such place around New York City. He was supposed to know from things like franks. The best frank I'd ever had was right in the New York subway system.

It was fun being with Ed at Fenway. We had box seats near the Yankees dugout on the third base side. They cost us less than a beer costs at Fenway now. It was a typical Fenway game, with lots of offence. Every time the Yanks would score a run, Ed would stand up and cheer. Every time the Red Sox would score a run, as for instance when Tony Conigliero bashed one over the Green Monster, the rest of us thirty-one thousand people would stand up and cheer. The Sox prevailed 8-4.

It's funny, I can remember that score, but I don't remember all the guys on the York Street Tigers. On the wall of my basement for thirty years in Vancouver, I had a drawing of the Tigers, maybe six of us, standing the way a ball team does for a yearly roster photograph. I hope that drawing is now with my stuff in storage, or with my stuff at the National Library.

I remember Hanford Woods, of course, but I don't remember any nickname. Maybe it was too obvious. He himself did name his daughter Georgia Woods, and I saw her years later, a terrific roller skater in the student ghetto.

Young Dwight Gardiner, a poetry student who would become a lifetime friend, was there, but I didn't give him his nickname "Expressway" until the first season of the Kosmic League. My other poetry student Artie Gold would sometimes ride out to Domtar with us, but Artie didn't presume to be an athlete. He could not catch a softball if you rolled it to him across the kitchen table. But he could recite the poems of Jack Spicer, one of the great baseball fans of all time.

Clark Blaise, who also taught at Sir George Williams University, was a couple of books into his terrific fiction career. Of all the fellow writers I have known, Clark Blaise and Hugh Hood were the most fun to do trivia with, especially sports trivia, and especially in Clark's case, baseball trivia. He has a prodigious memory. But during his few appearances as a first baseman for the York Street Tigers, he proved not to be a well-tuned machine made of coordinated parts. As for Hugh Hood, You could check out Robert Kroetsch's description of him as a would-be ballplayer at a writer's retreat by reading Kroetsch's *Crow Journals*. I saw W. P. Kinsella trying to throw out the first ball at a game somewhere. These successful fiction writers who love the Great Game were really what I was afraid I might be when I was younger. It took me till the York Street Tigers to find out that given a clean slate, I could do it. I had my father's DNA. My body knew what to look like.

One of my most popular nicknames I laid on Gordon Payne, the west coast painter. He had just caught a freighter to Montreal after a couple of years of hanging out in Afghanistan and Iraq and so forth, and was going to hang out in Montreal for a while before buying the west coast painter Roy Kiyooka's car and trying to drive to Vancouver. Gordon was a pitcher who would star later in the Kosmic League, a fireballing right-hander. I gave him the name "Excruciating" Payne. It proved to be an interesting challenge when it came to supportive infield chatter.

If my diaries were not in storage in Coquitlam, BC, I might go and have a look at a few of those Domtar games. I do remember that the York Street Tigers finished second in the league both years that I was involved. We did occasionally manufacture a 1-1 split on a Saturday, and rightly celebrated it during our post-game meal at the saloon in Ste. Anne-de-Bellvue.

I also recall consuming substances *before* the game, on occasion. As an *avant-garde* poet, I felt it my duty to experiment with the available resources. In fact, I thought of applying for a Canada Council grant for supplies and materials necessary for the production of art, in this case inspired poems. Would this mean that you were required to get a receipt from the person you bought your substances from, so you'd have something to show the Canada Council? And would you be helping your cause if you established, by way of a well-reasoned and prominently published essay, the relationship between good Panama Red and poetic inspiration? Inspiration, after all, means "breathing in."

One Saturday I played shortstop for the York Street Tigers against Domtar shortly after consuming something called "speed." Robert Frost might have called it joining my avocation with my avocation. You never saw such a hyper shortstop. I was all over the field, diving for balls I had no hope of reaching, backing up the play at every position you can think of. You never heard such non-stop chatter (not that I am known for my taciturnity on the diamond at the best of times).

"Let's play three!" I was heard to shout while the Domtar boys were gathering their equipment and the Tigers were trudging towards their cars.

Then the following Saturday I decided to continue the experiment by playing the first game at least with some very efficacious hashish that had made it to the province of Quebec from some country far to the east.

Now under the hazy sun on the West Island, the ball was grounded sharply between second base and third base, while a muscular Domtarian sped toward first. As the ball skipped nicely by the Tigers' shortstop, he gently turned his head, following the course of the spheroid, and pronounced on the small event.

"Beautiful," he whispered.

He was thinking of experimenting with LSD the following week, but his teammates conjoined to persuade him otherwise. It is, they allowed, the Age of Aquarius, but we have pledged to our far-flung fans that we will win our share of games this season.

The drive home was accomplished each Saturday afternoon after group experimentation with another substance, and I am sorry to say that I habitually engaged the Métropoilitaine in my six-passenger Chevrolet while carrying an unrecommended percentage of alcohol in my bloodstream. I apologize, and urge young people today to act in a more judicious manner.

Late in the season we were proceeding eastward into the city after defeat on the diamond and at least a tie in the bar, when we saw that the corn looked big and ripe. We were talking about the cornfield at Macdonald College in Ste. Anne-de-Bellvue, an agricultural school where Irving Layton once taught poetry or economics or something. The corn was high and relatively safe behind a high wire-mesh fence. But we were young athletes. We were supposed to perform highjinx. Think how delighted our spouses would be when we burst into the apartment with an armload of fresh corn!

I guess that drunk fence-climbing is better than drunk driving. And I'll bet that climbing and picking and tossing and climbing and falling and gathering and making it to the Chevrolet was enough to sober us up some. Oh, how we beamed, we gloated all the way home, laps piled with immense, perfectly-formed ears of agricultural school corn.

I think that our spouses knew it before they even tried to cook the stuff. This corn, though fat and fully developed as an experimental farm could make it, was inedible by human beings. It was animal corn. It was for cows and pigs and Yankees fans.

"We could use it for compost in the garden," offered Carol, eager to be helpful, a little drunk.

But none of us had a garden. We were losers for the third time in one day.

Before I get off the subject of the York Street Tigers, I have to tell you, briefly, about my most heroic post-game drive. I don't recall whether we were heading for the bar, or heading home after the bar. But we had Eytan Glouberman in the back seat, between two Tigers. Eytan was not a ballplayer, but more of a mascot, I suppose.

He was an eighteen-year-old with a severe diabetes problem, I think it was. He had been booted out by his parents, or so he said, because they couldn't put up with him. He was always having seizures because he didn't keep his sugar level where it ought to be. So here he was, living with Angela and me in our long narrow apartment. Our grocery bill had quadrupled. Once in a while Eytan would have a seizure, his eyes rolled back, his tongue all over the place, his limbs thrashing, things around him breaking. I would have to jump out of the tub or up from my writing desk, and wrestle him to the dining room floor while Angela fetched a candy bar from our stash and forced it down his gullet, hoping not to have her fingers bitten off.

What worked better than candy bars were these special pills about the size of a silver dollar. Eytan had to be reminded to carry them with him. On the occasion in question, I had a box of them in the glove compartment of my Chevrolet.

So there we were, two other people in the front seat, three in the back, Eytan Glouberman in the middle, and he had not had a proper kind of Saturday, spent as it was behind Domtar and maybe at the Ste. Anne-de-Bellvue pub.

Eytan started having a seizure, right there in the back of a 1965 Chevrolet Bel Air, between two ballplayers who had never seen such a thing and were only able to try to duck his flying elbows, and I, without losing the time it would take to find a parking spot and pull over, had my greatest day in baseball.

With my left hand on the wheel and one eye on the road, I leaned over in front of Dwight and opened the glove compartment, got a huge white pill out of its box, reached into the middle of the back seat, and shoved the pill into the mouth that was going "errk, errk, errk," and kept shoving so that Eytan could not spit it out, and after a while Eytan settled into a kind of doze, and I wiped my hand on the front of my baseball shirt, and hied us home, never more than one tire off the pavement, sure-handed shortstop of the York Street nine.

11

Prairie Parks

Canada is a country whose main exports are hockey players and cold fronts. Our main imports are baseball players and acid rain.

—Pierre Elliot Trudeau

A LOT OF GOOD BALLPLAYERS CAME FROM MOOSE JAW, or so I have been told, among them Roy Kiyooka and Fast Eddie, originally yclept Michael Barnholden. So it was not a stretch to make Moose Jaw part of our baseball odyssey. It *is* a stretch from Great Falls to Moose Jaw, though. On the way we could stop for lunch in Havre, Montana. It's pronounced "Havver," as Pierre, the capital of South Dakota, is pronounced "Peer." In my memory Havre was a quaint little dusty town on the plains, a long way from anywhere, keeping alive by clinging to the truck highway, a little old unpainted town with mostly wooden sidewalks.

Now it was just off Highway 2, and what was on Highway 2 was a line of colourful places called Kentucky Fried Chicken and Burger King. We parked in the middle of the little downtown, next to a new concrete sidewalk baked white in the sun, where no one walked in the heat. We found a wonderful unexpected eating place (and I wish I could read my handwriting about it), a kind of amateur-looking café with a lot of tables lined up, people at almost all of them this noon, and a twelve-page menu you wanted to stay in town to exhaust. Go there if you are around Havre between dawn and dark.

Then we proceeded to a store where I bought some underwear the likes of which I had not seen since my father was a young first baseman, and my laundry problem was solved, except for the embarrassment.

Then we nosed the Volvo north toward Canada. In an hour we saw some deer in a field not far off the highway. Except for the odd squashed thing, it was the first wildlife we had seen since entering the western United States. In western Canada we never drive from city to city without seeing wild animals. I was reminded of the time I drove from Mexico into Arizona. In our last few hours in Mexico we had driven through clouds of butterflies. Once we entered the United States, we saw a highway that was twice as wide and beyond that a vast silent emptiness, not one butterfly in the air.

For a week now, we had been away from Canadian news and media, getting by with local U.S. papers, no CBC on the radio. Our only connection had come as a kind of shock: as we were leaving Boise, trying to negotiate the roadwork that would turn us onto the freeway east toward Idaho Falls, my cell phone rang. I had run over this cell phone with my car two days after buying it, so it was a wonder that one could use it at all, though it was impossible to explore all its fancy gimmicks. All the while trying to keep the Volvo between highway repair barriers, looking for the numbers I desired, I scrambled to find the little machine that was chirping a plain chirp, and then scrambled to find the right button to push.

It was Canada, of course. A young voice that identified itself as part of the *National Post* team asked me for my opinion of the work of Carol Shields, the U.S.-Canadian novelist, and informed me that she had died the day before. I did my best to qualify my opinion, and talked longer than I thought I was able to, till the young voice was ready to let me go.

Now as we approached the Saskatchewan border north of Malta, Montana, we were able to tune in the CBC. The first thing we heard was that the Canadian Baseball League was going to "suspend operations until next year." They would hold the all-star game in Calgary, and that would be that. I was saddened, though not surprised. Now when Jean and I arrived in the Niagara region, the Niagara Stars would not be there. We would have no home team.

The Buffalo Bisons would not do as a home team.

We crossed into Canada just below Val Marie, no place at all, and drove on a very bad skinny dangerous highway out of 1943, between fields of canola, heading toward Swift Current, where I proposed staying the night, thus giving us a nice leisurely drive to Moose Jaw the next day, registration day for the seventh annual Saskatchewan Festival of Words.

But Jean was driving, and when she saw Swift Current, she just got onto the Trans-Canada and booted it the rest of the way to Moose Jaw, 755 kilometres for the day. For the second July in a row I got to stay a few days at the famous Temple Gardens Mineral Spa Resort Hotel in the middle of Moose Jaw. The whole fourth floor is a hotsprings pool (99 degrees), and you can even swim or wade outdoors (101 degrees), where there is a hotsprings balcony, people sitting around the pool out there, sipping on healthful drinks. Last year I didn't bother, which is usually my way, but this year I had Jean Baird with me. She got us into our river-rafting outfits and plain white bathrobes, and we headed straight for the mineral springs in the middle of Canada.

If you get a chance, do it.

Especially if you have a bit of a hangover. The mineral-smelling, body-embracing hot water has no other desire than to make you well. When we went for our second visit to the waters, we encountered the cause of said hangover. Shelagh Rogers and Alison Gzowski, the CBC ladies, were there too. The night before they had added tequila carousing to our late night vodka carousing with some poets, including the soon-to-be Lieutenant-Governor of New Brunswick, M. Herménégilde Chiasson.

The organizers in Moose Jaw always put on a good writers' festival. I didn't go to as many events this year as I had last year, partly because I was not as excited by the lineup of writers, partly because I had my *inamorata* with me, and partly because I chose to watch the season-ending Canadian Baseball League all-star game on television. As it turned out, the teams were tied after ten innings, so they decided to decide it with a home-run derby such as the one held the day before the major leagues all-star game. Five hitters from either side, the western division and the eastern division, were given ten outs each. The west won 1-0. It was pitiful.

I was feeling bad for Canadian baseball. What I saw next made me feel worse.

According to the *Moose Jaw Times-Herald*, there were baseball tournaments of all sorts going on in Moose Jaw, this writers' festival weekend. There were the Intermediate "B" Women's Championships and the Intermediate "C" Men's Championships. And there was the Junior "AAA" Provincial Baseball Championships.

Well, Jean and I reasoned, this is a baseball trip, not a literature trip, so we walked kitty-corner across Moose Jaw's very nice downtown Crescent Park and found two ballparks across the street from one another. We chose Ross Wells Field, and sure enough, that was where we would witness the Junior "AAA" contest between the Moose Jaw Eagles and the sadly undisciplined Regina Rebels. The score was 12-2 Eagles. Ross Wells Field is a little primitive, but there were good loyal baseball organizers there, though not a lot of other people. Despite the arguments I have always made, I felt doubt rising in me. I began to doubt that Canadians dig baseball the way that USAmericans do. There are some, such as I, who will know more about baseball than 99 percent of the people in any Tulsa ballpark, but I am beginning to suspect that my fellow Canadians will let themselves settle for hockey. Or as my good friend Victor Coleman put it in one of his poems:

There's no precision in hockey
all the tension is in losing the puck
I have talked to people
people who find baseball boring
They deserve hockey

I'd always thought that there were a lot of stout people in Manitoba and Saskatchewan, but after being in ballparks and hotels in the U.S. for a week, I found these people at Ross Wells Field to be just plain normal in size.

That's perhaps a little surprising. I was impressed by the number of folks opting for the "special" at the lineup concession booth —chicken strips with macaroni and french fries.

The quality of the baseball was not high, but these were young amateurs, after all, and we cut them some slack. Probably they could all skate like the devil.

Sunday, July 27, we headed on a hypotenuse back toward the States, and crossed at some forlorn spot southeast of Estevan. Portal, I think it was called on the map. There wasn't any town, just a house or two for border guards to sleep in. We pulled up to the portcullis of the little old U.S. border station and waited, windows open to the quiet prairie. Eventually a young guy with the inevitable U.S. handgun on his hip came out and looked at us through his sunglasses.

"Come on," I said to Jean. "Just this once."

So we showed him our ID and answered questions, where we are from, etc. We could see him trying to understand why I had BC licence plates if we lived in Ontario, but being where he was from, he really didn't know how far apart those places, states or whatever, were. He wanted to know my occupation. Just this once, I thought.

"I'm the Parliamentary Poet Laureate of Canada," I said, pride in my voice.

"Please step out of the car," he suggested.

"You bet," was my reply.

"Can I have a look in your trunk?" he asked.

I opened the Volvo's trunk, and the first thing in sight was a little cardboard box almost filled with copies of my thin pennant-shaped green poetry book *Baseball*.

"What's that?" the guy in the sunglasses asked.

"My new poetry book," I said, with great satisfaction.

"That's a book?"

"Yep. Just came out this spring."

"Okay, have a nice trip."

We were planning to sleep overnight, a baseballless stop, in Grand Forks, but Jean was driving again, and once more she decided to hump it, and we went all the way to Fargo, 909 kilometres.

The day was good and hot, but the heat and the country were beginning to change from west to middle west. The road still hung grey in front of our grey silver car all day, but now the ground was plain flat and sometimes green. I knew that it would be a while till I saw the arid territory I loved best.

We would not get to a ball field this night, but on the long fast run to the Minnesota border we listened to the Blue Jays-Orioles game, the Oakland-Anaheim game and the Winnipeg-Fargo game on the radio. Sunday is a swell day for driving across America.

We saw a crop-duster helicopter take off right in front of us. We ran over a million grasshoppers.

In Fargo we had our Mexican meal as usual, at a place filled with Chicano families, El Mariachi in the university district. This time Jean had *pollo con crema* and I had *pollo mole*. Then we retired to our room and watched the Yankees and Red Sox at Fenway. Baseball and my darling—what a darling to hang with this baseball guy.

Every time we entered a motel, we had to pass between U.S. flags and yellow ribbons. USAmericans love their dead young soldiers.

Next morning we were looking at a nice easy 330-kilometre drive to St. Cloud, Minnesota, where we were going to see the St. Cloud River Bats. In a sense this was going to be a highlight of our tour, because Jean had fallen upon the River Bats' highly animated website last winter. We knew that we could float down the I-94 in an easy three hours.

So we had oodles of time to continue paying our respects to U.S. literary Modernism. I knew that we were in Sinclair Lewis country, and when I saw the sign for Sauk Centre, I turned off the highway. The first thing we saw was the Sinclair Lewis Interpretive Center. If I were David McFadden, poet and travel book author, I would point out the spelling—the Center is in the Centre. This is a modest modern one-storey building in a little grassy park just outside downtown.

Though I had not been reading either Ezra Pound nor Ernest Hemingway when we were in southern Idaho, it so happened that I had been reading Sinclair Lewis's *Kingsblood Royal* for the past few days. It is a devastating fictional account of small-town U.S. racism, one of Lewis's strongest criticisms of U.S. social morals.

The Sinclair Lewis Interpretive Center displays photographs of the author and the town he grew up in, as well as clothing and other artefacts to offer a sense of a time and a career. It has not been added to for a few years, and it could use a little tending to. The brochures and the words behind glass inform us that Sinclair Lewis "celebrated small town USA." There is a plaque on the lawn outside the door, offering the information that underneath it rests a time capsule placed there by the local Rotary Club.

I am not making this up. Maybe the author of *Main Street* and *Babbit* is.

We went to the sun-baked middle of Sauk Centre and ate some midwest lunch, gazing out at the facades of Main Street.

When we arrived at St. Cloud we went and unloaded our stuff at the patriotic motel. There was a pretty prairie downpour, and I started to fret, worried that we would be deprived of our ball game. Jean laughed at me.

"It's not funny," I said. "We've been looking forward to the River Bats for six months."

"I was just remembering you in Chicago two years ago."

"God, that was neat!"

"It was raining, and you were beside yourself," she said. "Do you remember what you were whimpering?"

"I am 100 percent certain that you do," I said.

"'All my life I've wanted to go to a game in the bleachers of Wrigley Field,' you sobbed."

"Yeah, well … "

Well, we had joined crowds of Chicagoans dressed in the letter *C*, walking in the rain to the El. And that afternoon in the sun, people paid a kid one dollar to spray them with a little device he had that combined fan blades with a water pump.

There in St. Cloud it turned out that the weather was just fine, and the rain lowered the temperature to a decent 90 degrees or so, and 2,145 well-behaved Minnesotans came out to watch the River Bats take on the Rochester Honkers at Dick Putz Field. Honest.

You won't find the River Bats in the 2003 *Minor League Baseball Information Guide.* They play in the Northwoods League, in towns such as Duluth and Thunder Bay. These are not professionals, not yet. They are college players with NCAA eligibility left. They may use aluminum bats in college, but here they live the life of single-A pros, swinging wooden bats and travelling from town to town in team buses.

When a player came up to bat, the PA announcer told us what university he played for. The River Bats had an outfielder named Erstad, who must be related to the Anaheim Angels's outfielder. The latter I saw at AAA in Vancouver some years ago, and as soon as I saw him swinging a bat I said that he would be a regular in the bigs. He, like Roger Maris, is a rare major leaguer from North Dakota, so this college kid has to be his brother. Our theme of players' sons will have to expand to include other relatives. There was also a ninth-place hitter named Gardenhire. Maybe he will be a manager some day.

The list of great baseball names would have to expand, too. The Honkers had an outfielder named Nate Yoyo. I'd love to see him in a lineup with Elgin Bobo and Arquimedes Pozo. Oh, and another thing you should know about names. Every ball game we went to on this trip featured at least one ballplayer with the first name Drew. Here in St. Cloud it was a late-inning relief pitcher. A decade ago the name was Jason. A decade before that it was Kevin or Craig.

Perhaps because this is an NCAA development league, and because the student-players hail from the northern rim of the middle west, there were no African-American players or Latinos. None in the stands, either. These people were mainly nice white squares who high-fived each other *à la* 1970 when their River Bats did something commendable. These stands were nearly full, and folks bought posters and hats and sponge forefingers with River Bats on them.

Jean really liked their mascot. In fact, she would later aver that she liked this one best of all. It was a guy (maybe a woman) in a bat outfit complete with huge foldable wings. He even had a batmobile, which he used to ferry young student-reliefers in from the bullpen in left field.

I bought a River Bats cap, my second cap of the trip. I was going to stop at one, as tradition called for, but what could I do? Paul and Fast Eddie have never *seen* this cap. It's black, of course, with a nifty St C pattern on it, the *C* hooked on the bottom of the *S*. You can tell that the Northwoods League is not part of "organized baseball," as those general managers and owners like to style themselves. The St. Cloud cap has that preformed bend to the visor that you see in skateboard caps, and it is not a 59Fifty cap made by New Era, which has a monopoly on Minor League Baseball. Instead, it is a Richardson Pro model, whatever that is.

So I bought that, and at last I bought a bottle of beer. Now, I am a guy whose hair looks kind of silvery in some kinds of light. But when I finally got to the front of the long lineup, I was told that I could not buy a plastic bottle of beer unless I had a certain plastic bracelet around my wrist. I had to go and get into another long lineup and wait till I got to the front of that, and show the large person there my British Columbia driver's licence, on which there is a picture of me, wherein my face looks yellow. So, braceletted, I got back into another long lineup, and when I at last got to the front of that lineup, I was informed that for my six dollars U.S. I could get a plastic bottle of Miller's High Life or Bud Light. Eschewing the Light, I asked for a Miller's, and was informed by its label that the liquid therein was 3.2 percent alcohol. I was left to wonder whether the Bud Light had any alcohol in it at all. I take it that the state of Minnesota, or the county that the River Bats hang in, is just barely allowing the devil to the ballpark or anywhere else.

But the River Bat people do enjoy a little malicious humour involving beer. They pick a player on the visiting team and announce that whenever this individual strikes out, beer is on sale at half-price for an inning.

Oh, small-town baseball is fun, especially because you get to be so close to the action, as they say. But I long for the days when there weren't any flags on the backs of the uniforms.

12

Your Government in Action

In theory, there is no difference between theory and practice.
But, in practice, there is.

—Jan L.A. van de Snepscheut

TWO DECADES AGO I wrote an essay or at least an article on the famous
Kosmic League of Vancouver. For years and years I kept it in a pile of
stuff atop one of my filing cabinets. I gathered marvelous photographs
of the costumed heroes of the Kosmic League, and kept them in a
folder with the article. I never got around to finishing this job,
publishing it in a magazine or one of my books. Tch.

Now I don't know what has become of it. I wrote it before we all had
computers, so it isn't on a disk anywhere. It might be in a file box in the
National Library. It might be hidden in my stuff in storage in
Coquitlam. It might be among the dust bunnies under the bed of some
lout who borrowed it from me to check details for his own article or
book on the Kosmic League.

Darn it, it was full of details I don't remember now, and very funny
stories I will never be able to reconstruct or invent.

So I can't even recall dates. I could always check out my diary from
the seventies, but those volumes are in Coquitlam. I could look through
the game reports in the *Georgia Straight* in the seventies, but I am
writing this in the Niagara region of Ontario, where there is no file, as
far as I know, of the *Georgia Straight*.

Don't even mention the so-called Internet. The only reference I could find there was a passage in my book of memories about Greg Curnoe. And I have that book right here:

> I remember Greg Curnoe's reading at the Western Front during the spring equinox of 1974. I wrote in my diary, I have seldom enjoyed a reading more. Enjoyed. Earlier, during the afternoon, Greg was a guest outfielder on my ball team, the Granville Grange Zephyrs. It was considered a legal hiring because the team was made up of painters and poets. Greg contributed two off-field hits, but we lost 23-18 to Flex Morgan. I got one triple and two walks. Brian Fisher the painter played catcher for the Zephyrs. He came over to the house and got into an animated conversation with Greg. Boy, I liked that! They both stayed overnight. At one point we were all in the TV room. I had two-year-old Thea on my knee. I pointed to Brian and said he's a painter. Then I pointed to Greg and said he's a painter. Then Thea pointed to me and said you're a poet.

Sometimes my life seems to be a case of good timing. I was at UBC just when all those other young writers were there—Frank Davey, Gladys Hindmarch, Fred Wah, Lionel Kearns, Jamie Reid, Daphne Marlatt, David Bromige and so on, and we started *Tish* magazine, and all this just when the Beats and the San Francisco poets were hot, and Allen Ginsberg and Robert Creeley came and visited us, and hung out at Warren Tallman's house.

In 1971, Angela and I moved to Vancouver, mainly because the windowsills at our apartment in Montreal were piled high with black powdery dust. I had a Canada Council grant, and a fifty-fifty chance of getting a job on the coast after the grant ran out. We lived in a seven-person commune in our old neighbourhood in Kitsilano, so that each person had to cook dinner one night a week. Two of the people were pregnant.

These were, as they used to say, heady times. The sixties were still on, really, the prime minister wore a cape and a high hat, there was marijuana growing in the flowerbeds at Rideau Hall, and here in Vancouver straight guys were kissing gay guys while they set to getting the USAmericans out of Vietnam. We really thought that civilization had turned a corner. We had no notion that Nike and Wal-Mart were coming.

We were not Liberals, of course, but we were proud to have a prime minister who was disliked by Richard Nixon. Pierre Trudeau wanted to spend money on the lives of ordinary people rather than on the portfolios of financial hackers. His government picked up on Lester Pearson's idea for Centenary grants to local communities, and formed two programs that sought to improve domestic neighbourhoods the way that CUSO (Canadian University Services Overseas) had been trying for ten years to do in African- and Latin-American villages. These programs were OFY (Opportunities for Youth) and LIP (Local Initiatives Programs).

I was not involved in wangling funds. Some genius artists, used to filling out grant applications, got us a lot of softball equipment and playing time on diamonds around the city and its suburbs. I guess it must have been an LIP grant they got, because if it had been an OFY grant, there would have had to be a lot of looseness in the definition. I, for example, perhaps one of the older players in the league, was thirty-five, though only three years into my renewed playing career. It must have been an LIP grant. That, I thought, was wonderful—some civil servants in Ottawa thought that a bunch of softball players were contributing as much to the local and national culture as any childcare builders or folk-music facilitators.

I believe that the key we held was that we were going to save softball and maybe even baseball from the organized and the serious. As part of that campaign, we organized a Junior Kosmic League to rescue the kids from Little League.

The idea that brought us our federal funding was probably the theatrical nature of the league. Sure, we were ballplayers, but we were also artists and musicians, writers and actors. And loonies—one of the least successful teams was the Napoleons, who represented the Mental Patients Association, an activist group interested in liberating mental patients from the impersonal rules of the civil service, and other people from their stereotypes about mental patients. Their uniform consisted of a baseball shirt complete with an image of a hand tucked inside at waist level. Wonderful.

Two of the least subtle teams were the Afghani Oil Kings and the Flying Dildos. I think that they might have been in the rock 'n roll business, or some such lower echelon of the arts. One of them had a catcher who was always wrapped like an Egyptian mummy. Sometimes the Dildos would dress as dirty old men, in nothing but overcoats, sneakers and baseball gloves. They had a habit of picking on one member of their own team and chasing him to the far end of the field, overcoats held open.

Gill Collins played catcher on an all-female team called Nine Easy Pieces. They, too, had a habit of swarming a victim. In their case, this would be the youngest and cutest lad on the opposing side. If this (un)fortunate should happen to reach base, the nine baseballistas would descend upon him, shrieking like a combination of harpies and Beatles fans. Sometimes the game would be suspended, to be completed as part of a doubleheader the next time these teams met.

There was a team called Flex Morgan and the Mock Heroics, and another, mainly TV people, named the Teen Angels. When the league expanded late in its first season, there was a team in Burnaby called the East End Punks. I gave them their nickname, free of charge.

My team was the Granville Grange Zephyrs, a bunch of poets and painters from the west side. The name came from an artists' studio tucked under the Granville Street Bridge and next to the newly developed Granville Island market. This was the workplace, principally, of two fibreglass sculptors, Dallas Selman, a ne'er-do-well who later went into canoes and disappeared to Taiwan, and Glen Toppings, our first baseman and eldest player. He had a long red beard and an ancient ball cap that was way too small. I was amazed that this guy could still be playing ball on his fortieth birthday, little knowing that I would retire from the game at sixty-six.

Glen died during our second season, a victim of fibreglass dust. Unlike other sculptors, such as Roy Kiyooka, Glen had refused to wear a protective mask. At his funeral we filed by his open casket. He was the first dead person I had ever looked at.

Our catcher, and weakest hitter, was Brian Fisher, the painter of geometrical forms, whose exact mathematics led to nearly mystical advantages. Like Glen Toppings, Roy Kiyooka and Claude Breeze, he had come to Vancouver from Saskatchewan. He told me years later that he had got himself a catcher's mitt (in softball, you generally use a baseball first baseman's mitt behind the plate) because he figured that that was the only way he would make the team, volunteering for the position that offered the hardest work and least comfort. After about three weeks of the first season I got into a conversation with the young man I had dubbed "Cat."

"I wonder how many Brian Fishers there are," I said.

"What do you mean, Whip?"

That was the nom-de-baseball that I had perhaps assigned to myself, in derisive recognition of my throwing arm.

"Well, there's the famous painter Brian Fisher."

"He's me," said Cat.

Not knowing that my playmates were all famous—that was a lovely thing about playing ball, about gearing up in your non-poet, non-professor clothes, and leaping around in the dust or the mud.

You should have seen the mud at Capilano Stadium during the tournament that ended the 1971 season. Cap Stadium had been home to the AAA Vancouver Mounties when I was a university student forgoing history assignments in order to watch the San Diego Padres of the Pacific Coast League. The Zephyrs played well, and a little over our heads, in that tournament, to get into the final against the Teen Angels. I will never forget that I swatted a triple in the ninth inning of the semi-final to edge our friends the Punks—or something like that.

As the tournament went on for three days in the October rain, the mud of Capilano Stadium got deeper and deeper. In his grey sweat suit, Cat Fisher was caked with the mire he was squatting in. Our ace pitcher was artist Dennis Vance, whom I had rechristened "Dazzy," after the great Dodger pitcher (197-140, 3.24) from before my time. I think people still call him "Daz." During infield chatter he might be addressed as "Dogbreath," all in fun. He was famous for his socks. No one knew where he got them. They came up and over his knees, and were patterned with wide horizontal stripes, sometimes red and yellow, sometimes blue and orange. Opposing batsmen often appealed to the umpire, maintaining that such socks were illegal. Daz would then deck the complainer with the next pitch.

As I mentioned, our first baseman was ancient Glen Toppings, a middle-aged man with a long scraggly red beard and no shirt over his depressingly bony chest. Second base was handled for the tourney by Gerry Nairn, a radio announcer with a voice deeper than the mud in the Cap Stadium infield. He was permitted to play with us because he was a close blood relative of Gary Lee Nova, the incomprehensible painter and our left fielder. Third base was the purview of Lionel Kearns, the hockey player, saxophone player and poet. Lionel usually played in a hideous tie-dye shirt, the last one ever seen on the west coast. Lionel likes to do things impulsively, so our right fielder, for example, would have to be alert for a throw from third base, something never seen in organized baseball. He'd never seen, he complained, a play that went 5-9-3. Never would, either.

Having persuaded my mates that I'd been second-place all-star shortstop in Montreal, I won that position with the Zeds, as we called ourselves because the Oakland Athletics are styled the A's. Somehow or other I had acquired a reputation for very fast hands because my throw to first was, while accurate, and oftentimes pretty, a little rainbowish or soft. It was for this reason that my nom-de-diamond was "The Whip," or "Mr. Whip," or simply "Whip."

Our left fielder was the aforementioned Gary Lee Nova, or his substitute Lanny Beckman, who would later become a free agent and found the Napoleons. Nova had a strong arm, as did our other two outfielders. Centre was patrolled by Expressway Gardiner, who had served the York Street Tigers with distinction. (Excruciating Payne would also join the Zeds in the following year.) In right field we had poet Brad Robinson, who invented his own nickname, Engledink Birdhumper, which cognomen won the official *Georgia Straight* Kosmic League Stupid Name Contest for 1971.

If you look at our team photograph taken just before the championship game at Cap Stadium, you will see that most of us are wearing our team stickers. They were black on white, the word *ZED* in bold. I'm wearing mine on my famous old sweat-stained railroad engineer's cap, along with my Bobby Wine button.

In that championship game the Teen Angels beat us, kind of. I don't remember the score, but it doesn't matter. For one thing, it was thrilling to play on the field on which I had seen Brooks Robinson and George Bamberger disport themselves. Besides, as soon as the game was completed, our friends from other teams, especially the East End Punks, took a vote in the stands and declared that we, the Granville Grange Zephyrs, were the 1971 champions of the Kosmic League. The Teen Angels, they said, were not truly Kosmic. Their wives and girlfriends sat in the stands, wearing makeup, hairdos and heels. Their fellas played like jocks or Pentecostal picnickers, and showed displeasure when Dazzy rolled the ball in, or when we infielders went into our expectant crouches, but were facing the outfield.

Luckily, or unluckily, as it might be seen, there is a passage from one of Erich Blackhead's reports of a Kosmic League game in Roy Miki's annotated bibliography of my works, *A Record of Writing*. This from the *Georgia Straight*, 6–10 July 1971, a piece entitled "Zephyrs Gust into First Place":

> The Granville Grange Zephyrs took over full possession of first place in the Kosmik Softball League Sunday evening, with a convincing 20-10 defeat of a hard-dying Moose Valley Farms nine.... Another highlight of the game was the rookie umpire, Ronnie [She would later, as "Miss Ronnie," lead the women's team I defected to in the short-lived Kosmic Basketball League. She was a point guard who wore a coiled whip at her side. She once dislocated my thumb with a hard and unexpected pass]. She brought unaccustomed dazzle to the area behind the plate, and withstood the rude verbal attacks of the less civilized Zephyr players. Her only bad moment came when she was booed by women's lib members in the crowd for sweeping off home plate.
>
> ZEPHYRS   120 323 630 — 20 16 5
> FARMERS   110 035 000 — 10 11 9
>
> THREE STARS, as picked by the editors of Beaver Kosmos [my very minor publishing house]. (1) G. Bowering, whose four hits, including a titanic triple, and many runs batted in, led his team thru rally after rally. He also set a record for shortstops by catching three popups in one inning, pounding his mitt before each [a Zeds rule]. His only lapse was when he committed his first error of the season, letting a weak grounder by little Phyllis

skip by him with two out and the bases loaded in the big Farmer
sixth inning....

I feel that it is only fair to admit that "Erich Blackhead" was my pen
name, chosen to resemble that of Eric Whitehead, sports columnist of
the *Vancouver Province*. Well, while I am at it, I might as well mention
that Erich Blackhead was the final arbitrator of the all-star selections.
Whip Bowering made the all-star team for several years, despite some
stellar competition.

A few more of Erich Blackhead's headlines, just so that you'll get
a taste of his metaphorical weakness: "Zephyrs Storm Back to Rout
Rats", "Late Chinook Melts Punks—Zephyrs Hobble to Surprise
Victory."

Another artefact from the Kosmic League is reproduced in Miki's
award-winning book. There is a photo of my 1972 contract with the
Zephyrs. The original is of course among my papers at the National
Library of Canada. It was an impressive document, with fancy
scrollwork and a big red seal. It tells us with all the legal-looking
design and Gothic type possible that:

> It is hereby certified that George Mr. Whip Bowering, on July 9,
> 1972, has entered into an exclusive arrangement with THE
> GRANVILLE GRANGE ZEPHYRS in return for the sum of
> $70,000.00. This agreement gives sole playing rights of the above
> mentioned player to THE ZEPHYRS unless waived by either the
> general manager or the unanimous consent of the team.
>
> The above player will receive in the way of added bonuses
> $2,000.00 if his batting average is over .400 at the end of the
> playing season, $600.00 if his H.Q. is maintained and a
> Governor General's Award if he wins the Miss Kosmic League
> contest.

The contract is signed by Michael Quigley, G.M. and "Mr. Whip." It is officially dated and further signed by Engledink Birdhumper, O.K.L.K. and Killer Kelly Kiley, O.K.L.V.K.

You have to remember that $70,000.00 was a pretty good salary in 1972.

Each of the Kosmic teams was famous, in Vancouver and area alternative sporting circles, for a trademark comestible or beverage taken some time during any contest. Well, in some cases this happened *all through* said contest. Some squads went for the obvious choice, given the place and era. This choice, to speak of positives here, resulted in quite a lot of sharing, so that a baserunner might stop at first base, even though he seemed to have clouted a ball good enough for an inside-the-park home run; this because the first baseman was the only opponent who was, at the moment, toking.

Who can remember what we all ingested in those storied Local Initiatives days? I do recall the choice of the East End Punks. You used to be able to get a marvelously authentic-tasting hard cider that came from England in little actual crock bottles. Nicely eccentric. There was something bizarre and sixties-ish about Alban Goulden, a young fiction writer from Lethbridge, straight hair hanging behind him to his waist, tipping English cider on the playing fields of Burnaby.

As to the famed Granville Grange Zephyrs, the oldest and most respectable club in the league? In the fifth inning of every game we sent someone who was not expected to hit for a while to the nearest corner store for our signature popsicles. Other teams derided us at first, but as painters and poets we were used to that, and soon our popsicles became a legend that would endure as long as ball fans would trade stories of the Zeds and their romantic exploits on the diamond of Daisy Beanblossom Stadium (at Fifth and Collingwood), for example.

Boy, I loved being an all-star in the Kosmic League! I loved the real ballplaying, and I loved the theatre. We used to tailor our game to the ability of our opponent (though, in the spirit of the times, and emulating China's sports organizations, we never spoke of them as opponents). If we were playing a goof-off team with no real shot at the pennant, we would go heavy on the antics. We would invoke the Automatic Strike Rule (on a 3-0 pitch the next offering, no matter its trajectory, would be a called strike). We would pull off the famous Zephyrs double steal, in which the runner on first would steal second, and the runner on second would steal first. If we got the bases loaded the third base coach would signal the triple steal, in which all the runners would slide into the pitcher's rubber, sometimes joined by the batter. There were a lot of freelance plays and interpretations of plays.

The annual January 1 All-Star Game was a hoot, because the weather was always Kosmic. Most years there was a rain that came down at a forty-five-degree angle, but there was also a big fire made of railroad ties, and a tub of mulled wine. These went well with New Year's hangovers and sleep deprivation. The very first New Year's game was played after a snow fall. Someone used an orange spray paint bomb to draw the basepaths, and of course this route involved a big loop on the way to first. It was observed by all aspirants, I am glad to say.

During our second New Year's game I had the luck and skill to start a slick inning-ending 6-4-3 double play, but as I walked gently toward our mulled wine, the idiot first baseman, who was filling the spot left by the late Glen Toppings, was apparently unaware that the inning was over and fired a ball that hit me in the temple. I walked a few steps and then apparently toppled into the mud. As I told you in chapter one, I woke up on a gurney in the hallway of the emergency area of Vancouver General Hospital. Not a pretty sight in my *outré* baseball outfit, though I do not recall having any dog doo on my shoes. It should have been embarrassing, but there was too much pride involved.

But there were also lots of occasions when we would drop most of the shenanigans and go for the fun to be had when two pretty good teams were playing for the win. My favourite memory of this kind of game is about a few seconds of defensive fastball. I do not even remember whom we were playing, though I do remember that it occurred at Cricket Chatter Park, our home field. And I do remember that they had runners on first and third and nobody out. The hitter sent a one-hopper to short. I snaffled it, faked the runner back to third, and threw to second. While Engledink, who was subbing at second, relayed it to first, the poor sap on third broke for the plate. Stretch Toppings threw a low strike to Cat Fisher, and the guy slid into the tag.

It was the first triple play in the history of the Kosmic League, and the only one I have ever been involved in. In my last year in the Twilight League, in 2002, I saw a batted ball that could have been converted into an unassisted triple play, but our shortstop chose routine over immortality and flipped the ball to first after snagging a liner and running across second base.

There were certain exhibition games during which we would play the game pretty straight. These were the tilts we contested in the BC Penitentiary and at Oakalla Prison. At the Pen, which would have had a fine view of the Fraser River at New Westminster if the wall were just not so high, we played as well as we could, and got beaten by a respectable score. You have to figure that guys who get arrested for serious crimes are likely to be unbashful ballplayers. They all had tattoos and we didn't because this was in the early seventies.

It must have been 1973, because I was experimenting with what I thought might be a late-career move to first base. I had sunk half a C-note into the purchase of a trapper, but I hadn't got the stiffness out of it. The first baseman for the home team let me use his limp old trapper, and I was really careful with it.

But not as careful as Hans Fenger. Hans was a young, thin, sweet, innocent guitar-playing fellow with white skin, long hair and fine features. (In later years he got famous for teaching pop songs to elementary school choirs and cutting a record that went high on the charts.) He was also playing centre field for us. It happened that centre field in the BC Pen was next to the area where big muscular cons with long hair or bald heads and huge amateur tattoos collected to lift weights. We were a little afraid for Hans, as in what would happen if one of their sluggers lofted a fly ball over his head and in among the body builders? They were definitely not the Kosmic sort.

The Pen was where you went if your sentence was two years and up, like for example, life. Oakalla was the place for people who got two years less a day or under. Once, years earlier, I had accompanied my girlfriend Joan to Oakalla because she was taking theatre at UBC and was involved with a play being put on by the Oakalla Players. The officials were not keen on having young men play the female roles. What a strange visit that was! The father of one of my high school pals was there for a little embezzlement. He had also been involved in theatre in my hometown Oliver, and was now lending his expertise and English accent to this theatre behind bars.

A dozen years later I was back there with the Granville Grange Zephyrs, playing a road game against the Oakalla nine. These guys were younger than the Pen squad, and certainly younger than we. Their home field, where they played all their games, was not behind a wall but out in the Burnaby wilderness. There was a little rise beyond left field and a little rise beyond right field. On the horizon made by either rise stood uniformed non-players in possession of rifles and shotguns.

In the Pen and at Oakalla we did not have our usual fifth-inning popsicles.

Not far from Oakalla was the home park of the East End Punks. A diamond surrounded on three sides by forest was the jewel of Burnaby's Sperling Park, which, ominously, you will not find on the map. Beyond left field is Sperling Street, a major artery. Beyond right field are the woods. They are so close that anyone can be forgiven for swinging for the trees. Here was the site of my greatest moment as a Kosmic League batsman. Out of modesty, I was going to skip this story, but Jean insisted that I include it.

It is also very fondly remembered and often described by some of my best friends. Brian Fawcett was catching for the Punks that day. Paul Naylor was patrolling centre field, shading me toward right because he knew what sort of right-handed hitter I was. And Fast Eddie, then a young fireball specialist with a ridiculously long beard, was pitching against me.

I was our number two hitter, so in the top of the first I came up with one out and nobody on. Now, normally I am a canny artist with the Louisville Slugger, the kind of guy who lines sharp singles into whatever holes are left unattended by your infielders or outfielders. But there was no one on base, and those trees were so close. I wanted to see whether I could smack one to the opposite field and send Popcorn scampering among the cedars.

Fast Eddie appeared to be pitching me more carefully than was his wont. I was waiting for my favourite pitch, a fastball on the outside corner, but Fast Eddie kept just missing. I worked the count to 3-0. Fawcett went out to talk to his chucker. I took the next pitch, a delivery that was so high that Fawcett had to stand up to catch it. With the Automatic Strike Rule, I had Fast Eddie 3-1, a hitter's count. I could see Paul out there, pounding his glove and alternating his weight on his bent legs.

Then I got a change-up, thigh-high, out over the plate, toward the outside corner, nothing on it. I kept my head in and my weight back. I watched this poor fated pitch all the way from Mike's hand to the sweet spot on my bat. I stepped and distributed my weight perfectly, opened up my hips, and swung like a right-handed Ted Williams. I made perfect contact. I got all of it on the fat part of my aluminum weapon. It was the absolutely ideal moment at the plate that I had always desired.

There was an explosion that sent debris to all parts of the infield and the near outfield. I thought I must have actually knocked the cover off the ball.

Fast Eddie had served me not a Spalding but a painted grapefruit the exact size of a softball. I had hit it exactly the way they wanted me to, on the nose. A perfect grapefruit home run.

I was disappointed and yet thrilled as could be. I went into my Kosmic home run trot while seventeen ballplayers laughed and laughed.

13

Eastward Ho!

> If a woman has to choose between catching a fly ball and
> saving an infant's life, she will choose to save the infant's life
> without even considering if there is a man on base.
> —Dave Barry

WE GOT UP EARLY IN ST. CLOUD, because we had to drive eight hundred kilometres to Schaumburg, not knowing that once there we would drive great distances back and forth in Chicago's northwest suburbs.

We continued our hypotenusiastic driving, zooming southeast on I-94. Missing the bypass, we drove right through the middle of Minneapolis, but all we saw were the top halves of that city's various skyscrapers, because the highway was in a little canyon that snaked through town. Too bad, because though I have been there only once, for a few days ten years ago, Minneapolis strikes me as one of the most attractive cities in the U.S. You know what it has? It has a post office on wheels that goes around the city core, so that people and businesses can do their mailing right outside their front doors. It also has, of course, the Guthrie Theater and the Walker Art Center.

But the Twins were out of town, and we were bent on seeing the Schaumburg Flyers of the Midwest League. We zipped past a lot of places that I remembered reading about when I was a kid interested in baseball and otherwise in the world: Eau Claire, La Crosse, Madison—

two of my friends went from UBC to Madison, so I kept my eyes peeled, but from the I-94 all you can see is prairie, or whatever they call it down here.

On the radio half the stations were going on about that peculiar U.S. version of Christianity, involving rapture and miracle healing and patriotism. One guy, who was apparently able to hook up to a vast network of stations, explained that Communism desires to impose private bankers around the world. I thought that I was hearing his Texas accent wrong, but he repeated this news often. He was probably talking in code language about Jewish people and the United Nations.

One thing you often hear Canadians say in the U.S.: they really miss the CBC.

Okay, so it was a long day's drive, and then we were in the suburbs. These burbs looked pretty posh, made as they were of golf courses and architectured malls. Our normal procedure was to scout the ballpark, right? Make sure we know how to get there, then go and dump our stuff at a motel. Okay, so we finally found Alexian Field, a new stadium on its own little hill rising from a huge suburban parking lot. Then we had to drive forever to find the motels, off the freeway in a suburb farther north and west, a place called Hoffman Estates. The USAmericans have finally done it—created a legal community with a name invented by some developer, a name somehow both Jewish and boring. It is at times such as this that you wish that there were a neat ball team in Prairie du Chien, Wisconsin.

Okay, so we plunked our stuff in the Quinte Hotel in Hoffman Estates, Illinois, hauled in the cooler we bought in Oliver, put my glaucoma medicine on ice, plugged the laptop computer in, and headed back along the sidewalkless streets to Schaumburg, Illinois. The room at the Quinte was exactly like our earlier rooms at the Best Western, the Travelodge and the Comfort Inn. Even the remote control for the TV was identical to all the remote controls I had thumbed, looking for ESPN.

The lobby and the front door were festooned with U.S. flags. We never saw a UN flag anywhere. The USAmericans put their flag on everything. They wear stars-and-stripes hats and shirts and shorts and sunglasses. On the way to Schaumburg, Illinois, we had seen a road-paving machine with a U.S. flag on it.

Jean tried to use my phone card to make my computer pick up her e-mail. She is always doing things I don't begin to understand. But this one did not work. After a while we said to hell with it—let's go to the ballpark early.

It was a good thing that we did, because they started early. Apparently the Schaumburg Flyers and the Joliet Jackhammers (check their website for sound effects) had to finish a game that had been suspended in Joliet, so we got the finish as a bonus, and the scoreboard was upside down, of course, and the Flyers won. There was some applause.

Yes, during both games there was some applause. There are a lot of black people in Chicago, and lots of wonderful food often associated with the black people of the United States, but these northwest suburbs are very white. They look as if there is a lot of money in places such as Hoffman Estates and Schaumburg, and the white people have it. There were 5,749 people at Alexian Field, 5,740 of whom were white. They were wearing USAmerican leisure outfits, and hardly any of them were wearing Schaumburg Flyers stuff. They were pretty quiet, and many of them were holding cell phones against the sides of their heads.

Alexian Field is nice, in a stylish way. It is one of the new retro stadiums one sees more and more the farther east one goes, and it has an old-time hand-operated scoreboard. We splurged on reserved seats, but they were crummy, and after a while we moved to seats that had been vacated behind the plate. Wherever we went, however, the aisles were filled with flowing zomboid teenagers. There are no baseball fans in Schaumburg, only attendees.

I think that the crowd count was somewhat inflated because this was some sort of Boy Scouts of America night. In the U.S. the Boy Scouts are a paramilitary outfit, so before the second game began, we saw Boy Scouts from several suburbs parading with flags and their little military uniforms. After their parading and flag waving, they sat in the stands, these scouts, and whanged their thunderstixx together. As I think I may have said, I hate Thunderstixx Night. And it's getting to be that every night is Thunderstixx Night, because, of course, the people who like to find more and more new places for their advertisements slap some product name on these inflatable plastic tubes, and bang bang bang, away we go. A glance at the Flyers' schedule informs us: "Thunderstixx courtesy of Famous Dave's."

When the Liberal Party of Canada held its pretense of a leadership convention in Toronto in November 2003, Paul Martin supporters were slamming Paul Martin thunderstixx together. There were a lot of white people in *that* crowd, too.

I am not totally sure why the Schaumburg team in the Northern League is called the Flyers. Alexian Field was built so that all its dimensions copied those of Wrigley Field. No clue there. The mascot was a guy (I think) dressed up in a bear outfit, and called "Bearon." Is this a reference to the Red Baron, famous flyer of World War I? If so, I have a little more respect for this burg. Bearon was wearing WWI flyer headgear, *and* there were a lot of small airplanes in the air—low in the air. We were next to the Schaumburg municipal airport, and a lot of Schaumburgers can apparently afford small planes. I expect that the ball club has figured out what the ground rules are if a high fly ball bounces off a Piper Cub.

Okay, what about ballplayers' names? There were no odd ones to add to our funny collection, but there was one fairly interesting one to add to our other collection. Do you remember that a few years back, while his fans were petitioning the commissioner to let Pete Rose into the Baseball Hall of Fame, Pete Rose Junior was trying to get into the major leagues? The poor kid. Imagine being the son of the guy who holds the lifetime record for base hits and the reputation for gambling on baseball games. Now imagine having the same name but a lifetime

MBL batting average of .143. He went two for fourteen for the Cincinnati Reds in 1997. This was a kid who got his picture in the paper when he was five years old, looking eager in the Reds' dugout. Now he is in his fifteenth year in pro ball, and he has played for nineteen teams. In the spring of 2003 he was with Córdoba of the Mexican League. Now he is a thirty-five-year-old veteran corner infielder for the single-A Joliet Jackhammers of the Northern League.

In the regular game this night he went one for five.

Oh yes, and he now goes by the name P. J. Rose.

Oh, and another thing. By the time of the seventh-inning stretch, most of the Boy Scouts were gone, and Alexian Field was very quiet, except for the small airplanes. The Jackhammers won 6-4.

Cities are closer together the farther east you get, but for some reason we seemed to drive great distances every day now. I think that Jean wanted us home by August. On the morning of July 30, it took forever to shake loose the western suburbs of Chicago, and though the landscape was almost entirely highways, there were construction zones everywhere we went. That is another thing you find as you travel eastward—more and more of the Interstate system is made up of highway lane closures, bright orange traffic cones and cylinders, broken pavement, overly close transport trucks, jackhammers, paving machines and guys in hard hats.

Nevertheless, we left Illinois behind, and took I-65 south, actually bypassed Indianapolis, followed the I-70 to the I-75 and turned onto that lovely road in order to reach beautiful Dayton, Ohio, where you can buy a used parking meter for fifteen dollars or watch the Dayton Dragons play the Battle Creek Yankees of the Midwest League.

There in Dayton we altered our tradition and began a new one. Maybe the long drive between Schaumburg and Hoffman Estates had persuaded us. From now on we would drive directly to the ballpark, and after the game we would go and find a place to stay.

Mention Dayton, and your friends from Ohio will ask you why you ever went there. Ohio is peppered with cities that are famous for being ugly—Cleveland (this is changing of late), Youngstown, Akron, Toledo. But Ohio also has a hell of a lot of professional baseball teams. Anyway, we didn't see much of Dayton. We found a parking lot a couple of blocks from the stadium, and gave a few dollars to a guy in a suit who claimed that he was watching it. This is another thing you find more of in the east.

The Dragons are affiliated with the downstate Cincinnati Reds, and they play in a beautiful stadium with a silly name: Fifth Third Field. I thought that it was probably the name of a bank, but if that is true, it is also a silly name for a bank.

I come from Vancouver, where an AAA team used to play in a single-A stadium, called by the local boosters "the prettiest little ballpark in the world" because there is a treed hill beyond the outfield fence and usually a colourful sunset deep in foul territory to the right. Fifth Third Field is better than any AAA stadium I have seen, including Dunn Tire Park in Buffalo. Fifth Third is a new retro stadium surrounded by office buildings, a real park that is truly loved by Daytonians, a refuge, one imagines, in the middle of Ohio cityness.

And a single-A team plays here. In front of a lot of people.

The playing surface is splendid. That is why, after the 2003 season, Dayton's Ryan Kapitzke (he'd be Irish, given that first name) was named the "Midwest League Groundskeeper of the Year." When informed of the award, Kapitzke said that it was "more an accomplishment of the entire grounds crew at Fifth Third Field." There's a piece of pure sportsmanlike modesty from a man who has a degree in Sports Turf Management from Michigan State University.

Everyone in Dayton loves this place. We arrived an hour before game time and marched up to the ticket window. I could see through the wrought iron fence into the concourse, where beer and sausages and pitas and probably crêpes awaited us. I was going to look for a couple of good seats in the shade, because for the first time on this trip we were, as they say, feeling the humidity.

"Two in the shade. How about back of third base?" Our usual area.

"No seats available."

"Okay. What can we get?"

"No seats."

Come on, I was thinking. This is the biggest single-A stadium in the world, but it is still single-A, and while the population of Dayton is 165,000, this stadium must hold about 8,500.

"We drove all the way from the west coast to see the Dayton Dragons," I pleaded.

"This game sold out in February."

"My sweetheart is nuts about dragons. There are dragons all over our house."

"All we have left are lawn tickets."

There was a sloping lawn down the right field corner in foul territory. I bought two lawn tickets. I hate lawn tickets, especially when I am not carrying a blanket. I've tried to sit on sloping ballpark lawns in Everett and Phoenix. But what could we do? We decided to look around the whole building and then come back to the lawn. I was in a crummy mood. I am too old to sit for three hours on the ground. Here's what Jean wrote on the side of her scorebook page:

> George is fussy. He isn't happy he has lawn tickets.
> Now he is complaining about the beer guy. Now he says I'm full
> of shit.

I don't remember my animus about the beer guy, but I do remember that I was kidding about that last remark. Daringly. Oh, she also wrote:

> Attendance 8,494.

The Dragons gift shop is terrific, and Jean tried and tried to get me to add a Dragons cap to my collection. But I was already one cap over my customary limit, and the Dragons caps are thirty dollars U.S., the most expensive baseball caps I have ever seen. Jean did get a nifty D pin for her collection, though. This place was a lot different from Schaumburg. Here there were lots of people wearing Dragons stuff and Reds stuff. We were in Ohio. If Indiana is the basketball state, and Florida is the football state, Ohio is the baseball state.

Back to the lawn we went, and tried to get set for three hours of agony. I mean, I am in my late sixties. I don't even go to picnics. We tried the little curb at the top of the lawn. Then we got lucky, and then some. Just above the lawn there was a row of plastic patio chairs, where people who had brought wheelchair patients got to sit. A regular told us, at the top of the second inning, that it could just be that the two remaining empty seats would not be occupied today, this being the middle of the week.

Some years back a woman who accompanied a wheelchair fan robbed me of a foul ball in the Kingdome. All this time I had been waiting for recompense.

We plunked our tired bones into those chairs and waited for wheelchairs that never came. How could I know that in two months I would be in a wheelchair myself? After about three innings I let myself relax a little and enjoyed as much as I could the Yankees' 11-0 pasting of the locals. I hate the New York Yankees, but I have to admit, once again, damn it, that they have the best uniform in baseball. Now I have to add that maybe those Battle Creek Yankees have the best cap in minor league baseball. You could look it up. I wouldn't wear one, though. I own a lot of baseball caps, but not a Yankees' cap, and no Yankees farm team caps. I will not wear Nikes, and I will not cheer for U.S. Steel.

Being in this big new park, with such a packed crowd, was a lot different from being in the drive-up crowd in Missoula, that's for sure. Either the people of Dayton have nothing in their lives but baseball, or the Dragons' officials know a secret that is not understood in Montreal and Ottawa. According to the Dragons' printed schedule, their games are on ESPN Radio 1410, WING-AM and the Time Warner Cable channel. If you "surf on over" to their website, you can sign up for the waiting list to buy a non-lawn ticket.

This was a big crowd, yes, and a varied one. There was an African-American guy on the lawn in front of us, with ten little black kids, all of whom were loaded down with popcorn and sodas and immense basketball shoes. To their right were a couple of women wearing Harley-Davidson leather jackets. One of them was a double for Erin Mouré, the great Canadian poet.

The Dragons were down 4-0 after the first inning, and 8-0 after six, but these 8,494 people did not show any displeasure. Out here, on the lawn, we heard the crack of the Yankee bat after the hitter had taken two steps toward first, but we were having fun, even in the humidity of late July. The U.S. can be a swell place sometimes.

While the between-innings nonsense was carrying on in there beside the infield, we hobnobbed with our neighbours on and back of the lawn. But we paid attention when the mascots got going. These were Jean's favourite mascots of all. They consisted of a boy dragon and a girl dragon. Their highjinks were more creative than usual, the highlight being the moment when the girl dragon persuaded the home plate umpire to do the Hokey-Pokey with her as the music came over the PA.

Dayton is a wonderful place in which to go to a baseball game. At one point there was a young woman in a tutu, dancing *en pointe* along the third base line. There was a galoot in some lighter-than-air inflatable suit, who bounced on his head, and landed on an umpire, flattening this unfortunate individual.

I suppose it is not surprising that we got two new entries for our great baseball names collection. These were both postmodern ethnonyms. The Battle Creek Yankees have a second-string catcher named Kaazim Summerville, and the Dayton Dragons feature a first baseman who answers to the name Travis Wong.

It was also at Fifth Third Field that we came closest to nabbing a foul ball, that greatest of all baseball prizes. If you are going to sit on or just above a lawn just foul of the fair pole, you have to expect that at least once in the game, some left-handed hitter is going to send a genuine Midwest League ball in your direction.

It took a while, but in the eighth inning a high curling foul fly ball came our way.

"I got it!" I intoned, as I always do.

It was headed straight for Jean, or rather on an arc toward Jean. She had to do three things. She had to put down her pen and scorebook. She had to stand up. She had to reach up with her bare hands and snag that spheroid, now descending at a rate explainable only by a physics teacher.

A crowd converged on Jean, heavy guys wearing ball gloves, kids with caps on sideways, motorcycle dudes with crinkly facial hair. Most of them vocalized.

"I got it!"

"Mine!"

"Unggghh!"

"Urk!"

"Ow!"

Jean was at the bottom of the pile, her hand still holding her pen but jammed now in the fold of her chair. Out of the corner of my eye I saw the ball bouncing high toward the wrought iron fence and Patterson Boulevard.

The pile of human body parts unpiled, and Jean got situated in her chair again, but she was going to have a very sore hand for a while. The look in her eyes was terrific. She was having fun and pain at the same time. The contradiction of a Cubs fan, I thought later.

147

"You know all those people who bring ball gloves to the stadium?" she asked.

"Yeah. You want to borrow one of my gloves?"

"I'm bringing a bat," she said.

14

Billy and Rodney

We are always the same age inside.

—Gertrude Stein

I SUPPOSE THAT ONE KNEW that the Kosmic League was in its dotage when teams could not find a whole roster, and started to forfeit games or borrow individuals from the opposition, or play children and dogs in the outfield.

I am sort of kidding about the dogs. There were always lots of dogs at Kosmic League games, because so many of the players and fans were ex-hippie types (to employ a short-hand nomenclature). In fact the KL had a universal ground-rule about dogs: dogs were "in play." That is, there would be no stoppage of play if a ball hit a German shepherd or if a baserunner fell over a chocolate lab retriever. Scorekeepers sometimes awarded an assist to Ol' Shep if an infielder retired a runner on a ricochet off him.

Another way you could have sensed that the Kosmic League might not last forever was the number of amalgamations. My team, the renowned Granville Grange Zephyrs, first merged with Flex Morgan and the Mock Heroics, and the team became known as the Flex Zephyrs, which was pretty hard to say, and we were relieved when we were joined by the few East End Punks who had not moved out of town.

Somewhere among my shirts that are in storage in Coquitlam as I write, there is a long-sleeved tee-shirt with a loose number 8 on the shoulder and a lot of words on the front, proclaiming the wearer to be a member of the "All-New Punk Style Zephyr Flex Morgan."

Well, the Kosmic League had to come to an end, even as the sixties did (except for a lot of holdouts in minor valleys of the West Kootenays and various enclaves among the older trees of Vancouver Island). The prime minister, after all, was now wearing polished oxfords instead of sandals in the House.

There was no era in my lifetime less Kosmic than the late seventies and early eighties. Mayors were wearing sideburns. Major league ballplayers (and their managers) were wearing double-knit. The World Series was played in those horrible circular stadiums in Pittsburgh and Philadelphia. Every time you turned on commercial radio you got Kool and the Gang or the Bee Gees.

In terms of writing, this was my period as a novelist, which would be followed by my period as a history writer (note that I did not say "historian"). As the long poem gave way to the novel, as the early Trudeau era of LIP grants gave way to the late Trudeau era's slide toward Mulroneyism, so the lovely theatre of the Kosmic League would become a memory.

Long hair would now belong to non-reading petty criminals instead of peaceniks.

I know that I kept on playing ball in the years between the Kosmic League and the Twilight League, but I don't remember all that much about my Sundays from 1975 to 1985, let's say. If I had access to my diary, kept in black hardbound scribblers like the one I am using for this manuscript that you will not see unless you visit the National Library under its new name years from now, I could look some of this stuff up. I could check the entry for Sunday, June 14, 1981, for example, and find out how my team did that day and what I did at the plate, as well as my current batting average.

I can remember this. If I woke up on a Sunday and saw that it was raining, I would become anxious, then irritable, then depressed. I would have to spend the day marking papers. On days when there was just a light drizzle, or wide puddles left over from an all-night torrent, I would put on my ballplaying duds and drive to the designated diamond and sit in my car for an hour or so, the only player to show up. I might have a Gilbert Sorrentino novel with me, but Gilbert Sorrentino is not baseball.

I do remember the ten-foot fence that separated left field from King Edward Avenue. This was at the elementary school that a guy named Spinelli had got a permit for the summer. Big strapping young males enjoyed cranking high flies over that fence, excited by the chance that a softball might scare the heck out of an asshole or bar-owner driving a BMW.

That fence and fences like it (across town there was a left field building called "The Brown Monster") raised a conflict in my soul. I have always seen myself as a National Leaguer, as an anti-Yankee, as the kind of competitor who likes to beat you by hitting behind the runner breaking for second or laying down a perfect squeeze bunt—further, as the kind of player who knows *when* and when *not* to do these things.

But that fence! I was in my late forties. When would I get a better chance to crank one out before I got too frail to hit a long fly ball at all? Yeah, but won't swinging for the fence put a hole in my batting average and hurt the team? Would I sacrifice my on-base average for the chance to pop one? I fretted about this problem for a few weeks before coming up with a compromise that I would never tell anyone about.

It had almost always been my practice to take the first pitch, even if it was belt high on the outside corner. Now I decided that if it came over the inside half of the plate, I would go into my home run swing.

Then if I didn't belt a long ball, and if there was now a strike on me, I would go into my batting average stance and routine.

Aw, even little Paul smashed a few over the twelve-foot fence in left field.

The odds are that some time that round bat will hit that round ball on just the round centimetre you need, at just the speed and altitude you might desire, just this once, to loft a Ruthian clout and permit you the home run trot you have been practising in your mind all season.

Then one Sunday my fantasy came true.

Well, no, it didn't.

But in a sense it kind of did.

No, not really.

But it almost did.

All right, here's what happened. I went into my home run stance, and when I got a pitch down and in, I went into my home run swing. As I remember it, I must have looked a lot like Joe DiMaggio. I got ahold of one. I could feel it, that almost imperceptible contact that means that you have nailed one.

Up the ball went. And far.

Spinelli, the chucker, turned like Ralph Branca to follow the flight of his share in a legend. I started into my trot.

The ball rose, and then it fell. The left fielder had given up on it. The ball fell, and landed on the aluminum rod that was the top of the fourteen-foot fence.

It hit the rod and bounced out of the park, onto the grass this side of King Edward Avenue.

Foul.

Maybe a foot foul. Maybe two feet.

For the first of many times, I said, "I'll take it."

Then I trotted back to the plate and picked up my aluminum bat and went into my batting average stance. I looked like Pete Rose.

There are things written in my diary that I do not otherwise remember, and I don't keep my diary faithfully as I once did. Foolish, isn't it? Just when my memory starts to get old and unreliable, I neglect to tend to my written version. Well, mainly I forget to do it. So some memories of the sandlot days between Kosmic and Twilight leagues will remain unmoored.

I do remember Billy Wills fondly, though. I met Billy Wills through David Kerfoot, who was the centre fielder for Duthie's, the main bookstore in Vancouver. Billy was a fairly little guy, medium maybe, a good ballplayer, went all out, sort of like Paul, zoomed. Whenever a foul ball went uncaught at Nat Bailey Stadium, home of the AAA Vancouver Canadians, one of us louts in section nine would shout, "Billy Wills would have had it!"

Billy used to drive my daughter Thea, then ten years old, nuts. He had some sort of job that involved troubled kids or kids in trouble, and one year he was situated on Forty-first Avenue a few blocks west of Ruby's, where Thea and I liked to go for lunch.

Thea usually had a grilled cheese sandwich, and I usually had a greaseburger. On the days that Billy Wills would meet us for lunch, he would always—always—have a plain burger and a vanilla milkshake.

I forgot to mention that Billy Wills was at the time a guy with a slender masculine build and blond hair. All the little girls on my girls' softball team had crushes on him. He was always puzzled by his success with the hearts of young girls. They would sigh when he walked by. But he was always devoted to someone named Nancy. I mean, he was always falling for another girl named Nancy. I think he might have married one at last.

Billy Wills was a creature of habit. He'd be happy sharing a plain burger and a vanilla shake with a woman named Nancy.

Both Fawcett and Fast Eddie were married to women named Nancy. But they weren't worried about Billy Wills. He was a straight shooter.

But he drove Thea Bowering nuts.

"Billy Wills," she finally got the nerve to say one day at Ruby's, "I can maybe understand why you always order a plain hamburger—"

"Given what your father, Whip Bowering, eats."

"Exactly. But I have to ask you. Why do you always have a vanilla milkshake?"

"Such as the one I am enjoying now," added Billy Wills.

"Precisely. This is Ruby's. It is the most successful ice cream parlour on Forty-first Avenue. I don't know how many flavours there are here. I, for example, am enjoying a bubble gum milkshake today. Why don't you at least try chocolate?"

"A chocolate milkshake?"

"Chocolate is very successful," said Thea, helping herself to the only french fry on my plate that did not have HP Sauce on it. "Why do you persist with vanilla, week after week?"

"You want to know why I always have a vanilla shake?" asked Billy Wills.

"That's why I'm here," said Thea.

Billy Wills put his empty milkshake cup away. They made nice milkshakes at Ruby's in those days.

"You see, it's like this," he began. "When I was a few years younger than you are today, my dad took me to a place a lot like Ruby's and bought me my first milkshake. It so happened that this was a vanilla milkshake—"

"Oh, no!" said Thea, covering her ears for a moment, then uncovering them.

"Well, that vanilla milkshake was the most delicious thing I had ever tasted. I could not imagine anything tasting better. What if next time I tried, say, a strawberry milkshake, and it wasn't anywhere as good? It would have been an opportunity lost forever. I made a vow then and there that I would always order a vanilla milkshake."

"Yeah, but Billy Wills—"

"Oh, man! The most delicious thing I'd ever tasted!"

After that I could never get the father-daughter conversation around to Billy Wills.

"Don't talk to me about Billy Wills," Thea would say. "I love him, but he drives me crazy."

The reason I brought up Billy Wills is that I want to show you what I mean when I say that he would always go all out. The hell with logic.

One fine day after a lot of rainy days and a few fine days, at the northeast diamond at the park on Sixteenth just west of Macdonald, Billy Wills was up to bat, he being our leadoff hitter, and I was on deck. The ground was hard, having been roiled into mud ruts and then baked by the July sun. So when Billy Wills got ahold of one and lined it to right, it hit the ground and kept on going.

Billy Wills went *tearing* around the bases, in that sharp-turning counter-clockwise course we love so much. The right fielder had finally run the ball down and got it to the cut-off person in shallow right, and this individual was turning now to fire the ball to wherever it was needed. It turned out that this was home plate, because Billy Wills was running through the stop sign at third and aspiring to an inside-the-park home run.

The smart baseball veteran in me questioned his decision. There were none out. There was no doubt in my mind that I would score Billy Wills from third. I would loft a sacrifice fly, or stroke a ground ball to the right side, or lay down a bunt, or pop a flare over the infield.

But oh no, here came Billy Wills home, blue eyes as open as those of a hen fleeing an intent, silent, chicken-eating dog.

The ground around home plate was composed of hard-baked ruts.

The ball, though, bounced true into the catcher's hands.

Billy Wills went into his slide. I would never have done that on a surface like that.

I was in the on-deck circle. I heard Billy Wills's ankle break. A little later, I did not want to look at it.

I hate hearing injuries. I've never heard one of mine, but I'll always remember hearing Billy Wills's ankle.

The year after that I heard Trudy Richter's ankle. Every time I think of this one, right now for example, my toes tighten and I want to close my eyes.

At the time, Trudy Richter was Paul's wife, and she was both highly pregnant and one of our starting pitchers. On the day to which I am alluding, she was warming up prior to our game against someone, maybe Ronnie Tomato's Central Park Perverts. I was in the same area of somewhat scrabbly grass, playing long-toss with someone. Then I heard Trudy's ankle.

Or to be more precise, I heard her Achilles tendon. Trudy was a short, good-looking, muscular German-Canadian pregnant woman in shorts and an Oakland A's hat. She had taken about three warm-up pitches, and on the next one stepped into some little unseen hole in the grass.

I heard her tendon go. First it snapped. Then it rolled up like a window blind. I do not want to hear that again.

Trudy and Paul's kid Tyson is a terrific young ballplayer and jazz pianist. I wonder how he feels about his mother's pitching when she was eight months gone. Tyson can handle a hard hit ground ball pretty well.

I seem to have returned to the theme of baseball injuries.

Well, baseball injuries are more dignified than dogfight injuries (my present broken hip) or falling-in-the-bathroom injuries.

Still, the injuries I hated the most were the ones my kid Thea incurred. Angela used to give me hell for not watching her closely enough, but when you're playing, say, an important playoff game, it's hard to be watching your kid all the time. Besides, it's not as if my ballpark was the only place where she got whacked. At pre-three day care she got pushed off the climbing thing and wound up with a huge swollen eye. When we went shopping, Thea riding on my shoulders, I always told people no, I didn't do it. Once she swallowed a bottle of lemon-scented furniture polish while her mother was on the telephone, and had to have her stomach pumped. Once, I heard, from the bottom of the stairs, that sound I'd been warned about, the one babies make when they have a sudden super-high temperature, and I had to drive her to emergency during rush hour, wheels high over the curb.

Her first baseball injury came while we were playing a Kosmic League game at Cricket Chatter Park, off Twelfth Avenue. She was running around with the other three-year-olds and their dogs, and some boy slugged her with a board that may have had a nail in it.

Well, I had to take her with me to those games. It was either that or stay home. Besides, there were generally other kids to play with, and the ballplayers all had helloes to say to "The Gump."

One of the injuries that kind of bothered me was the one to her chin, or rather that tender area just back of the chin before we can start talking about the neck. We were playing across town at the diamond beside Trout Lake. There was a huge parking lot there, with those concrete gizmos you nose your front tires up against. Apparently Thea had taken to playing among those concrete things, jumping from one to another or something.

What a good idea! Child plays in the parking lot, difficult to see over the hood of your typical ballplayer car.

So she came crying and dazed and bleeding, to our field of dreams. Luckily, our catcher for the day was Rodney Gage.

Rodney, a refugee from Los Angeles, was one of the few African-Americans in and after the Kosmic League. Once the quarry of Nine Easy Pieces, he escaped with his virtue more or less intact, and enjoyed a career in the movies, playing a guard in a white helmet in a dystopia fittingly filmed at Simon Fraser University (where the screen

157

adaptation of *1984* would be filmed). This was, if you are interested in checking it out, *The Groundstar Conspiracy*, starring George Peppard and Canadian actor Michael Sarrazin.

There were rumours that Rodney had been a studio musician in LA, and other rumours that were just rumours of rumours. But he did seem to be able to do a little of whatever was required. One of his skills was first aid, and when Thea showed up with a bleeding behind-the-chin, Rodney pressed his beautiful dark finger on the wound and held it there while I drove in my ballplaying outfit, as usual, to emergency.

Ever since that day I have been urging everyone to rent *The Groundstar Conspiracy*.

15

Home Again, Home Again

I don't love baseball. I don't love most of today's players. I don't love the owners. I do love, however, the baseball that is in the heads of baseball fans. I love the dreams of glory of 10-year-olds, the reminiscences of 70-year-olds. The greatest baseball arena is in our heads, what we bring to the games, to the telecasts, to reading newspaper reports.

—Stan Isaacs

AT FIRST I WASN'T WILD ABOUT OUR NEW ROUTINE, but after a few days and nights I thought it was pretty efficient—especially after all that driving back and forth to Hoffman Estates, Illinois.

So after the Dayton game, Jean drove with her bruised hand eastward, till we bypassed Columbus, then turned south off the I-70, found a sweet anonymous little Ohio town and pulled into the parking lot of a Red Roof Inn. We were now at the exact opposite of that old-timey auto court in Riggins, Idaho. Here at the Red Roof, we didn't know what to do. It was like visiting someone at a small prison. Finally, we figured out that we were supposed to wait at a bulletproof window with a shallow open space at its bottom for someone to show up.

I was thinking: okay, this open space is just about big enough to slide a credit card through, but couldn't you poke a pistol through, just as easily?

After a while a huge woman with short and sparse orange-pink hair appeared and asked for my driver's licence. I asked her whether she meant that she wanted my licence plate number. Hers was a face that had probably never experienced an emotion. No, she wanted my driver's licence. That's what the hole was for.

"Boy," I whispered to Jean, "there must be a lot of crime in Ohio. Or maybe just at Red Roof Inns." I had never before been to a Red Roof Inn.

Now I was a little scared, as you sometimes get in the U.S. There was a Tim Hortons doughnut place just the other side of the parking lot, the first we had seen on this trip, but I was still at least nervous.

Once in a while when you are driving in the U.S., you remember that a lot of the cars you see have pistols in their glove compartments. In the U.S. a lot of people call them pistol compartments, I think.

I don't know whether we were locked in all night. We were wrung out after driving 680 kilometres through three states and watching a ball game in the warm evening air. In the morning we had a shorter drive, though again we went through three states. We were headed for a day game in Pittsburgh.

Pittsburgh was a new city for me. But even better than that was Wheeling, West Virginia. When I was really young I knew that wonderful phrase, Wheeling West Virginia, as a site on the radio for country and western music, or as we called it, shit-kickin' tunes. It is a hell of an interesting-looking city as you zip through, tucked in between coal-seam hills, I figured, with big old serious bridges across the Ohio River.

I'd like to have stopped in this interesting little city. I had been a six-year-old boy in Greenwood, BC, a former mining boomtown with old mansions, and there was a certain recognizable *scent* or something in the air above these gorges and things. I think that I was also drawn by the first non-flat country we'd seen in a long while.

Douglas Fetherling (now George Fetherling), the Canadian poet and journalist, was brought up in Wheeling, West Virginia, and in his autobiography he says that the Mob was well-ensconced there. But if you go to the city's official website, you will see the claim that Wheeling has the second-lowest crime rate in the country. I guess things have changed since Doug/George was a USAmerican boy.

Anyway, hooray, I had acquired West Virginia, my thirty-third state. Even though it takes longer to write about crossing the West Virginia northern panhandle than it takes to drive across it.

As we drove out of West Virginia and into western Pennsylvania, I thought of Stan Musial, third of the three great hitters of my boyhood. Stan Musial was a Polish-American lad born in Donora, Pennsylvania, a tiny zinc town near Pittsburgh. Its other claim to fame was a zinc-smog in the summer of 1948 (otherwise the greatest year in civilization) that killed a hundred people and felled a lot more.

Stan Musial of the St. Louis Cardinals hit .376 with thirty-nine home runs and 131 RBIs in 1948.

Driving into Pittsburgh, at least driving into Pittsburgh from the west, is strange, and I'll bet that it is even stranger when there aren't road construction cones all over the place. You just have to surrender yourself to the road signs, forget logic, and stop fretting over how close you are to game time, as the road takes you around hills and over river gorges, always promising that there is a city nearby, no fooling.

Once you are in the middle of Pittsburgh, as improbable as that seems, you have to get used to driving around these streets that are absolutely filled with traffic, trying to figure out how to get to the nice new baseball stadium you can see between the bridges, to which a lot of people are walking, lucky folk.

Then when you miraculously get across the Allegheny River, you drive around and around, looking for a parking space, until Jean says

"Turn here, and follow those cars," and then you hand some unattractive guy a U.S. twenty-dollar bill. This action allows you to park the Volvo between a couple of SUVs, get out into the lovely humidity and hike toward the stadium on the horizon.

When we lived in London, Ontario in 1966-67, I could watch the Pittsburgh Pirates at Forbes Field, centre field kind of dark in black and white on the ABC television station from Erie. Forbes Field was replaced by one of those horrible round multipurpose parks, this one called Three Rivers Stadium, in 1970. Now, Jean and I walked into PNC Park, "a classic-style ballpark, an intimate facility that embraces the progressiveness of Pittsburgh while saluting the spirit of early ballpark originals such as Forbes Field, Wrigley Field and Fenway Park." That's what it says on the ballpark's website. It doesn't tell you what PNC stands for. I'm thinking a bank.

Gotta be a bank. After a nice drive to northern single-A parks, here we were, at last, paying major league prices. The stadium might be "intimate," but it seemed so big, so well-filled with stores and booths that want to sell you something at ballpark/airport prices, so ... USAmerican. We were no longer in Idaho, Toto, nor even Ohio; we were in the United States of America.

I found myself rubbernecking. A few years ago someone erected a statue of Stan Musial at the park in St. Louis. Then there was a Michael Jordan statue in Chicago. Now all the new parks are getting into the team heritage act. As soon as we got to PNC Park, I was gawking at big photographs and statues of the Old Pirates. The most striking had nothing to do with Honus Wagner's legs, but rather the cast metal hands of Ralph Kiner and his bat. Brilliant.

I was seduced. I would recommend a visit to this stadium. There on the last day of July we sat in shaded seats above the first base line and saw how baseball had saved nineteenth-century America. These cities full of European working-class immigrants were not mindful of the spirit—they were satanic mills out of which plutocrats lifted fortunes with which to purchase the gold faucets for their bathtubs. Immigrant families lived in the grey, in the noise and the foul-tasting air. But in the middle of these Pittsburghs and Buffalos and Brooklyns there were walled-off greenswards, and on Sunday afternoons you and your children could assemble there with your few coins and pretend that the New World might have a little Eden left in it after all.

In 1845 the New York Knickerbocker Base Ball Club began to play games in Hoboken, New Jersey, at their new grounds called Elysian Fields.

"I've died and gone to Heaven," I announced.

There were hardly any advertisements on the outfield fence. There was no deluge of military patriotism. There were no phalanxes of hypnotized teenagers plodding up and down the aisles. All the between-innings nonsense was done on the big screen in centre field.

Best of all, this was a National League park. There would be no designated hitter! Hoorah!

So we settled down to see how the hapless Pittsburgh Pirates would fare against the hopeless San Diego Padres.

Things looked good for the home nine (not the home ten—hooray!) as 18,045 Thursday-afternoon fans watched. The leadoff hitter got a single in the first inning. He was advanced via a sacrifice fly. Then Brian Giles was walked, and the scene was set for right fielder Matt Stairs, that big scruffy bopper from New Brunswick. Stairs whacked one, and only the right field stands kept the ball from plopping into one of Pittsburgh's three rivers.

3-0 Bucs. The requisite noise and smoke rose from the gaudy scoreboard.

"Daytime fireworks just don't cut it!" exclaimed Jean.

The Pirates' mascot, that famous green parrot dressed up in a pirate outfit, cavorted on top of the Pittsburgh dugout.

"Mascots with beaks just don't do it for me," Jean informed me yet again.

"The pirates' parrot is a little pirate—that is pure genius," I urged with a tone of informedness, puffed up as I was by a fellow Canadian's home run.

"Shiver me timbers," she said, sarcasm as thick as Matt Stairs's physique.

I was, I said, getting my seventy-four dollars' (U.S.) worth. Vendors sought more, old guys repeatedly hollering indecipherable words, perhaps in a western Penn accent. More yelling was coming from a guy to our right, who hollered "Swing!" just about every time one of the many Pittsburgh pitchers delivered the ball. I thought that I'd left this small-town idiocy behind in Oliver, BC in 1953.

The Padres fielded two more players who would be included in our list of former players' sons. Sean Burroughs I had seen play in Tacoma, last year. He had been a star for the U.S. champion Little League team a few years back, had played for the U.S. Olympic team, and had been up and down between Portland and San Diego. He's going to be a good singles hitter and has a chance to get his OPS over .800. His father Jeff Burroughs won the American League MVP race in 1974, six years before Sean was born. Jeff's lifetime OPS was .794.

In this game, Sean went two for four, with two walks and two runs.

Gary Mathews Jr. went two for five, as his Padres came back to win the game 10-7. His father was a good hitter for four teams in the National League. Sports writers were always spelling his name wrong, so most people called him Sarge. In 1987 he was traded to the Seattle Mariners, and he got into forty-five games with them before hanging them up.

One day at the Kingdome, I was leaning against the left field fence, watching Sarge warm up.

"Didn't you use to be Gary Mathews?" I asked him.

He nodded and smiled.

But his lifetime OPS was .803.

When you are at a major league game, there is another player list you may enjoy. These are the guys on your fantasy team. As we were dealing here with two last-place teams, you can be sure that a lot of my fantasy players got into the game. Three of my pitchers did, and my rookie first baseman. My rookie first baseman went zero for five, of course. My pitchers were not exactly engaged in a pitchers' duel, but here is an indicator of the kind of season the Pittsburgh Pirates and I were having in 2003: in the fifth inning they sent one of my pitchers, Kip Wells, up to pinch hit. He smacked a 2-2 pitch off the wall in centre field and later scored.

"That's my guy," I announced to all around me. I didn't even get any inquiring glances. This was Pittsburgh.

All in all, if you can ignore the rapidity with which U.S. currency flies from your hands, PNC is a nice experience. My only regret is that we didn't pick up a Pirates' schedule. I do love to collect tickets and those little folded schedules at ballparks.

The latter are free.

I thought that we were going to head up toward Erie and stay overnight somewhere around there, but once Jean got hold of the controls there was no stopping her. Even though the rains of the east had replaced the relentless sun of the west, Jean sat as she always does on the freeway, comfortable in the passing lane, in this case determined to get us home to Port Colborne before the dawn of August. And so she did.

And on August 1 I began to write my baseball book: "While helping me pack, Jean found a zip-lock bag containing a pair of mangled aviator glasses—"

So we had finished our drive across most of the wide continent. So we had arrived in my new home, and the long hot July was contained in our diaries and scorebook. The story of our baseball parks was over, wasn't it?

Nope.

Five days later we were at Lynx Stadium in Ottawa, watching the Lynx drop a tough little defensive game 2-0 to the Scranton Wilkes-Barre Red Barons (one of my favourite team names in AAA, the other being the Colorado Springs Sky Sox).

It's a utilitarian AAA stadium, with no particular character, and no roof, which is something to think about. It seems that every time we go to a game in the International League, the skies are either threatening rain or dropping a thin shower all through the set.

Not that a lot of people would have got wet. We had been warned that the Lynx were the Expos of the International League, even now that they were an Orioles affiliate rather than a Montreal one. In fact, the tiers of seats were so deprived of human bums that we moved down to the second row behind the Lynx dugout. We were surrounded by friendly fans, and all through the game I shared a conversation with an old coot (who, I'm afraid I have to say, was probably at most five years older than I) who knew his baseball pretty well. You know—one of those "remember when Rube Marquand won twenty games three seasons in a row?" conversations.

In Montana the stadiums were surrounded by pointy mountains, in Ohio and Pennsylvania by skyscrapers. Here the prospect was the usual square buildings of Ottawa. I think I understand the square buildings of Ottawa. The Houses of Parliament are tall stone HP Sauce labels, so no one else was allowed to make anything but square buildings. In the downtown core of Ottawa the buildings are all twelve stories high and square.

I felt bad that hardly anyone was going to baseball games in the nation's capital. (Well, in the USAmerican capital no one at all was going. But that was sure going to change, alas!) In the winter, which is a great deal of the year in Ottawa, they drive a prodigious distance to spend a few hundred dollars to watch a hockey game against Columbus or Nashville. Even the once-abandoned Canadian Football League is operating here again.

I wondered: is there anything the Parliamentary Poet Laureate can do to make people from Ottawa and Hull go to the ballpark? Naw.

But it was interesting to be at a ball game in Canada. The outfield distances were in metres and feet. The scoreboard was bilingual, and so were the PA announcements. The crowd, or let us say the group in the stands, sang "O Canada!" in two languages.

Seeing that we were in Ottawa, where there were employees and others puffing on cigarettes in front of every store, restaurant and government building, I was surprised to see that no one was pounding a butt in the stands.

The person they appointed to sing the national anthems had to be stylin', of course, just like nearly all the others we had heard. I don't know why every young white country girl these days has to warble urban diphthongs as if they were the natural children of Shaka Khan. Just sing the song and get out of the way, I say. I mean if we must have an official national anthem at a ball game. It could be worse, I guess. At least here in Canada we don't have guys in military duds, with rifles on their shoulders, marching with some damned flag in the outfield while fighter jets roar overhead.

But here's something I'd like to know. How come every Lynx player is wearing a U.S. flag as well as a Canadian flag on his back? The baseball park started off as a place to get away from the factory for a couple of hours. It should also be a place where a person and his family can seek refuge from flags and rifles.

Aw well. It might not be 1948, but it is baseball. At least when you have a sparse turnout as you do here, you don't get little kids running around ignoring the game, or zombie teens trying to compete with it. At least here in the nearly frozen north we can see the talent of the black players we didn't see in the Midwest and the west.

Two of them added to our sons-of-the-famous list. Garry Maddox II patrolled the outfield for the Red Barons. Tim Raines Jr. did likewise for the Lynx. Maddox batted eighth and went one for five this night.

Raines led off for the Lynx and also went one for five in this pitchers'
game. He also made an obvious attempt to steal second and was safe
only because the throw went looking for a bag in some other division of
the International League.

It was a pretty decent game, if you like 2-0 games as I do. And
afterward we had a late dinner and a few beers at my favourite dive in
Ottawa, a smelly upstairs beer parlour called the Glue Pot.

16

The Twilight of the Gods

Since baseball time is measured only in outs, all you have to
do is succeed utterly; keep hitting, keep the rally alive, and
you have defeated time. You remain forever young.
                                                    —Roger Angell

I GREW OLD IN THE TWILIGHT LEAGUE.

At first the Twilight League was made up almost entirely of people involved with published words. There were reporters for the *Vancouver Sun*. There were magazine editors. There were magazine distributors and booksellers, columnists and movie reviewers. Then there was my team, made up of poets. Boy, we had fun! Boy, we lost a lot! Not that poets are not good ballplayers. Poets are the unacknowledged batting champions of the world.

Boy, the years went by!

Maybe it's a good thing that my diaries are packed away across the country. The stuff that happened in the Twilight League would fill a book and then some.

Remember that back in the days of the Kosmic League I admired Glen Toppings for playing at the age of forty? I played in the Twilight League when I was fifty. Hell, I played in the Twilight League when I was sixty.

I'd switched the direction of my admiration from Glen Toppings to David Alfaro Siqueiros, the great Mexican muralist. People know that

Siqueiros was an artist and a labour organizer and an assassin, and a communist, but most people do not know that, like Glen Toppings, Siqueiros was a first baseman.

Siqueiros spent a lot of his life in jail or in exile. When he was out of jail, he was machine-gunning Trotsky's house, or organizing miners, or painting great Marxist murals. When he was inside jails they would not let him paint the walls, so he did thousands of easel paintings that will cost you a lot of money these days.

In the late 1950s Siqueiros was given the project of creating a grand mural on the walls of Maximilian's magnificent castle in Chapultepec Park. It was a perfect setting. Maximilian's magnificent castle overlooking the city was the place from which that Hapsburg ruler was hauled to his execution by the Mexican insurgents. The castle was headquarters for one of the U.S. invasions of Mexico, the one in which the invaders were decimated by the armed Mexican children now remembered in the name of the grand boulevard called Insurgentes. And Maximilian's castle was the residence of the hated dictator Porfirio Díaz. Siqueiros's mural would take as its subject the overthrow of Porfirio Díaz.

Well, Siqueiros had to do a lot of his sketches for the mural while he was a prisoner in the nearby Lecumberri Penitentiary. The sixties were a time of dissent in Mexico as they were elsewhere. In Mexico they would culminate in the army's 1968 murder of university students whose protests, the president thought, might endanger the success of the Olympic Games and suggest to the world that it had been a mistake to grant the games to such a volatile nation.

A lot of people were going to be coming to these games, and tourism is very important to Mexico City. It would not look good, then, to have a half-finished mural at Maximilian's castle and the artist in jail. So it was decreed that David Alfaro Siqueiros should be let out of jail again in 1964.

Thousands of people were waiting for him outside the jail. Four thousand people were waiting to throw him a party at the biggest movie theatre in town. I wanted to go downtown, but I have a problem with crowds, so I stayed home in Churubusco.

But Siqueiros did not show up at the prison gate at the advertised time. The huge crowd that was waiting to carry him to the cinema theatre had to wait a couple of hours. Why?

Because Siqueiros's ball team had an important game that afternoon, and he was their starting first baseman.

He was seventy years old.

That's even older than I am now, if you can imagine.

And to think: I officially retired from the diamond when I was sixty-six.

Glen Toppings died in 1972.

David Alfaro Siqueiros died in 1974.

There were changes, amalgamations and withdrawals over the years in the Twilight League. For years I didn't even know that it was called the Twilight League. If it was mentioned in the newspaper, if, say, a player was being written about in his other disguise as an artist, the organization was just referred to as the "Media League."

A lot of former Kosmic Leaguers were around: Leaky Fawcett, Fast Eddie, Gill Collins, Popcorn Naylor, Laura Stannard. Sometimes there was a great temptation to do something goofy and theatrical, and I do remember that there was a pitcher who had never worn shoes in his life, and that there was a team that played a game under protest because the opponents' team dog had peed on someone's glove, and that once in every game I would pull the old snot-ball routine.

The snot-ball. This would entail my approaching the pitcher's position (we always called it "the mound," though a softball pitcher throws from the flats) from my infield spot, and taking the orb from

Fast Eddie or Jim Allan or whoever was hurling that day. Then I would hold it under my nose and make a huge snotting noise, and holding the ball delicately between thumb and middle finger, hand it back to the chucker, who himself would then hold the ball with great respect. The disgust on the faces of the batter and his companions (and our catcher) made the manoeuvre one of the highlights of any game tape.

We do not have reliable stats, but it is believed that batters facing the snot-ball fared significantly worse than dry-ball batters.

In general however, the Twilight League did not feature the theatre (or circus) of the Kosmic League. Because its main organizer, *Vancouver Sun* movie critic Marke Andrews, was a kind of anal-retentive pitcher-commissioner, the scores and standings were kept in a big book, and the season-ending championship tournament insisted on a clear adherence to league rules, whatever they were.

So skill was met with approval. But jockism was still frowned upon. There were obvious signs that companionship was more important than competition, especially in the clothing favoured by the pitchers. There was the barefoot boy, of course. And there was Marke Andrews's hat. Opponents would routinely protest the hat, but as Marke was the league's ultimate authority, such protests always met with failure. It was a kind of fuzzy hunter's hat, I guess, a heavy wool item in a brown plaid, with a peak, earflaps, and a big bushy ball on top. Marke wore this atrocious headwear on the hottest July day, along with shapeless cotton shorts of no colour known to designers, and a torn and faded Red Sox tee-shirt.

Three pitchers, Jim Allan, Fast Eddie and a southpaw from Richmond named Steve, wore tiny gloves from the earliest days of baseball, flat little leather items without padding or pocket or even laces. These gloves were said to be designated for the Hall of Fame.

Actually, clothing was always one of my favourite things about the TL. A lot of players were known for their signature items of attire. My friend Darryl always wore pants that had distress rips and holes in them. In addition to his tiny ancient glove, pitcher Jim Allan wore operating room greens, and who knows what in his enormous afro.

Back in the day Jim had been a rock and roll promoter. Now he was the most prominent gink at the Granville Book Company, a cooperative that was sort of my team's sponsor. We were officially the Paperbacks, but because of our age and physical imperfections we were generally known, by ourselves and others, as the Bad Backs.

The Bad Backs. Sometimes we won. More often we blew an early lead. (I'll never forget the fun some Kosmic League teams had with my *Georgia Straight* headline: "Zephyrs Blow Early Lead." They kept asking who this lucky lad was. I guess they were thinking of the great American League pitcher Early Wynn, 300-244, 3.54.) It didn't matter. Everyone made the playoffs, just like in the NHL.

We all grew old in the Twilight League. But there came a time when I figured that I had to be the oldest person in the seven-team loop. I was our David Alfaro Siqueiros, but I couldn't paint. I once remarked that if I were to retire, the average age of the league's players would drop by five years. Sure. I remember games in which I was four times as old as our left fielder. With Jim Allen, Brian Fawcett, Fast Eddie and me, we had the slowest baserunners on the North American continent. There was a lot of talk about issuing walkers.

Often the vocalizing on the diamond would go like this:

"I got it!"

"Oh, Jesus!"

Our home venue, which we shared with the Friendly People, was the famous Needle Park. Well, a lot of the parks on the east side of Vancouver are called Needle Park, I suppose. Ours was one of the older Needle Parks in town. Its real name is Woodland Park. It sits between McLean Drive and Woodland Drive, and is marked off north and south by Frances Street and Adanac Street. It's the two blocks of grass that sit between the hip working-class Commercial Drive and East Hastings, the most heroinized street in Canada.

It wasn't the sixties anymore. We didn't say Cricket Chatter Park and Daisy Beanblossom Stadium. Needle Park is not funny, but we said it as if it were, sometimes. Most of our games were on Sundays, which occurred shortly after Saturday nights, which are big around Woodland Park. When we arrived at our home field we would have to groom the playing area, meaning that we would search the outfield grass for hypodermic needles and carefully dispose of them, near but not inside the garbage barrel, in case anyone should rummage through it with bare hands.

Playing ball in Vancouver in the late twentieth century.

People might have lived dangerously around Woodland when it came to drugs, but they must have practised safe sex. We found an awful lot of used condoms every Sunday. We also found high-heeled pumps and undies and the odd pair of slacks.

We also found a lot of dog kaka. There were, of course, signs posted, advising citizens that dogs had to be leashed, and that dog owners were responsible for gathering their pets' kaka. But the people who lived around Woodland and Commercial were known for their low opinion of authority. Dogs around there tended to be big, and unlike their relatives on the west side, they ran or squatted free in the park.

Outfielders at Woodland Park had to keep their eyes on the ball *and* on the grass.

Jim Allan kept the team equipment—bats, balls, bases, orange plastic cones, catcher's armour—in his horribly beat-up car. During the history of the Twilight League he had a series of grotesque cars, including a yellowish van that had the door on the wrong side, a blue pickup truck that would not start on level ground, and a little nondescript hatchback that may have been made in Latvia. In these vehicles Jim Allan carried the Bad Backs' equipment—along with a shovel, a hoe and a pickaxe.

It rains in Vancouver, and after it stops raining, it is still wet. In the nice high school diamonds on the west side there is drainage. A day after a week's rain, these grassy diamonds are ready to go. On the east side, however, where none of Vancouver's alderpersons lives, there are wide puddles at home plate and elsewhere on the soil diamonds such as the one at Woodland. Jim Allan and the other early arrivers dug little trenches in this soil in an attempt to encourage the wide puddles to run along behind the backstop. Then they tried to find some relatively dry soil to fill up the muddy hollows where batters left-handed and right will be required to stand.

We all liked dry spells.

There were other characteristics of Woodland that made it a special place in which to conduct sporting contests. There were, for example, many immigrants from non-baseball countries, who did not know that it is perilous to conduct picnics or *tai chi* sessions in left field, kaka or no kaka. There were people of many national heritages who had consumed some product that alters the level of awareness in their brains and bodies and causes them to walk in imperfect gaits across areas also occupied by relatively still outfielders. It was even worse when these folks were pushing or pulling heavily laden grocery carts, because these latter were difficult to wheel over uneven soil and grass, kaka or no.

Luckily, we also played road games across town, even in leafy BMW country, Kerrisdale, site of my second eye injury, and above False Creek, site of my first eye injury. The Kerrisdale diamond, back of Magee High School, was also the site of my broken left wrist, come to think of it. A lot of my injuries happened in the Twilight League. They say that between your early fifties and your mid-sixties, your reflexes might start to go.

One of my favourite moments in softball happened at the Magee diamond. The Magee diamond was just about the exact opposite of our home diamond. It had thick, well-mowed grass. It even had grass in the infield. It had no proper bench, but there was a lovely big tree near third base, a place to sprawl and look good. In the Twilight League a pop-up that hit a tree limb in foul territory was a foul ball, while a pop-up that hit a tree limb in fair territory was declared no-pitch. At the Seventh Avenue diamond above False Creek, home diamond for the Write Sox, whom we all called the Soreheads, the nearest tree was in deep right field and up a little hill.

Magee was home park for the Secret Nine, an athletic and pretty young crew who had team shirts—each with the number 9 on the back. Their centre fielder was a tall young guy who had lots of talent but not much in the way of smarts. He could really hit the long ball, despite the fact that he had but one working eyeball. Not much perspective on the game, we said over and over among ourselves. Once he stroked an impressive home run, and on crossing home plate, he missed the high five, delivering a palm to the face of his congratulator, and taking one in his own mug.

But this guy, like a lot of individuals who are bothered by the perception that other people know more than they do, had a surly attitude. There are genial men who have natural baseball talent but lesser knowledge of the game. But this guy seemed to resent any unspoken suggestion that he was short on savvy. Well, one of my great joys as a player or fan is to know more than the other guy, and, if possible, to convert that greater knowledge into victory. That is, in all likelihood, a flaw in my character, but one that I manage quickly to forgive.

Once, in the TL championship tournament, I was playing first base and had to dive (all right, flop) to my right to snag a skipping grounder. Unable to rise to my feet in time to retire the hustling runner in a conventional fashion, I flopped back to my left and touched the base with my bare right hand. I beat him by a heartbeat. This gink loudly maintained that he was safe because I hadn't touched the bag with my glove wherein was nestled the ball. I guess he was confusing the situation with another in which a tagging of the baserunner might be involved. The umpire hesitated.

"What," I inquired with professorial calm, being as to how I was a professor during the weekdays, "would be the case were I, the first baseman, to have touched said base with one of my feet?"

There were a lot of such moments on the sandlots of Vancouver and Burnaby in the late twentieth century.

But back to my treatment of the ignorant young athlete who patrolled centre field for the Secret Nine.

There are a lot of admonitions to ballplayers, simple bits of lore that they should commit to memory. Many of these have to do with running the bases, perhaps the most likely activity to show the intelligence of a ballplayer. Do not make the first or third out at third base, we runners are told.

If a ground ball is hit in front of you, and you are not forced, do not try to advance, we are advised. Well, the guy I have been describing was on second base, having smacked a nice double to left centre. There was one out, and we were in the middle innings of a tied game. I was playing shortstop, just waiting for my chance, and praise be to Marty Marion, here it came. I grabbed a one-hopper and went into throwing mode. Ho ho, the galoot took off for third, and I had him cold. I tagged him politely, and then turned my attention to the business at first.

Boy, he was pissed off!

I did not smile.

I'll bet that he has forgotten all about it.

I made one concession to geezerhood on the diamond. After the age of sixty I quit playing in shorts. This happened shortly after my daughter, subbing at second base that day, asked the now famous question:

"Are those your legs, or are you riding a chicken?"

At about the same time, my team, the Bad Backs, started giving me retirement presents. I got a framed photograph of the team, all in our nifty team shirts. I got a giant-size bottle of Geritol. I got a lawn chair. For the first several years my teammates would present me with my gift right after we got eliminated from the season-ending tournament. After that they started giving me my retirement present at the *start* of the season.

In the pre-season of 2002, *Vancouver* magazine ran a story by Guy MacPherson about me and the Twilight League. First he quoted me on my second eye injury: "Smashed my glasses to smithereens and blinded me for a few days. But I don't care. Baseball's important. More important than eyesight."

Then MacPherson quoted league commissioner Marke Andrews to the effect that I was "the biggest bench jockey in the world," which is, I guess, true. I could never stop the flow of witticisms that passed through me. "It's like having a stand-up comic for the game. You get this cheap, live entertainment."

It's all true. That's why I was so proud of my kid and her chicken remark.

I gave MacPherson a shot at the end of the piece. He wondered what would happen if I were to retire.

"I think the league would just more or less disappear without me, to tell the truth," I am quoted as saying.

I was, mostly, just kidding.

In the summer of 2002, I kept waiting for my skill at getting the ball out of the infield to return. Then I felt that sad realization I had read about so often—they always say, the real ballplayers, that there comes a time when you know it's time to hang them up.

In July 2002 I quit the Bad Backs.

In early August I was coaxed out of retirement by the Friendly People, our opponent pals, and played a few more games. Then I hung them up for good (I think).

During the off-season the Twilight League folded. There are rumours that Jim Allan is trying to get it going again, in some form.

But they'll have to do it without me.

I'm headed for the Hall of Fame.

17

A Trip Around Lake Erie

> To get to know a country, you must have direct contact with the earth. It's futile to gaze at the world through a car window.
>
> —Albert Einstein

IN 2002 WE WENT TO GAMES IN THE AAA PARKS in Buffalo and Syracuse, but we really wanted to go to Batavia and watch the Muckdogs. We were encouraged by the silliness of the idea, the Muckdogs' website, and the sad little Batavia Muckdogs seat cushion that our pal Jack Cardoso gave Jean that year.

The Muckdogs are in the single-A NY-Penn League, along with such heart-stirring outfits as the Aberdeen IronBirds and the Mahoning Valley Scrappers. When I was a kid this was called the PONY League, sporting teams from two U.S. states and Ontario. Or was it Ohio? The last Ontario team was the St. Catharines Stompers, who are now the Brooklyn Cyclones. So it goes.

Batavia is a little burg just off the New York Thruway, not far from Rochester. We can't tell you anything about the town because Dwyer Stadium is on the outskirts. You do drive down a few typical upstate residential streets to get there, but you don't even know where downtown is.

You are probably dying to know what a Muckdog is. The team logo presents a ferocious mutt climbing over a board fence in the shape of an

M. It is one of the worst logos in organized baseball. But the team name has, really, nothing to do with any variety of canine. It signifies the hard-working farmers of the area, who toil in the generative muck that blesses local agriculture.

As for Batavia—well, there is a Batavia, Illinois and a Batavia, Ohio as well as Batavia, New York. The Batavi were an ancient Germanic people who inhabited the area around the mouths of the Rhine. So the Dutch have always named things—ships, stores, apartment buildings—Batavia. They named towns in their overseas colonies Batavia, hence Batavia, capital of Java, now a city known as Jakarta. Lots of muckdogs there.

We arrived at little Dwyer Stadium on August 13, an 89-degree day, to see the Dogs entertain the Tri-City ValleyCats. Okay, we know about Batavia, but what about Tri-Cities? These could not be the three towns that house the Tri-Cities Dust Devils of the Northwest League. Those are Kennewick, Pasco and Walla Walla, Washington. Sitting in Dwyer Stadium, I didn't have a clue as to where these ValleyCats were from, much less which river, even less what a valleycat could be. Some time later I tried to look them up. They seem to come from Troy, Albany and Schenectady, New York, which would make the river the Hudson in two cases and the Mohawk in the third.

We parked the Volvo in the free dirt parking lot, as usual in a single-A town, and beyond reach, we hoped as always, of a pop foul. When we got to the entrance we were pleasantly surprised to hear that tickets were free tonight. Why were they free? Because this was "Substance-Free Night," just as it said on the little folded Muckdogs schedule. After some inquiry, we found out that this did not signify just any substance, but only the kind that alter one's consciousness. That meant that I would not get a beer at all during this game, and later we were to find that the game would go for thirteen innings.

Just as well. Batavia is in Gennessee County, and I remember Gennessee as one of the worst store-bought beers I have ever tasted.

So in the 89-degree humidity I would have to make do with a pop, or a soda, as they say down here. I got into a lineup at one of several tents behind the little grandstand and saw that ahead of me in the lineup were two full-uniformed ValleyCats. Boy, they were young! Boy, this was old-timey USAmerican smalltowniana!

Here's another thing I saw while I stood in this lineup: everyone else was carrying little yellow tickets, which they exchanged for pizza or hamburgers or other upstate New York cuisine. All I had to exchange for these substances was some of that funny U.S. paper money.

"Where did all you lucky people get those yellow tickets?" I asked a fat woman in flowered shorts.

"They were handing them out at the gate," she said, in perfectly understandable English. "Free food for the first three hundred people in the park."

"Dang!" I replied. "We were about the tenth and eleventh people here. No one told me about any free food."

"Oh yeah, there's always free food on substance night."

"This is all Jean Baird's fault for not picking up the yellow tickets."

"Ah well, you still get free baseball," she said.

Yep. Thirteen innings of free baseball.

When we got inside, we found very little shade, and what there was was going to disappear. Some nitwit had decided to situate home plate in the southeast corner of the park. Did he think that a left-handed pitcher was called a "northpaw"?

Well, in Vancouver, home plate at Nat Bailey Stadium is in the northeast corner, but the sun in Vancouver is seldom a great problem. And I think the builders wanted fans to have a nice view of Little Mountain.

We did sit as high as we could get behind home plate (about eight rows up, under the broadcast booth), but the shade was soon gone, and we were too, because of the kids who were being noisy in a non-baseball way. We went and sat as high as we could in the uncovered seats on the first base line. There a fat woman in a Muckdogs shirt hollered "Heads up!" every time a foul ball went back of the stands—for thirteen innings.

I made up for her by employing my usual high wit for most of the game. This was apparently a little-known skill at Dwyer Stadium. I wonder whether Substance-Free Night always brings out the folks with funny-shaped foreheads and bib overalls. Anyway, in about the eighth inning, a tall fat boy with poking-up natural orange hair was standing in front of Jean and me, urging his weird-looking parents to give him U.S. money for his tenth snack. I touched the lad gently on the elbow.

"Were you to sit down, we might be permitted to see what is transpiring on the field of play," I said.

The lad sat down. But now his father, a man with a face like a coal shovel, complained that he was tired of hearing me say things when he was trying to watch a ball game. I said that I didn't know that games were supposed to be watched in silence. For an inning or two, I said "shhhh" every time the woman beside us bellowed "Heads up!" I would tell people that in Batavia the dads get miffed if you use the subjunctive on their kids.

It was a pretty quiet and obviously a rather dull crowd. I wondered whether this was the usual group or just the substance-free group. I noticed that some of the ushers and other employees were stepping into the space between the stands to suck on cigarettes. I would have thought that Camels were included among the chastised substances.

After a year of anticipation, Batavia was turning out, at least for me, to be a bit of a letdown. Dwyer Stadium was no great shakes, either. The infield grass did not look as if it was going to make it through the single-A short season. The canned music was particularly bad white rock. The lights were the worst we had seen yet. There were just as many fat people as one had seen in the west, though I must say that there was more of a pleasing ethnic mix, as they say, with people who looked Polish, for example. And there were black players being watched by a crowd with some black people in it. But most of the spectators were pretty unknowledgeable. By the thirteenth inning, there weren't many of them left. Farming folk get up early.

Only once in my life have I left a game before it was over. Once, in Vancouver, I took off after eight innings because I had been experiencing intense chest pains since the fifth. I could not figure out whether they were due to a heart attack or to the entire store-bought bag of unshelled peanuts. I was, as usual, watching the game alone—I was one of those geezers you see sitting alone in the grandstand, wearing an old baseball cap, filled with knowledge. I drove home. Next day I was in Vancouver General Hospital with a blocked bile duct. I stayed in that hospital during three weeks of the baseball season that year. What a waste!

So even if we had to drive all the way back to Port Colborne, a small city without a movie theatre or a baseball stadium (though it has two ice arenas), we were not going to leave this late-season single-A game before it was decided.

Just in case you think that the Batavia experience was all punk, let me tell you that the U.S. national anthem was, for a change, sung by a classical soprano rather than by a white stylin' Motown wannabe.

And the mascot did not have a beak. In her notes, Jean opined that he was wimpish. He was nice, she wrote, but dumb. He was a guy in a dog outfit, with the giant feet that mascots always have. He wore a Muckdogs shirt, with the number 1 in the shape of a bone, and he had a collar. Jean warmed to him in the later innings, when he took up residence in the stands, his forelegs around the shoulders of his neighbours. Every time a member of the home team would strike out or be deprived of a base hit by a nifty ValleyCat fielding play, he would let out a long doggy whimper. Jean liked that.

But for thirteen innings, the Muckdogs stranded runners in scoring positions. For thirteen innings they muffed grounders or throws—but here in Batavia all such eventualities are deemed "hits" by the local scorekeeper.

Finally, in the top of the thirteenth, the Muckdogs' centre fielder kicked the ball around for a while, the Cats defeated the Dogs 7-6, and we remaining fans got into our cars and drove home, unimpaired by any substances.

We spent most of a week of the precious 2003 season in Port Colborne without seeing a live baseball game. Then Jean piped up.

"Let's make a trip around Lake Erie."

"That's the title of a famous book by David McFadden," I replied.

"I mean a baseball trip," she continued.

"There's a novel idea," I rejoined.

"No, a non-fiction idea," she countered.

"You know what I mean," I groused. "Besides, McFadden's book was written before he had his temporary baseball *thing*."

"McFadden could teach you a thing or two about travel book writing," said my sweet roommate.

"And imaginary dialogue," I added.

This time we took Jean's car, a plain maroon Mercury Sable, because the Volvo guy in St. Catharines said that with a shagglepin like that the last thing I wanted to do was to take my Volvo on a long trip. Hmm.

We went to Buffalo and turned right. The south shore of Lake Erie is grape country. We saw millions of vines, but not the signs indicating wineries that you see beside all the roads on the Niagara Isthmus in Canada.

We zipped by Erie, home of the AA Erie SeaWolves of the Eastern League. The SeaWolves were on the road, and we were on our way to see the Cleveland Indians. This had been our single-A summer, that's for sure. We saw no AA games, and the three major league games we would see involved five nowhere teams (the Pirates, the Padres, the Indians, the Tigers and the Angels) plus the Minnesota Twins. The

184

Twins have proven, as have the Kansas City Royals, that it is possible to be champions and completely dull at the same time.

In the late eighties and early nineties, I went to Cleveland three times, as a poet, as a baseball scholar and as a professor-fan. In his *A Trip Around Lake Erie*, David McFadden called Cleveland the most beautiful city in the U.S.; but then he is also on record as calling Hamilton the most beautiful city in Canada.

Of course, I was eager to go the first time. My father was a Cleveland Indians fan, and I remember the starting lineup of the 1948 Tribe. How clever it was of them to be World Series champions in the greatest year in the history of civilization! As a Red Sox fan I should for all time hate Cleveland and 1948, but I also loved my dad and the colourful baseball magazines that fall.

Besides, in "Yards," my long poem about baseball parks, the best piece is the one about Cleveland's gargantuan Municipal Stadium, the biggest baseball building in the world.

I saw quite a few games there. It is something to sit with seven thousand people in a place that could seat eighty-four thousand. (Once in the summer of 1985 I sat with twenty-five hundred other people, five hundred of them policemen, to watch a soccer game in Hitler's seventy-six-thousand-seat *Olympiastadion* in Berlin). After a few innings of my witticisms in Municipal Stadium, I had a clear view in front of me. There I could hardly believe my eyes as from the second deck back of the first base line I saw Cecil Fielder of the Detroit Tigers strike out on a Tom Candiotti "fastball," a pitch that may have attained seventy-five miles an hour on its course to the plate. Candiotti would go weeks without throwing anything but knuckleballs. Fielder had stroked fifty-one home runs the season before.

It happened that on this occasion I was in Cleveland for a conference on literature and baseball. The next morning, Carl Willis, the pitching coach for the Indians, was to address us scholars. Now, ever since Big Daddy had whiffed, I had been telling everyone that Candiotti got him with a fastball. You know that some knuckleballers throw 100 percent knucklers, and others throw 99 percent knucklers.

"No way the Candy Man got him with a fastball," averred some associate professor from Ball State University. "He doesn't even *have* a fastball.

"You shouldn't call him the Candy Man," I objected. "Candy Moldonado also plays for the Indians, and he's the Candy Man."

"Yeah? They were both called the Candy Man before they came to Cleveland. How you going to decide which one has to, uh, drop the nickname?"

"It's a stupid nickname, anyway," I argued.

Now we were in a dining room at Cleveland State University, and Carl Willis had just finished an interesting talk about the ways in which a pitching coach has to coddle his ten or twelve young arms. He wanted to know whether there were any questions. I put up my hand.

"What did Candiotti strike out Fielder with last night?" I asked.

"Fastball."

He wasn't even smiling. I was. It was my greatest moment in baseball, again.

On the same weekend I was walking down East Sixth Street in Cleveland, with W. P. Kinsella. Bill was at the time in his full Richard Brautigan mode—hair dyed yellow and pretty long, mustache dyed yellow and waxed into a Buffalo Bill configuration. Walking beside him, I just looked like some faithful poet companion. It was nice and hot in that Lake Erie way, and a dump truck pulled to a stop for the red light at Superior. The driver stuck his head out the window and shouted:

"Hey, Shoeless Joe!"

Bill didn't know, but several years earlier I had been the judge responsible for his winning the Alberta Best First Book Award. The other two novels weren't bad, but they weren't about baseball, eh?

Now, it so happens that Kinsella and I are the only two novelists in western Canada who write about baseball and about Indians.

One time I was in Ottawa for some conference or festival, staying at a Swiss bed and breakfast with Bob Kroetsch and others. In my spare time I went to see the people at Oberon Press, publisher of Kinsella and me. Oberon was in the Delta Hotel building, and after my visit I was on my way to the National Library. This involved crossing the lobby of the Delta Hotel. In the middle of the lobby, in front of the fireplace, were two guys in chairs. One was W. P. Kinsella and the other was the guy who wrote about books for the *Ottawa Citizen*. I hadn't known that Kinsella was in town. He wasn't there for our conference or festival. I guess he was touring his new book from Oberon Press.

In any case, I did not slow my pace on my way across the lobby of the Delta. As I strode by this interview in front of the fireplace, I spoke a few words to the *Citizen*.

"This guy may know a little about baseball, but he doesn't know anything about Indians."

An enigmatic strider.

It was one of my greatest days in hotel lobbies.

Now here we were in Cleveland, Jean and I, unwilling to see our great baseball tour come to an end.

It was a decade since I had been in town. The basketball Cavaliers had moved into downtown. The last time I was here the ground had just been cleared for the Gund Arena, where the Cavs would play, or maybe Jacobs Field, where the Indians would move from the Mistake by the Lake. Even the NFL Browns were now playing in a new structure where Municipal Stadium had been, where Lou Boudreau had calmly thrown to first.

A decade and more ago, though, Cleveland had started recovering from the neglect and blight that had made its name an essential part of

USAmerican jokes. I remember sitting in a nice new heritage bar beside the river that used to catch fire. Then there were pleasure boats on the river, and I was sipping Rolling Rock beer with Donald Hall.

Back in the day, Donald Hall had been the co-editor of the enemy poetry anthology. In 1960 we hotshots carried around Donald M. Allen's *The New American Poetry*, the amazing anthology that brought together Charles Olson, Allen Ginsberg, Gary Snyder and other younger poets in the hip tradition of Ezra Pound and William Carlos Williams.

Donald Hall and someone else had brought out *New Poets of England and America* in 1957. No poets appeared in both books. Hall's anthology was for the squares, the academics, in the tradition of Robert Frost and Edwin Arlington Robinson. I can't remember who-all was in it, but I'd guess folks such as Donald Justice and W. D. Snodgrass.

But the Donald Hall I found myself having a beer with was a different and later man. He had been visited by cancer and dire predictions. He was not interested in academic poetry anymore. Now he was interested in baseball. His most enjoyable accomplishment of late was the design he had done for a lovely centennial edition of *Casey at the Bat*.

See? Baseball brings enemies together for a beer later in life.

Anyway, here we were in renovated downtown Cleveland, and there was lots of time before the first pitch. So we went to the gaudy Rock and Roll Hall of Fame and Museum. It too had been built since my last time in town. We plunked down forty-two U.S. dollars and spent a good part of an afternoon. The Rock and Roll Hall of Fame and Museum is mainly old record jackets that you still have at home, and Jimi Hendrix's pants. The biggest room is the gift shop, which you are compelled to go through to get outside, into the humidity.

We changed parking lots and headed for the ballpark. For the first few years after Jacobs Field was built, you could not get into the building unless you ponied up to a scalper. During the nineties it must have been the most successful stadium in major league baseball. I'd seen it often on television, but I'd never seen empty seats in the Jake. I guess northern Ohioans have twigged to the fact that you need a good team, too. The Indians were American League pennant winners in 1998, but the 2003 Indians were out of the basement only because the 2003 Detroit Tigers were the worst team in the history of the league.

I soured on this park early. On the way there I bought a little bottle of water for about two dollars. But on arrival, I was told by a big USAmerican security officer that I could not bring it into the Jake. I informed this person that I could not believe my ears. Water? Water! You cannot bring water into Jacobs Field, folks. It wasn't even the famous Lake Erie water. Ho ho, I thought, this tall young Nazi does not suspect that I am also carrying a little roll of Mentos in an inside pocket. Heh heh. I thought about inquiring whether he had ever heard of Flip Rosen. Instead, I took a little swig of the *verboten* liquid and tossed the plastic bottle into the handy nearby barrel.

We got into the park pretty early, and because I wanted to experience cheapskate nosebleed seats for a change, I plunked down twenty U.S. dollars for a pair of ducats, and we began our climb—to the fifth deck, section 572, way up in the corner out over left field. I have always been scared of height in man-made structures, and for the past year I had been taking Serc, an anti-vertigo pill. Jean was looking concerned, checking the hue of my face. I felt a little better when other cheapskates showed up in our section. There were not a lot of them, but half were wearing Minnesota Twins regalia. I was wearing my Tacoma cap. I tried not to look at the equivalent seats high in the right field corner. There was a lot of stadium to be seen from way up where we were. The Jumbotron got us to a sad start, showing a parade of famous moments in baseball, including too much time on Bill Buckner's booting that slow roller from Mookie Wilson.

The game itself was short, only two and a half hours despite the fact that the Twins, even without a few of their starters with unspellable names, got nine runs. The Indians scored two, and I was in the men's room while they did it. Apparently Jean's favourite player, Coco Crisp, led off with a triple, and scored ahead of some gink named Blake, who popped a home run.

Ho hum. There were a lot of pigeons in this park, and they were at least as interesting as Slider, the tribe's mascot.

Jean didn't get beaten up chasing a foul ball, because no Indian or Twin since Harmon Killebrew could hit one this far. But we did hear a neat story from the people to our left. This was a guy with his two sons, maybe ten and eleven. Every summer they drive around, going to ball games. Apparently their mom was more of a fan of shopping.

"So do we," I told him.

"We were thinking of going to Toronto, but we're worried about the big SARS epidemic," confessed the dad.

"Aw, just don't hang around any hospitals," we told him.

So we exchanged ballpark stories. I showed them my Rainiers cap. They were all wearing brand new Cleveland Indians caps. Those lucky kids must have a neat collection.

"Last month we were in a game in Beloit."

"Aw, we missed Beloit," I said.

"Their grand-dad was with us."

"Neat."

"They started throwing free hotdogs into the stands."

"Ah, the minor league parks!"

"Their grand-dad trampled the living dickens out of them, going after a hotdog."

"Whew!"

"Got it, too."

18

My Favourite Things

> Would a football fan listen to one hundred games a year
> *on radio?*
>
> —Thomas Boswell

I WAS GOING TO SAY, "INDULGE ME." But to heck with that. I'm going to indulge myself.

This decision has nothing to do with the fact that I am writing this during the week before Christmas and New Year, when the newspapers are printing their best-of-the-year lists. Best fusion restaurant soup of the year—chili raspberry surprise, etc.

Nope, I made my decision weeks and weeks ago, as a promise and reward for all the long hard toil I have bent myself to in these hand-written pages.

So this chapter is going to be about my favourite baseball things. Oh, and by the way, I hate whiskers on kittens.

Being as to how I am a Canadian, not a USAmerican, I will lead off with my favourite teams rather than my favourite individuals.

AMERICAN LEAGUE TEAM: The Boston Red Sox. I told you about the 1945 World Series when I was nine years old and heard part of it on my Uncle Red's big console radio in Penticton. I decided then that the Detroit Tigers were my favourite team, even before they won the Series.

The following year I decided that the team I really liked was the Red Sox. The 1946 World Series introduced me to the heartache of being a Bosox fan. The 2004 World Series had me cheering for the St. Louis Cardinals after the third game. I was not ready for the idea that my team could be the champions. It would be like being a Yankees fan, and who could face the drabness of that? I knew, when the Sox won the fourth game, that there would be baseball illiterates wearing Red Sox gear all next year.

So 1946 would be the last time I'd be a front-runner. The late forties was an absolutely wonderful time to follow the races in the American League, and a character-forming time to become a teenager.

It was also kind of sad as well as secure to be a tad in a treefruit valley in the Interior of British Columbia, so far away from the eastern USA, where major league baseball was carried on. In the paper or one of my baseball magazines I would read about some team making a "western trip," and the writer meant Chicago and St. Louis, cities I knew to be way back east.

So I would never see them, Ted Williams, Bobby Doerr, Johnnie Pesky, Dom DiMaggio. But for that reason, I would never forget them. I also know who played for the 1948 Cleveland Indians, such a glamorous crew, my lovely enemies and my dad's team that he would never see.

When the Toronto Blue Jays came into the American League, they skewed things a lot. I have trouble now, rooting for the Sox when they are visitors at SkyDome in Toronto. No baseball fan could ever root for SkyDome, though. Not even under its drab new name, the Rogers Centre, or something along that line.

But if anyone asks me who my team is, I always say the Red Sox.

Which is bothersome, because I like the National League better. When I was a kid, the American League always won the all-star game and always won the World Series, except when the Red Sox were in it.

When I was a kid, the other kids touted the Yankees, so I supported the underdogs, namely ...

NATIONAL LEAGUE TEAM: The Brooklyn Dodgers. In a sense, you could call this front-running, at least for a while after 1946. But remember, the Bums were loveable losers. They were not yet the rich entertainers of the Hollywood set that they have become. They had a demi-logo of a hobo in need of a shave. They had the Sym-Phonie Band that played Spike Jones music at Ebbets Field. In U.S. war movies, when a soldier was dying in his sergeant's arms, he always asked, in a Brooklyn accent, how the Dodgers did yesterday.

The Red Sox were sorehead losers. The Bums were loveable losers. When they scrabbled their way into the World Series, they got swatted by the Yankees in those glowing white pinstriped uniforms.

Besides, my father liked the Giants and the Cardinals. What could I do?

Since moving to Los Angeles, of course, the Dodgers are no more loveable than the Los Angeles Lakers, whom I hate in a healthy manner, though I liked them when they were in Minnesota, where their name made sense. (Don't get me started on that one. When Toronto got into the NBA and called their team the Raptors, some Toronto sports writer actually wrote that at least the team was not named after some bird.) And when the Montreal Expos (a name so terrible that you had to kind of like it) came into the National League, I was living in Montreal, or Heaven, as we called it that year. So though I do not throw away my lifelong allegiances (well, okay, I did throw away the Celtics), you could not expect me to enjoy a Los Angeles win over the Expos. And when the jerks who run baseball succeeded in giving the Expos to their moneyed friends down south, I grudgingly went back to the Dodgers full time. Though I am still not sure that I approve of that red number on the front of the shirt.

One Dodger that I will never forgive is Rick Monday, a bonus baby who had become a journeyman outfielder. On Sunday, October 19, 1981, he came up in the ninth inning with two out and hit a home run over Olympic Stadium's centre field fence, thus taking the NL pennant away from the Expos. The Expos would lose another pennant to a players' strike. Despite being the best team in baseball for a few years, the Expos would never get into the World Series. What Whip Wilson (vs. Lash LaRue) fan could not love them?

All the other kids liked Frank Sinatra, but I went with Bing Crosby. They all cheered for Joe DiMaggio, but I dug Ted Williams. Nowadays, most people talk about Williams first, but in, say, 1949 it was Joe DiMaggio.

FAVOURITE PLAYER: Yes, Ted Williams. The Kid. The Splendid Splinter. He's on the cover of one of my books. I have two different Ted Williams tee-shirts. Of course, I liked him partly because he was always a Red Sock, and because he was not Joe DiMaggio. I liked it that he would not tip his hat after he trotted out a home run, and the newspaper writers hated him, and he would not wear a tie, and he would not swing at a pitch that was two inches wide, even if the winning run was on second. I've written about him often. I am proud to be quoted at the beginning of Leigh Montville's big biography of him. I think that if he hadn't fought in two wars, and hadn't run into the fence in an all-star game, he would have had well over seven hundred home runs. He probably was the best pure hitter ever, and he would probably have agreed with that statement. If you asked me who I thought was the best ballplayer of my lifetime, I would tell you Willy Mays. But Ted Williams was the best hitter.

And most of that time Ted Williams was my favourite. If I'd known him in real, as they say, life, I'd probably have disliked him big time. Like Richard S. Prather.

YARD: The park I liked being in the most was the one in which I saw my first major league game. It was called Tiger Stadium, but when I was a kid it had been Briggs Stadium. The other kids liked Babe Ruth, but I liked Ty Cobb. The great Detroit outfielder played half his games at Briggs Stadium, before going to the A's, but in those days it was called Navin Field. If I had known Ty Cobb personally, I know I would have despised him.

Once my mother saw me trying to sharpen the spikes I inherited from my father, and I was doing that in emulation of Ty Cobb. And Eddy Stanky. They were two guys who did not care for African-Americans. Screw both of them, I say now.

Briggs Stadium just looked like the definition of a baseball park. It was green and old, and had a second deck all around. It was a square with rounded corners. It was where Ted Williams hit a two-out, two-on home run to win the 1941 all-star game 7-5.

I was with Greg Curnoe the great Canadian painter and lacrosse enthusiast when I saw my first major league game on July 9, 1967. The Red Sox were in town, and Carl Yastrzemski was on his way to the Triple Crown and the MVP Award. The Sox would win the AL pennant, beating the Tigers (and the Twins) by one game.

In the game we saw Dick McAuliffe hit a home run that entered our area in the second deck overlooking right field. It came our way as a line drive, but we were not close enough to scramble for it. The game we saw was the first of a doubleheader, but I could talk Greg into only one inning of the second game. I felt uncomfortable because he was not really a baseball fan, not the kind that could hunker down for two games. Years later he said somewhere that he hadn't really appreciated how meaningful and exciting this visit to Tiger Shrine was for me. Well, I didn't get to see Al Kaline play because on June 27, he had broken his hand jamming his bat into the bat rack after striking out against Sudden Sam McDowell as the Tigers lost to Cleveland 8-1.

Still, being there was like a moment eighteen years later, when I stood at Keats's grave in Rome.

Oh, and here's another thing that happened in that game (and I hope that you remember that my diaries are locked away five thousand kilometres to the west). The very good African-American pitcher Earl Wilson, who would go 22-11, with a 3.27 ERA that year, hit a home run on a rope just over the low fence in left field. He also won the game 10-4. The Sox won the nightcap 3-0.

Well, Briggs Stadium is a thing of the past now. So is San Francisco's Candlestick Park, the worst place I ever saw a game played. It hasn't been torn down—it has just been left to a football team, and had its name changed, in that hideous new way, to 3Com Park. A candlestick was a bird that used to live there. I don't know what a 3Com is.

I went to Candlestick by bus. I was the only rider on the bus, and when I got there I did not wonder why. I got patted down by some sort of cop on the way in. When I took my seat I had to get ready for a few hours of freezing in the summer wind. Around me were greasy people cursing in sleeping bags. I tried to concentrate on the team my dad liked so well.

UNIFORM: I hate to admit it. The New York Yankees have the best home uniform in baseball. The Tigers' home outfit is a close second. But those Yankees pinstripes are classic, calm and authoritative at once. They even managed to make a weasel like Billy Martin look okay. When the Yankees played their season opener against Tampa Bay in Tokyo, the Yanks were officially the away team, but the Japanese said that they had to wear their famous pinstripes.

In the National Football League the despicable Dallas Cowboys have the best uniforms, especially their white jerseys.

In the National Hockey League the Detroit Red Wings have the best home whites.

In professional soccer the uniforms are there simply to advertise businesses. I usually cheer for Guinness to defeat Sony.

In the National Basketball Association there are some nice uniforms. I'd say that the Boston Celtics have the best one.

Do you see the constant here? As far as I am concerned (and people will tell you that I have impeccable taste and a sense for such things) the best uniforms are clean and simple, and do not change every few years. The Yankees pinstripes are pretty well the same ones that Lou Gehrig wore. The Yankees do not have a different hat for road games.

Unfortunately, just as we are now living in a time when stadiums are named after banks or pet food companies, so we are seeing an era in which the team uniform is a matter of marketing. When Michael Jordan changed his number after one of his retirements, the Chicago Bulls sold a lot more of his jerseys, to people who had to keep up. Same thing happened when the Toronto Maple Leafs developed long blue epaulets.

Have you noticed that the New York Yankees uniforms do not have any names on the back? I hate the Yankees, but they have class.

You want to know something about marketing? Some teams now have *five* different caps—the home game cap, the road game cap, the special days cap, the spring training cap and the batting practice cap. Tell me: does a team have to have a different cap for batting practice? And tell me this: where did I lose my New Orleans Zephyrs batting practice cap on my last visit to Vancouver before I moved back there? You watch—one day your kid will be telling you how much he needs a Houston Astros television interview cap.

You have seen the games in which the teams wear "throwback" uniforms, outfits from 1960 or 1935. Do you think that they are doing this to "honour" old-time baseball?

And when was the last time the Chicago White Sox wore white socks?

BASEBALL NOVEL: Have I mentioned how much I hated *The Natural* by Bernard Malamute? Bernard Malamute was a professor novelist much admired by professor novelists. Even my friend Clark Blaise the baseball short story writer was a willing acolyte of Bernard Malamute. All right. I know that I have told you about that phony academic book. But really, I mean geeze ...

BASEBALL MOVIE: When I was a kid they were always making baseball movies, and any baseball kid would go to them, but you know, they were all pretty bad, hardly worth the fifteen cents. William Bendix as Babe Ruth? Ronald Reagan as Grover Cleveland Alexander? Reagan playing a guy named after a president? Might as well ask him to play a president. Burt Lancaster as Jim Thorpe?

As one got older, one saw fewer Italians as Apaches, and more cinema ballplayers who appeared to have seen a ball or a bat before. Kevin Costner would be persuasive as a catcher in one film and a pitcher in another.

If you look at chat groups on the Internet, you will see a lot of people listing their favourite baseball movies. I've looked and looked, and I've often seen *The Natural* or *Field of Dreams*, but I have never once seen my own favourite, which is *Major League* (1989). *Major League* is, I always claim, a remake of Mel Brooks's *The Producers*. A woman buys the Cleveland Indians and tries to make a terrible team worse by getting her general manager to sign a bunch of proven losers. She wants to move the team to Florida, and figures that utter failure is her chance to alienate Cleveland and her ticket out of town.

This is a rowdy, obscene, irreligious, loud, impolite and thoroughly enjoyable comedy. As in *The Producers*, ownership's plans go awry, and the misfits, voodooists, legally blind and demented come together to go on a winning streak, and fill Cleveland's stadium with jubilant fans. Bob Euker parlayed his numb major league career, via a bunch of beer commercials on television, to a role here as a dipsomaniac play-by-play announcer with no skills for diplomacy.

There were two sequels. The first one was a bummer. The second probably was, too. They should have moved them to Florida.

BASEBALL ANNOUNCER: Someone my age is supposed to be regaling you with the wonders of Dizzy Dean in the TV booth.

"The runners return to their respectable bases," he said.

"He slud into third," he said.

"There's a tall can of corn," he most famously said.

Sure. But I grew up in the Interior of British Columbia, fifteen miles from the Washington border. At night the left coastline of the U.S. was mine. I listened to radio from Seattle, Sacramento, San Francisco and San Diego. This means that I heard the hit parade from KGO 800 in San Francisco. But I heard the Pacific Coast League from KRSC 1150 in Seattle.

That is, I listened to the grinding voice of Leo Lassen. Leo broadcasted the Seattle Rainiers' games from Sicks' Stadium, or when the Rainiers were in, say, Los Angeles, he sat in front of a ticker tape and "recreated" the games right there in the Seattle studio, with sound-effect click of the bat and dialed-up crowd noises.

Leo sometimes forgot the name of the San Francisco shortstop— "The shortstop knocks the ball down, gets to his feet and fires to first."

Leo used to say of the pitcher, "He whines and throws," and my dad would pantomime, but with an audible whine.

But Leo never forgot to mention the name of his sponsor, Hansen Bakery, Seattle's big rival to Langendorf Bread.

I really liked the way Leo would call the play, and then go back and give you a second version with more details. But he was most famous for his home run call.

"It's back, back, back, back, back, and it's a home run," he would say, the last words a kind of anti-climax if it was an opposition homer.

Now the guy in Seattle says, "Bye-bye, baseball."

What is your favourite announcer's homer?

"You can kiss it goodbye."

"That one's not coming back."

"It's outta here."

"He can touch them all."

"It's long enough."

"It could be. It might be. It is."

I still like Leo Lassen's "back back back back back" the best, and I'll never forget the way his voice kind of brayed while he was repeating that word.

Oh, and if you want to know the worst announcers ever, they are those guys who do the Toronto Blue Jays games. It doesn't matter which TV network you're looking at.

BIG LEAGUE MANAGER: Leo Durocher. Are you kidding me?

19

Dark Satanic Mills

I don't know anything about baseball.
                                    —David W. McFadden

FOLLOWING OUR NEW ROUTINE, we left Cleveland after the game and drove along the non-toll Ohio highway as far as some featureless place called Elyria. There we pretended we were USAmericans, having a late dinner at Applebee's, where we saw the resignation in the eyes of the waiter when this big tough guy came in to have all the chicken wings you can eat for a buck and a half.

"We're closing the kitchen in twenty minutes," said the waiter. "Should I just order up four pounds?"

The big tough guy was totally silent, a kind of methodical *presence*. We left while he was mowing his silent way through his preparatory salad.

In the morning we had a late breakfast at IHOP #5507, and pointed the Mercury Sable westward, toward Toledo, Ohio. So I had time to reflect on USAmericans and food. The country is dotted with fast food joints, and each one is full of hefty families stuffing their faces. The knife and fork have nearly disappeared from U.S. life—too slow, I would imagine. In cafés and restaurants the servings are gigantic. I think that they do this because they want to show the world and themselves that they can. The U.S., they have been told all their lives, is the most successful country there is, land of abundance. Eat up!

They can be seen getting something new to scarf down after every inning of the ball game: peanuts and Cracker Jack and hotdogs and ice cream and potato chips and pizza and fries and Pepsi and Coke and beer and bratwurst and pretzels and hamburgers and sno-cones and cheese dogs and drumsticks and wings and cotton candy and sundaes and sushi and pork rinds and nachos and corn dogs and Philly steaks.

I had one of my headaches (as I do now at this instant of writing [though not at this instant of rewriting], [but I do have one now that I am re-rewriting] on the last day of the year) all day, and by late evening I would also be shaky. How fitting that we would spend that day in Toledo, Ohio, and the night in Monroe, Michigan.

The Toledo Mud Hens are probably the most famous minor league team in baseball. Since childhood, I had wanted to go to Toledo and see the Mud Hens. I went to Toledo, Spain with my wife and daughter late in the twentieth century. It is a Gothic stone city on top of a little mountain, one of the most beautiful cities in the world. I didn't expect that much of Toledo, Ohio, though when I was a teenager I'd heard that the *Toledo Blade* was a great crusading newspaper.

My pal Fast Eddie wears Toledo Mud Hens caps and shirts and so on, because his wife Nancy comes from Toledo, Ohio. There was no doubt: I was going to acquire a Mud Hens cap. This was a new trip, after all, and I already had Indians and Tigers caps.

Downtown Toledo is pretty sorrowful. As Jean says, it looks as if it used to be something. I like that in international seaports such as Trieste or Puerto Limón. And it can be sadly interesting, as in Butte. But this mid-sized city is a spill off the highway to Detroit, and the air is humid, and there are 86 Fahrenheit degrees, and hardly anyone on these sidewalks, and too much of downtown is made up of no-attendant parking lots with many available parking spots.

In fact, in the area of the ballpark, most of the human figures on the sidewalk are made of bronze, these being the four sculptures of the knothole gang gathered around a few specially made knotholes in a small wooden section of the stadium fence. Of course I got a few photos of me joining them to look through a knothole. No one is bothered by the fact that a metre to our left is a section of fence made of wrought iron. To our right is a section of brick and stone. The outfielders will be backed by postmodern architecture. This, too, is Fifth Third Park, and it is by some distance the best thing going in downtown Toledo.

We were there to buy tickets at 1:30, and a good thing, too, because there weren't many left. Ohioans really fill up their Fifth Third Parks.

Then we had an afternoon to kill in Toledo, Ohio. Okay, I said, we can start by finding me some aspirin for my headache. We went tooling around forlorn Toledo. Often we found ourselves on long, wide, obviously once-regal Collingwood Street. Collingwood Street is edged by tall deciduous trees, big churches of every conceivable denomination and some you'll never hear of again, and old mansions that seem to be mummified, the grass not quite covering the ground, the automobiles all USAmerican, large and a few years old.

What we did not find on Collingwood Street was a drugstore or any other store that might purvey aspirin. Jean was driving.

"Okay," I said, "despite the fact that I am a human being of the adult male persuasion, I will deign to ask for directions."

"Ask whom?"

There was not a person to be seen on the streets of this city of 314,000 souls, but I had a headache, and I told Jean to keep driving. At last we saw a man standing at a curb, smoking a cigarette. I reasoned to myself that cigarettes are often purchased in places where aspirin are for sale. Behind this man was a hospital. He looked like a survivor.

"Ask him," I replied.

Jean scooted up this little one-way street with a couple of arrows on signs pointed in the opposite way. She zipped the window down, and in tumbled the hot humid air. The guy was the first white USAmerican we had seen in Toledo.

"Hi," I said, because he was on my side of the car. I was feeling kind of brave because I hadn't quit smoking all that long ago, and here was some temptation to resist. I was after analgesic, not nicotine.

"How ya?" He did not even comment on the one-way street with his eyes.

"I'd like to know where I can buy some aspirin," I said.

"Downtown?"

"Well, yeah."

Behind him was this big hospital. It was full of aspirins, I was thinking, or probably Tylenols.

"You won't find any downtown," he said, looking over our heads to an imaginary horizon. "You have to go out to one of the malls."

I was at the point of asking whether *he* had any aspirins on him.

"Thanks," I said.

We drove and drove. We got stuck between a hubcap shop and the freeway. Eventually we found a cost-cutter supermarket for black people that were not well-off, and I bought about five hundred aspirins for two dollars. I was the first person in our lineup to use U.S. currency instead of food stamps.

Then we drove some more, feeling grounded once we got back to Collingwood Street. My friend George Stanley the superior poet lived on Collingwood Street in Vancouver. My girl Jean was born and brought up in Collingwood, Ontario. In *A Trip Around Lake Erie*, David McFadden mentions the Collingwood poetry festival.

As a reader you are doing what we were doing, killing time before the ball game between the Toledo Mud Hens and the Louisville Bats. Mainly we wanted to be somewhere with air conditioning.

"Oh my God!" I said. It was a phrase you usually heard from a clot of teenage girls in a mall.

"What?" She jammed on the brakes.

"No. I just remembered that like Buffalo, Cleveland and Detroit, Toledo has a great art gallery. When these northern industrial cities got rich they started art galleries and symphonies. Now that all the money has gone to the southwest, the galleries remain as repositories of great art, standing among the ruins."

After a little more driving, we arrived at the long low white Toledo Museum of Art at 3:30. Perfect. It closes at 4:00. Okay, skip the pottery and fabrics. But make sure that you have a look at that big beautiful ceramic Matisse on the wall when you enter. You could sit and look at that for your half-hour. That alone will tell you that this is a great gallery.

Nicely Matissed, we went back to the ballpark area, parked in a lot that was nearly empty, and went to the Spaghetti Warehouse, where we sat inside a real old streetcar inside the restaurant and looked askance at the sheer size of our entrées. Jean decided to sneak a doggy bag into Fifth Third Park. Why not? It was advertised as Pooches at the Park Night, said so right on our tickets.

We got to the park early and had our customary stroll before settling into our seats. This consisted partly of my whining about the fact that I didn't have a hotdog and a basket of fries, Jean patting my tummy and putting on her "ahem" look.

When we sat down, we found that the seats in this Fifth Third Park were really narrow. A lot of people around here were not going to be able to fit their backsides into them. I had a look around—some folks were sitting on the front edge of their seats, padded knees and stomachs up against the seat in front. Just about all of these people were white folks—Polish-Americans, maybe, German-Americans. All the rest of downtown Toledo is populated by black people, but the ballpark in the middle of downtown Toledo is full of white people. Big white people.

A few of them had brought their dogs. Behind us for a few minutes there was a spotted Great Dane trying to make its way between the bare human legs in the concourse. The year before, Fast Eddie, Paul, George Stanley and I had gone to a day game in Everett. As we were approaching the stadium, we kept seeing dogs on leashes. When we got inside the park we saw that people were sitting behind tables piled with gratis cans of dog food. It took us a while to learn that this was an event called "Bark in the Park." After the fifth inning there was a big parade of dogs across the outfield, and for the seventh-inning stretch there was an excitable border collie or some such animal catching Frisbees. Paul and I started barking—what the heck?

There were about 150 dogs in the park that day in Everett. Here at Fifth Third Park, a generous estimate would put the canine attendance at about 15. The parade, along foul territory on the first base side, was ragged, with tiny hairy dogs tangled around the feet of the two Great Danes. Pooches at the Park wasn't much to look at.

Neither were the Mud Hens. These were, after all, the AAA hopefuls for the Detroit Tigers, who were on schedule to attain the worst season's record in the history of big league baseball. If these guys were not good enough to replace the losingest Tigers, they should not be expected to show much against the Louisville Bats, who were the AAA hopefuls for the moribund Cincinnati Reds. Sure enough, the Hens got six hits and lost 3-1.

Too bad. At the outset the PA announced the appearance of "your world-famous Toledo Mud Hens," which is, I think, true. Their players may be pretty punk, but the franchise is renowned. They can also be respected for their logo, that old-fashioned tough-but-scrawny bat-wielding bird that has always been there. He's the opposite of the Muckdog.

Well, I love baseball, all baseball. Even when I have a headache. But this was not a thrilling game, and the humidity would discourage much jumping up and down. The teenaged girls in our region of the stands showed their first interest in anything other than their own appearance when the hotdog race started up on the Jumbotron.

Jean thought that it was kind of cute that the reliefers walked in from the "hen pen." She liked the logo a lot, and likes her Mud Hen pin better than any other in her collection. But she didn't care a whole lot for the mascot, a big yellow-feathered guy named Muddy. He had a beak. Even worse was his female companion, Muddonna.

Imagine. We had a half-hour in the Toledo Museum of Art, and three hours at Fifth Third Park.

We motored in the dark as far as Monroe, unable to see the bucolic beauty of America, but noting the irony that here in the middle of that part of America devoted to the history and the continuing creation of the automobile, appeared the worst highway in the Great Lakes region at least. It is more like a strip-bombed target than a freeway, this I-75 that joins Toledo to Detroit. Your automobile is banging up and down, and the lanes get narrower and narrower, with stained concrete walls lit, it seems, only by the fires of Hell that have broken through the crust of the Earth.

So in Monroe we ignored the dark Satanic mills and tucked into a big Holiday Inn Express room with a Jacuzzi. I didn't use the Jacuzzi, but Jean did. I surfed the TV for sports news. Here we were, in Michigan, the state in which I got the two best slices of pizza I have ever had, one in 1956 in the Upper Peninsula, the other in 1967, passed in through the window of a Volkswagen Beetle on a street in Detroit.

Neither slice was from a pizza chain. A pizza chain called Little Caesar's, which makes TV commercials saying that gangsters are amusing, is owned by an ex-ballplayer named Mike Ilitch. In 1982 he bought the Detroit Red Wings ice hockey team for $8 million. In 1992 he bought the Detroit Tigers for $85 million. In recent years the Red

Wings have been a powerhouse, loaded with players who will go to the Hockey Hall of Fame. None of the 2003 Tigers is headed for Cooperstown.

In Toledo last night the nice old lady who was sitting with her nice old hubby to our left let it be known that the reason for the catastrophe of the Tigers and the tragedy of the Mud Hens was simple: "That so-and-so" was spending a fortune on the hockey team, and pinching every baseball penny.

We took our time banging and crashing our way up to Detroit. When you leave Monroe you also leave Lake Erie, and you despair of ever seeing Canada again. The sky is filled with precipitate air metal, and the ground is made up of three things—thousands of industrial chimneys with horror leaving them at the tops, great expanses of entirely used-up dirt and broken-down highways.

You would think that a country with an auto industry would try to have smooth open highways leading into and out of the region where the autos are made. But drive to Dearborn or Pontiac. You will see that big industry doesn't give a shit. You want a car, pal? If you don't, get the hell out of our way.

Jean had never been in Detroit. The last time I had been there was in 1967, when Canada was a hundred years young, and the Motor City was already really old. You'll be shocked by the downtown, I told her. It looks like Beirut after the civil war. Detroit is a code word for urban disaster. It makes Toledo look like a momentary glitch. It makes Hamilton look kind of pretty. It's desolate. It's the peeyoo of America. Downtown is all holes and boarded-up windows on buildings that used to be the verve of modern architecture—most of a century ago.

In 1997 the city sold permits for 86 construction starts and 8,432 demolitions.

Comerica Park, named after some kind of financial services outfit, along with Ford Field, the new home of the Detroit Lions football team, is supposed to start downtown Detroit on the road to postwar recovery. We'll see. It is not Tiger Stadium. It is more Disney than Briggs. There's a Ferris wheel, giant sculptures of tigers, a water extravaganza, a carrousel with tigers instead of horses, stainless steel statues of Ty Cobb, Charlie Gehringer, Hank Greenberg, Willie Horton, Al Kaline and my favourite boyhood pitcher, Hal Newhouser, all in splendid action. There's a lot more.

When the workers at Disneyland finish their staff softball tournament, the winners shout, "We're going to Comerica Park!"

Between 1966 and 1967 Detroit was for me a poetry city. When I came down here from London, Ontario, I hung out with John Sinclair and his gang in an old semi-condemned building in an area where all the storefronts were broken or boarded up. I was involved with their poetry magazine *Work* and John's jazz magazine *Change*, and the underground newspaper *Guerrilla*.

That Detroit is all gone now, but as in Toledo, we had time to kill, so we headed for the museums out on wide Woodward Avenue that still seemed to retain at least a remnant of its grandeur. It was so hot and so humid, that our principal aim was to find a parking spot as close as possible to any door that would lead to public air conditioning. How age and America had diminished us!

First the Detroit Institute of Arts. This is a grand museum, comparable with Chicago's Art Institute. I wanted mainly to see the great Diego Rivera mural that I had last seen thirty-six years ago. Imagine that those pictures have remained visible all those months and years, open to love while we were away, somewhere else, in Osoyoos or Copenhagen.

In 1932 Rivera painted all the walls, twenty-seven panels in all, of a large court inside the DIA. The work is called "Detroit Industry," and in Rivera's usual way, shows the relationship between workers and bosses. It is a wonderful place, the middle of that court, to stand for, say, forty-five minutes. Here is a great mural that was not painted over or demolished when the U.S. capitalists found out that Rivera was still a socialist, ungrateful Mex. Good for Detroit!

If you are really lucky you will see the Siqueiros mural at Maximilian's Castle and the Rivera mural at the Detroit Institute of Arts.

We also went to the Detroit History Museum up the street. There you can find out a lot about the guys who made cars, but nothing about the Artists' Workshop, John Sinclair's outfit.

When we got to Comerica, having said no thanks to the old black guy outside who had some crack for sale, we did our usual stroll, and we could see that though this one had a Ferris wheel and all, these new downtown parks with their retro kinks were starting to look alike to the baseball traveller. In my opinion, the one in Seattle, though named after some bank or insurance company, sets the mark. Its seats are banked so steeply that all fans are close to the field—and every once in a while you can hear a train horn from the nearby railroad station.

We lingered long in the air-conditioned gift and souvenir shop. Everywhere we went, from the ticket window to the deli-sandwich bar, people were happy to make jokes about supporting this team. Today was August 21, and unless the Tigers were to go on a tear during the next five weeks, well, you know what the Tigers were going to be.

But in fact there weren't all that many people here to do the supporting. We had bought seats in the front row of the left field bleachers, good home run ball location, except that homers were hard to come by at Comerica. But it was so damned hot in that Midwest humidity way that we never went there. Instead we found some nice expensive seats in the shade on the terrace along the left field side and plunked ourselves down there. These were neat little comfort stations, two wide armchairs linked by a table for your drinks and scorebook. The crowd was so small and the security so lax that no one in an outfit asked to look at our tickets. Compare SkyDome, where the ushers will chase away kids who come down in the ninth inning to see what the game looks like from the good seats that some businessmen have vacated.

Jean was so cute, sitting there in her red Niagara Stars cap. She was fascinated by Ben Weber, the wired-looking Anaheim relief pitcher with the nerd eyeglasses. She was scornful of the Tigers' mascot Paws, who never showed up, either because it was inhumanly hot in a tiger outfit, or too embarrassing to be any kind of tiger in Detroit in August 2003.

In any case, the feckless Anaheim Angels defeated the disastrous Detroit Tigers 10-7, and our ballpark season was now really over, though I did not know it. On Labour Day I would try to referee a dogfight, and wind up in the hospital in Welland with four spikes in a broken hip. Now, having written much of this book while sitting in a wheelchair, I am second-guessing my plans to come out of retirement on the sandlots of Vancouver next summer or even the one after that.

20

Cricket and Pesäpalla

> They (Expos fans) discovered 'boo' is pronounced the same in French as it is in English.
>
> —Harry Caray

SO, AS YOU HAVE NOTICED, that baseball trip that Jean and I took occurred mainly across the top of the U.S. map. The main reason for this is that organized baseball, as it terms itself, keeps moving out of Canada. Despite the fact that we Canadians were playing baseball at least as early as were the USAmericans, and maybe earlier, we keep losing our pro teams. The Calgary Cannons went south. So did the Medicine Hat Blue Jays. The Vancouver Canadians fell out of the Pacific Coast League. The St. Catharines Stompers became the Brooklyn Cyclones, of all things. The Expos are nostalgia, and the Ottawa Lynx don't look all that permanent. The Edmonton Trappers had a neat name, but that didn't save them. The whole Canadian Baseball League vanished into the northern air.

Sometimes I think that the whole country should be condemned to hockey. It's such an *angry* game. One evening lately I was in London, Ontario, and the air was at minus 15 degrees, and a guy was skating on this little patch of ice at the market. He was going fast as hell. He should have had a stick in his hands, he seemed so *angry*, just skating by artificial light in the cold night.

Baseball is played on the grass, if you have grass, in flannels. I think that part of the reason for all the anger and violence in hockey is the fact that hockey players are forced to wear embarrassing clothes. Hockey players are high school dropouts with too much hair on their bodies. They have to wear *shorts* over high knit stockings. And how are these stockings held up? Garter belts. How are the shorts held up? Suspenders. Hockey players have to be cross-dressing fur-bearers. No wonder they are always ready to bash somebody.

So, despite the fact that I get down on my knees every day to thank the Lord that I was born north of the forty-ninth parallel, I will cross that line to see a baseball game any day of the week. Until the magic summer of 2004 I had never been in San Diego when the Padres were home, but I had gone and taken a look at their ballpark. Same thing with Shea Stadium when we got stuck in Queens one New Year's Eve.

I've never been to a hockey rink outside of Canada. I have been to soccer games in Central America and bullfights in Mexico, but these are only local colour. If I am in Tahiti or Serbia, I want to see the baseball park.

My old pal the poet Lionel Kearns is still playing hockey with all his sons, and probably some grandsons now. Decades ago he played some ice hockey at an arena in Mexico City. Maybe if I'd been there at the time, I would have gone to see him play. The only time I was in Mexico City with Lionel, he was on his way to Cuba. The lucky son of a gun got to play catcher in a game in which Fidel Castro was his pitcher. Now that I think of it, I'm as angry as a hockey player that a hockey player got to play baseball with Fidel in 1964.

In high school Lionel was also a bagpipe player. He got used to wearing embarrassing clothes. I was a tuba player. Maybe that explains something.

In Mexico I got to go to a baseball game with my pal Sergio Mondragón, the poet and Yoga teacher. In Mexico City, you could go to see the Diablos Rojos or the Tigres. Sergio and I went to see the

213

Tigres play Puebla. Harry "Suitcase" Simpson was playing outfield for the Tigres. He had played in the Negro Leagues, gone to the majors when USAmericans figured that money could be made by integrating baseball, and come to the Mexican League in his old age. He got his nickname because of all the times he changed teams.

Casey Stengel once called Suitcase Simpson the best defensive outfielder in baseball. You'll remember that Ted Williams gave that accolade to Jim Piersall. In any case, playing the outfield in Mexico City is a specialized job. Because the city is 7,700 feet above sea level, a decently hit fly ball tends to carry. Thus the outfielders have learned to stand on the warning track, and never have to go back on the ball.

As you know, the spectator usually feels ready for a hotdog around the fourth inning. In Mexico one feels ready for a taco, of course. I volunteered to go and get the tacos, and this caused a certain anxiety in the *corazón* of Señor Mondragón. As a Yoga teacher and practitioner, Sergio was a vegetarian. I was a Canadian, and Spanish is not the language of Canadians, so Sergio was concerned that I might get him a *taco con seso* instead of a *taco con queso*. Those two words sound quite a lot alike, but *queso* means cheese, which is what Sergio was in favour of, while *seso* means brain, which he did not allow himself to eat. Two other factors were conjoined to the facts that I was a newcomer to Mexican Spanish and that the words resembled one another. One: the tacos you got at the ballpark were closed and deep-fried in vegetable oil. Two: even when you force them open, you have to be careful, because cooked cheese and cooked brain are the same shade of off-white.

"Don't worry about a thing." I said to Sergio, as I trundled off to the ballpark's *taquería*.

When I got back with the tacos that I was pretty sure had to be *queso* because I had my own reasons for not desiring to eat brain, Sergio was delicate, both with his movements and with my sentiments. He carefully opened one corner of the warm taco, and carefully held it to his nose.

I did not take a bite of mine till he took a bite of his.

One could write a whole chapter on ballpark food, and one probably has done so.

And various ballpark foods in various countries would be a neat subject. Tacos in Mexico. Sushi in Japan.

Once I went to a baseball game at Aloha Stadium, out by Pearl Harbor. This was way back when there were teams from Pacific coast cities in the Pacific Coast League. But I was not there to watch the PCL Hawaii Islanders. They were over the water and on the road. No, I was watching a contest between the University of Hawaii Rainbow Warriors and a team from some university in California, maybe Chico State.

Aloha Stadium was interesting. It had artificial turf, for football and baseball and God knows what other sports they play in the former paradise. I saw them changing the configuration from football or soccer to baseball. This involved moving an entire section or two of stands. These sections are on wheels, and they move with the slow majesty you see in the closing of the roof at the former SkyDome in Toronto.

I had seen a lot of baseball being played in parks around Honolulu. Most of it was being played by Japanese-Americans, or maybe Japanese-Hawaiians. Now here at Aloha Stadium, there was not a big crowd, but what crowd there was was made up mostly of Japanese-Americans. I suppose that I could have got a hotdog, this being part of the U.S. empire, but when I looked around, I didn't see anyone eating hotdogs or popcorn. I saw old Japanese guys manipulating chopsticks (*ohashi*) and styrofoam versions of the traditional Japanese lunch boxes (*bento*). The stuff inside was pretty basic—rice, shrimp, *miso*; and these ballpark *bento* were about as far from, say, a fine Meiji lacquer lunch box as ballpark nachos are from the nachos you might expect to get at the Tampico Restaurant in Everett, Washington.

Maybe there is a direct inverse relationship between the quality of the food and the quality of the baseball being played. I say this because the best frank I ever had at a baseball game I got in a small suburb somewhere in the hills above Basel, Switzerland. What can you expect? Maybe the best ballpark franks are in Austria, but let me tell you, this very moment I am picturing that huge dog I had while watching the Eagles play the Bears on that hillside diamond. It was a sausage to write home about, packed into a real Swiss bread bun, with real European mustard, real Alpine sauerkraut, and onions to die for. Man, it was good.

The Eagles and the Bears were not so good. My friend Ela and I were part of a very small group standing in a drizzle, watching these eager young Swiss men, encouraged by their USAmerican managers, make a stab at the North American game. We may have been the only watchers who were not related to someone there. I had found out about the game in the Basel newspaper. It would not stop drizzling, so after the franks (oh, Lord, they were good!) were devoured and the final score reached 17-8, we went to the tram station.

I was pretty happy, though a little damp. I'd added a new baseball country to my collection, and I'd taken Ela to her first baseball game in Switzerland, though she had been living there for ten years.

In Melbourne the hotdogs were not as good, but the baseball was better.

In the good old days, starting in 1984, I got to New Zealand and/or Australia every second year or more, but usually I was half a world away from baseball, or so I thought. I did catch sight of the road to the Perth Heat's home park, because it is visible from a vehicle taking one to or from the Perth airport. Once I was sharing a taxi to the airport with Doris Lessing, the famous English novelist from Rhodesia. I pointed to the road in question.

"That's where the Perth baseball team play their home games," I explained, using the poor pronoun reference and verb agreement favoured by the British.

"Is that so?" Ms. Lessing wanted to know.

I'm thinking that baseball never caught on in Rhodesia.

But a few years later I was in Melbourne with a bunch of my Aussie friends and a few Canadians I had got to know. My favourite in this latter group was Alison Gordon, the famous baseball crime novelist from Toronto. Ms. Gordon is the perpetrator of the best baseball crime novel title of all time: *The Dead Pull Hitter.*

Alison used to be a baseball reporter for the *Toronto Star*, the best newspaper in Canada, and though she is not a big fan of professional ballplayers, she loves baseball. We were in Australia during the infamous baseball strike of 1994, and Alison told me that she was starving for baseball. I know, I told her, though because I lived in a minor league city, I at least had some box scores to look at. She told me that she had taken to following the Intercounty League in southern Ontario much more closely than ever before.

I suppose that we could have gone to a one-day cricket match, but I didn't even know whether it was cricket season. It was winter down under, after all, though the idea of a winter in Australia is pretty comical to someone such as I, who am at this very moment looking out at a snowy wonderland, as in "I wonder what I am doing here."

But at least I *played* a little cricket. Okay, not real cricket, but a nice family outing that the Aussies have created, called beach cricket. You know that the Aussies have a big island, and they have a folklore about the "outback," as they call their interior, but almost all of them live on the coast, and they spend as much of their lives as they can at the beach. For beach cricket you get those little wooden wicket things, a cricket bat, and a tennis ball, the same kind of object that shinny players imitate ice hockey with. Part of the fun is whacking the ball into the Bass Strait and watching your friends go after it, especially if they are attired not in "swimmers," but in the outfits they'd go to a barbecue or a church service in.

I know a little about cricket, I guess. I will never figure out what is meant by "unlimited overs," but I do know that the batsman is supposed to stand stiff like an Englishman, with the bat pointed downward, and swing stiff-armed when he wants to strike the bowler's googly or something. I tried the stiff approach, but got impatient, and it was not long till I was hitting fly balls into the chuck or toward the sandy cliff at the top edge of the beach.

Couldn't get Alison to play, though. I guess she's a reporter at heart.

But cricket is not baseball, though it is more interesting than all those other British games. Luckily, Alison found out that the Australian League baseball semi-final playoffs were happening, and even better than that, the Sydney Blues were in town to play the Melbourne Reds. It was a sand dune for a drowning man! Six of us wedged our bodies into a little Australian car and went in search of the Reds' home park. Three of us were Australians, but no one knew where the game was to be conducted, not even Beryl Langer, the great sociologist and expert on Canadian crime fiction writers.

We just drove around in the gloaming, left turns, right turns, in likely parts of Melbourne, a city surrounded by suburbs, and suburbs often, we knew, play host to ball teams. It was getting late. The game had started a while ago. We were getting hysterical with baseball starvation. The car felt small.

"Look for light," I said. "I'm going to find the park. Look for lights."

And sure enough, that's how we did it. By the fifth inning we were settled into the grandstand, ready to ignore anything that didn't seem like real baseball. Alison bought a truly beautiful Reds tee-shirt that featured an illustration of a baseball bat with a bite taken out of it. I wish that I had got one, too; I'd be wearing it right now instead of the Bristol University one I have on. But I was a purist in those days—I would buy only a baseball cap, and they didn't have one big enough for me.

Yes, the hotdogs were pretty Australian, but the Aussies were better ballplayers than were the Swiss. I think that they are allowed two foreigners per team, but I've been told that there are quite a few ballplaying Australians who used to be USAmericans. I can't remember which former big leaguers we saw, and I can't remember the score or who won. But I do remember the relaxed look on Alison Gordon's face as she sat back in her grandstand seat, with a tee-shirt in one hand and a hotdog in the other.

Uh huh, the hotdog was pretty Australian, but it was okay.

On the way to finding the ballpark, we had got to discussing our favourite movies. I went on smugly about *The Tall T*, a wonderful oater starring Randolph Scott, the greatest Hollywood actor of all time, with Richard Boone as the head bad guy, ably abetted by an eerie Henry Silva. The love interest is Maureen O'Sullivan, and the director is my guy Budd Boetticher.

I said, oh so smugly, that the other five people in the car would not only have never seen it, but would never have heard of it. But I was underestimating the marvelous Beryl Langer. She knew the movie well, and even agreed with me that it is a great film that cuts right into the heart of loneliness and its relationship with good and evil.

Two weeks after I got back to Canada I received a tube in the mail from Australia. It was from Beryl. Inside it were two of those old poster stills they used to put in front of the movie theatre. They showed two scenes from *The Tall T*.

A lot of my adventures in baseball around the world have nothing to do with food. Take Costa Rica, for example. In Costa Rica the national cuisine is the hamburger, and the best hamburgers in the country come from a joint called *Hamburguesa Big Boy*. And if you find the baseball stadium in Puerto Limón, Costa Rica, in, say, February 1979, you will discover that this concrete structure across the road from the soccer stadium is called *El Estadio Big Boy*.

I was at the time wearing a sort of baseball cap. Puerto Limón is a lot closer to the equator than one usually is, unless one is in Honolulu, and so the sun is, in February, still pretty high in the sky, certainly a lot higher than it is back home in Vancouver, where you probably will not catch sight of it anyway, or even Trieste, where one began to write the novel one was now writing in Costa Rica.

So I got a line of sunburn along the part in my hair, and decided that I should have a hat for protection against the unrelenting sun. The sun in Vancouver is not only a lot lower, but is also well-concealed behind grey clouds. In Costa Rica one finds out that it wants to burn up everything in sight.

I went looking for a hat. They have some neat hats in Puerto Limón, straw hats, Hemingway deep sea fishing hats, light blue plastic cowpoke hats. But they all come in tiny sizes. People along the Caribbean coast of Central America grow smallish heads. I finally bought the largest hat in Limón, a baseball cap with an illustration of a rock band called Kiss on the front. It was three sizes too small, so I got out my Swiss Army knife and made a few strategic cuts. The hat did cover the bright red part in my hair, but it kind of … perched on my head.

Years later I got the largest Mexico City Diablos Rojos cap I could find. I could not bear to slice it with my Swiss Army knife, so it lay for years in the trunk of my car, along with my other emergency baseball gear.

I wore my Kiss hat on my walk to Big Boy Stadium. Like a lot of Puerto Limón, the stadium had seen better days. By the waterfront there is a little triangle of park, with white paint on the trunks of the palm trees. This is where Cristobal Colón made one of his landings on one of his voyages.

It looked as if he could have played ball at Big Boy Stadium. There were a lot of weeds and old banana skins outside the park, stains in the concrete of the stadium, imperfections in the wood that one saw from time to time.

But here and there in the stands were a few old black men sitting apart and still, chins on hands folded on walking sticks. On the other side of the chicken wire were one older black guy and four young black guys. I took a seat and wished that I had a walking stick, maybe the one I would pick up in Mexico City eight years later.

It was pre-season. The infield was a little muddy. The grass in the outfield was a little long, and not very even in its lengthiness. The kids' gloves were not very recent in their manufacture. Their instructor did not have a basket of white baseballs. I felt as if I recognized him, just as I'd felt as if I recognized all the old black men and women sitting on the verandahs of their little unpainted houses along the track of the Northern Railway built late in the nineteenth century by Canadian money paid to African-Jamaican gandy-dancers.

The old coach, if that's what he was, hit fungos to the young men, and they often caught them. Then he set them up as infielders and hit grounders to them, and the four young guys pounced on them inexpertly but with panache. I was reminded of the young black college soccer team I had seen in San José, the capital of Costa Rica. Okay, it is true, and it isn't a racist observation: wherever you go, most black guys just play sports with more pizzazz.

I was a lonely middle-aged Canadian guy looking at a remnant of my favourite game, maybe some pre-season workout at a weed-grown ball yard on the tenth degree north of latitude.

Once in Berlin I looked from the window of my yellow subway car at an above ground station, and saw a white baseball lying on the grass halfway up a slope that no one could climb without running afoul of German law.

Looking from an Italian train window just before arriving in Bologna from Padua, I saw two kids playing ball, one pitching to the other. I presumed that the pitcher was, every second pitch, the one that went to chase the ball.

Once, from the window of a train going from Oslo to Lund, I saw an unpeopled baseball diamond near the coast of Sweden, not far from the place where they make Lego.

Another time, from the window of a car returning to Rome from Viterbo, I spied an abandoned baseball diamond. The car was a Fiat being driven by Annalisa Goldoni. Annalisa translated my very long poem *Kerrisdale Elegies* into Italian. For the baseball part of *Elegie di Kerrisdale*, she got help from her brother, who was involved with Italian baseball. Every year the European baseball championship final is between Italy and Holland.

But the strangest baseball I ever saw was in Finland. Early in the twentieth century a man named Lauri Pihkala went to the U.S. for a while and fell in love with the great game. He brought baseball home with him and tried to teach it to his countrymen. There already were ancient ball games in Finland, of course, and some of these were combined with what Pihkala could remember of the New World game, the result being a popular summer pastime called Pesäpallo.

Pesäpallo is very big in Suomi. One in every ten Finns is a ballplayer. All children play it at school, and there are hundreds of little league teams. The game looks a lot like our game, but there are significant differences. For example, there are no fireball pitchers, because the pitcher stands beside the batter and tosses the ball up for him. It's sort of a cross between slo-pitch and pepper. There are four bases, as in our game, but first base is part way down the third base line. Second base is sort of where we would have first base. And just as there are no power pitchers, there are no huge power hitters, because there are no fences to hit homers over.

It's a really neat game. In 2003, as in most years lately, the men's championship went to Sotkamon Jymy. On the women's side, Jyväskylä Kirittäret won their first ever title.

Oh, and when Sotkamon won the championship game? The team and its fans celebrated in the traditional way by running into Lake Sapso. This happened on September 14. Lake Sapso is on the sixty-third degree north of latitude.

21

What's in *Your* Trunk?

Fanaticism? No. Writing is exciting and baseball is like writing.

—Marianne Moore

SOMETIMES I THINK ABOUT HOW MANY ASPECTS THERE ARE to your life, and then I think about the sheer number of ways the game of baseball, uh, impacts on your day, and I have to wonder how a person finds any time to think about anything other than baseball.

Even with all that fervent attention, I still cannot answer any of the classic questions about the game. Why is a fly ball that hits the foul pole declared fair? How come the people at the ball game sing "Take me out to the ball game"? What do people mean when they say that some unexpected thing has come straight out of left field? I gave some thought to the things that can come, more or less straight, out of left field. One would be a ball thrown by the left fielder after either a catch or a hit. But wouldn't everyone at the park be expecting it? The same thing goes for the left fielder, who trots in, out of left field, after the third out.

Are we supposed to think that left field is by its own nature some weird place that we normally don't think about? I've always thought that of all the positions in baseball, left field is the least exciting. Of course, if a muscular person such as Sammy Sosa used to be comes up to the batter's box that is closer to left field, he is said to be taking his stance on the right side of the plate. He is likely to hit a ball to the left side of the infield or down the left field foul line—which is in fair territory.

I think that the guy who decided all that left-right stuff was the grandfather of the guy who started the business about being a certain number of games over or under .500. This talk started in the 1980s. It just gave this baseball fancier one more thing to fret about. According to sportswriters and their fellow Mensa members on television, if the Red Sox are 7 and 6 after the first two weeks of play, they are a game over .500. But if the Yankees, please, God, are at 6 and 6, the Sox are a *half* game ahead of them. Given that the Yankees are at .500, I do not see why someone hasn't done something about this years ago.

Can you go ahead and live your life and follow your team, and not let this sort of thing bother you?

Is it all right with you if there are no Pacific coast cities in the Pacific Coast League (unless you want to argue for Tacoma, at the southern end of Puget Sound, which is all salt water, eh?)? After all, Atlanta is no longer in the western division of the National League. Think of it: the state of Tennessee has two teams in the Pacific Coast League, the same number boasted by California.

But there is a lot of relativity in the minor leagues, teams moving or changing working agreements and names. Already, one of the teams Jean and I saw on our trip has changed from the Idaho Falls Padres to the Idaho Falls Chukars. This will not make Jean happy. She liked that mascot at McDermott Field, the guy dressed up as a padre, with robe and tonsure. The new mascot is sure to have a beak.

I told you how unhappy we were when the Canadian Baseball League went seams up, and our "home team" Niagara Stars (at

Welland) disappeared. Welland is only fifteen minutes away from our semi-rural home in downtown Port Colborne. And St. Catharines is only a half-hour away. I have a St. Catharines Stompers fan hat and an authentic St. Catharines Stompers jersey. It is expensive-looking and beautiful. It is very white with burgundy pinstripes, and the word STOMPERS incorporates the logo—a bunch of grapes, honouring St. Catharines's position as the biggest city in Ontario's Niagara wine district. It's the wine capital of Ontario.

I won the hat and the jersey for being the smartest guy in a two-man baseball quiz at the Port Colborne High School. A guy from Stompers management presented me with my prizes, and I looked forward to a game in St. Catharines Community Park against some NY-Penn League opponent, maybe the Muckdogs.

How natural to have a St. Catharines team play those towns just down the road—Batavia, Auburn, Oneonta. But the Toronto Blue Jays would not spend any money on their single-A team down the lakeshore, and what was bound to happen, happened. The Stompers could have been my home team, but they are now in Brooklyn, playing in a nice little stadium at Coney Island. My buddy Fast Eddie and one of his sons got to watch them there. They may have been playing the Staten Island Yankees.

In a very small sense I am glad. It is always even more cool to have a jersey from a defunct team. At least it was until the business boys started manufacturing St. Louis Browns shirts and Brooklyn Dodgers caps. It is especially neat to have an authentic jersey from a defunct minor league team.

"Stompers? What the hell are the Stompers?"

And then you get to tell them.

A completely different satisfaction is the one I get from my baseball pants. I used to wear them to play ball in sometimes. For the past few years I have worn them while exercising and pushing on machines at the gym. They have stitched-up rips from before I got them years ago at the Cleveland Indians store. They are the grey double-knit road pants of the 1984 Indians, and they were worn that year by number 8, Carmen Castillo, an outfielder who never got more than 220 at-bats in a season. In 1984 he had 211 at-bats, and hit .261.

I must have been at least 100 points higher than that in 1984.

The question of a team name and shirt can be complicated when you are trying to coach a team of young girls.

I don't know how these things happen, but I got involved with my daughter Thea's team when she and the rest, mostly Traceys and Staceys, were ten years old. The league was sponsored, minimally, by the YWCA, which means that they paid for balls, bats, bases, catcher's equipment and batting helmets.

The league was more or less organized around schools, so my charges were Thea's classmates at Quilchena Elementary School, and they played their home games at the school and road games at other schools in our part of Vancouver, Volvo country.

I looked around, and no sponsor, YWCA or school board, seemed to be taking care of uniforms, so I thought that I might take up a collection, and then I thought about how much of a hassle that would be, so I decided that my devotion to the game that had enriched my life was enough to cause me to foot the bill for adjustable caps and shirts with logos on them.

I went to an outfit that would sell me shirts and transfer an image onto the fronts. I looked at their choice of images and selected a cardinal standing on his back legs, arms (wings) crossed, looking tough. They'll love this, I thought, my Cardinals.

They hated those shirts. They took to wearing them backward or inside out or under another tee-shirt. They said that the cardinal was stupid. That was their word, stupid.

"But look at him," I said. "He's so tough. He was the best logo in the shirt store."

"Stupid," said Stacey.

They didn't want to be called the Quilchena Cardinals.

"Cards," I said. "Cards for short. That is so neat."

"Dumb," said Tracey.

I remained puzzled and hurt and a dad while my non-Cardinals discussed a name they might call themselves. In short order they came up with a consensus.

"The Mitts."

"What?"

"We're going to be the Mitts."

"What? Impossible. You can't call a ball team the Mitts."

"We were thinking of the Bats."

"That might be a little better."

"But people might think of Batman and those kinds of bats."

"That's why it might be—"

"So we're the Mitts."

"You can't name a team after something you wear."

"Yeah, you can," opined the other Tracey. "What about the Maple Leafs?"

"That's—"

"Go, Mitts, go!"

Eleven little girls chanted and ran out onto the grass for fielding practice.

The Mitts did not win many of their games, and never developed much in the way of a competitive personality. They were the daughters of pretty well-off youngish west-siders, and none of them had parents who knew anything about baseball, except for Thea, of course. Their parents were more of a sailing and skiing crowd. Occasionally my girls would go up against a team of girls from the working-class east side, and the devotion to skills would be a study in contrasts.

So I was a little frustrated. But I had come to real adulthood in the sixties. I told myself, "Competition is temporary; friendship is eternal."

And I did have fun. I liked these little people, including Kirsty Smith, Thea's best friend all through school. Once in a while they would even do something I had advised doing. I'll tell you my favourite instance of that.

Thea had to tread a fine line. As the coach's kid, she did not want to appear as anything but one of the girls, the Mitts. But she *was* my kid, and our bond might show up in her passed-on canniness.

I noticed how often a ball four pitch eluded the little equipment-covered catcher and went to the backstop in this league, and how often the catcher, because of her cumbersome chest pad, face mask and shin guards, or just a dip in attentiveness, took a long time to go and retrieve the errant ball. If such an occasion should arise when you are the batsperson, I suggested, take off on a run for first, have a look, and if the catcher is dawdling, keep on going to second.

I gave this advice to other girls, but Thea was the only one who remembered the idea.

But what was my most-often repeated bit of advice to these young diamond dames? Was it keep your eye on the ball? Always hit the cut-off girl? Charge the ground ball? No. My most-often uttered request was "Please stop chewing on your glove!"

That was then. This is now. It is really a later then, but let's call it now. According to now there is snow on top of everything I can see from the four windows of my ground level writing tower here in Port Colborne. The fir trees across the street, the wrought iron fence, very beautiful, you might say, the Pontiac Sunbird, the Maximum 40 km/h sign, the unattended high school, the discarded fast food containers all around the high school. Snow on top of everything. It is still a month until the pitchers and catchers report in Fort Myers and Sun City. The *Toronto*

Star is full of pictures of people covered with snow in Toronto streets you can't recognize.

But right beside me, as I write these forlorn words with a Pilot Hi-Tecpoint V5 in my hardback scribbler, is a Mac G4 computer, and it brings me my fantasy baseball league! I am getting ready for my eleventh season of fantasy baseball, and I must be having fun, because it seems like my fifth season. I know I've told you about this, but you don't mind if I go on a bit, do you? If you aren't interested in my fantasy team, skip forward to "The Twilight League playoff tournament.... "

I subscribe to an outfit called Scoresheet Baseball, and I guess they earn that name by sending you their completed scoresheets of the six or seven games your team played that week. Scoresheet runs a lot of leagues. Ours is called the Seaver League, and is made up of ten teams in two divisions. We are constructed of National League players (though you are allowed to keep two AL guys if they've been traded to that loop since you acquired them), so there are no #&*%!%&!# designated hitters and no New York Yankees.

I'm matching wits and pitchers with guys from Ontario, Alberta and British Columbia, mostly guys I have never met. I joined in 1996 at the urging of my old writing pal Brian (Leaky) Fawcett of the old East End Punks. What a wonderful year that was! Brian finished first in his division, and I finished first in my division. How hard is this, I asked myself. Then my team, the High Sox, wiped him out in the playoff, and a few weeks later my mantelpiece trophy arrived in the mail. I had to assemble it, and the little golden batter doesn't face the right way when you screw him all the way in. But my name is spelled correctly, and this trophy will always stand on the mantel of my writing room.

Brian has finished atop his division four times, but he has never taken home the trophy. A couple of years back, his son Max, in his second year in the league, beat him in the finals. I finished a distant second to Max in my division. I have finished just about everywhere, including another first in my division, but I have only the one trophy—till this year.

As I have said, fantasy baseball really changes the way you read the daily box scores all summer. And when you are watching a game on television? How about when your pitcher in the real world, say Kazuhisa Ishii, is pitching against your fantasy team stalwart Albert Pujols, and the game is on the line? This is when you feel confused, even a little dirty, somehow. You start hoping for scenarios such as this: Pujols gets a single, but the runner, say Jim Edmonds, gets thrown out at the plate.

It is impure. But they started it. They brought in the designated hitter, the skyboxes, interleague games, the Nike ads, the endless super-slo-mo replays.

And I get punished sufficiently. My key players are almost always on the season-long disabled list. A couple of years ago my number one starting pitcher *died* during the season. In recent years my first draft has always turned out to be a bust. I carried Roberto Alomar for three years. Or my number two starting pitcher gets traded to the Colorado Rockies and has to pitch half his games in Coors Field, where ERAs go to die.

Fantasy baseball is a corrupting love, I suppose, but it is also one of those things that give your secret inner anticipation/pleasure receptors a quiet thrill—like the arrival of a new Jerome Charyn novel, or waking up to realize that tonight is pub night.

We get our weekly results on Tuesdays. So Tuesday is even more important than Wednesday, the day that the new *Baseball Weekly* arrives in the stores. Almost as important as Sunday, the day you play the Friendly People, if it is not raining.

The 2004 season was especially sweet, because one of our owners bailed, and I bought his team for Jean. It was an early Valentine's present. What romantic guy would not think of that? Already, before the annual draft had started, when we were figuring out which thirteen ballplayers we would protect, she was grabbing the *Toronto Star* sports section before I could get my hands on it. She found out that her third baseman Aaron Boone had blown out his knee playing basketball, and her closer Rob Nen couldn't throw off the mound, and one of her starters, Ryan Dempster, probably wouldn't pitch for the Cubs till next year.

I got to say "ah, hah, hah, hah!" Summer was going to be fun.

The Twilight League playoff tournament used to consume the Labour Day weekend, so it was always impossible to enter the 3-Day Novel Contest.

Then we were on our own.

What happened after that we die-hards would call the "Real Season."

Usually Jim Allan would make a lot of phone calls to see whether we would be coming out, but if you were a ballplayer, you just knew that you should make it to Needle Park at noon on Sunday. To play some ball. Chances were it might not rain, and you'd get to play ball all through September and October, at least. This was why you lived in Vancouver instead of Edmonton or Ottawa.

All we had to do was get eighteen people to the park on Sunday. Or sixteen, anyway.

Throw the ball around. Smoke a cigarette if so inclined. Try to explain the fundamentals of the game to some Spaniards or Englishmen someone had brought along.

Then we would all toss our gloves into one big pile, and Jim Allan or Fast Eddie would stoop over the pile, quickly flipping the gloves into two new piles. That's how we chose up sides.

This was fun, and a lovely slow way to spend early Sunday afternoon. If you are over fifty, you are highly conscious of the fact that the sweetness of playing this game will not be available forever. If you are in your sixties that sweetness is especially sweet because so many parts of your body hurt.

If there were only fourteen people there because it was October, you would have two outfielders and three infielders.

If there were twelve people, you would play scrub, and that was fun, because you got to play all the positions.

Someone found a game you could play with eight people. I think we might have called it Belgian baseball.

Or if there were only four of us, and the early November sun was glinting on the wet brown leaves all over the ground, and there were a few alkies sitting around watching, we could sort of have infield practice.

Next week I would sit in my car beside Needle Park, reading a novel by John Hawkes. I would give it an hour.

In the snow belt, where I spent the winter of 2003–2004, people carry this sort of thing in the trunks of their cars: a container of sand, a container of salt, a plastic jug of windshield fluid, chunks of wood for jamming under tires, tire chains.

A decade ago, this is what I had in the trunk of my Volvo: a canvas bag of softballs, a catcher's mask, several ball gloves, including Thea's blue suede glove that fits on a right hand, a few aluminum softball bats, my white turf shoes with fading blood stains, several very ugly ball caps, elastoplast bandages, batting gloves with the fingers cut off, and a cup that someone must have worn, sometime.

Now I have stripped down. In the trunk of my present Volvo I have the turf shoes, my black infielder's glove, my brown trapper, and one bat.

You never know. You might be driving around on a day when it's not raining, and you might see some people who are trying to play a game with just two outfielders.

Afterword

Never Get Back

THAT EPIC TRIP WAS NOT TO BE THE LAST EXCURSION with my baseball love. The following June 30, we packed our beer chairs and water bottles into the Volvo and headed east. We were moving to our new home in Vancouver, and you might maintain that such a trip is westward. Ho. Buffalo, New York is thirty kilometres east of Port Colborne, Ontario, so east we went, then turned right at the pointy end of Lake Erie, and aimed south and west. Our plan was to drive to Vancouver, British Columbia, via San Diego, California. Our first stop was a pretty ballpark in a mall in Niles, Ohio, where the Mahoning Valley Scrappers of the New York-Penn League lost 4-3 to the Auburn Doubledays.

Oho, the open road. We saw the Mets prevail 7-5 at the Great American Ball Park in Cincinnati, then drove into and out of tiny Sparta, Kentucky, the scariest little town I have ever seen. I have to say that Xenophon was right about the Spartans. In Sparta the only place to eat could have used some paint. There was a sign in the window offering catfish sandwiches, but there was also a wreath of black flowers on the door, along with the information that "Daddy Bill" had died the day before.

So we crossed a few more Midwest states to see a rain-delayed game in Busch Stadium, where my pal Woody Williams beat the Seattle Mariners and my chum Albert Pujols got three hits. But more exciting was the day in St. Louis. All we saw was the St. Louis Art Museum. What a beautiful building, on a hill in a big park, where the entry is free ("Dedicated to Art and Free to All") and the marble is as shiny as it was just after the World's Fair of a century ago. I love the great art museums of the eastern U.S., in the cities that were once so highly aware of their growing grandeur. We decided to start a new tradition of picnics along the road, the first one of which was on the grounds of the St. Louis Art Museum. Our second took place on the following day, in the deserted central square of Sarcoxie, Missouri, old buildings around us in the Midwest heat, one of them containing the Jubilee Christian Fellowship. One hillbilly truck bore a bumper sticker that proclaimed "It's a dog eat dog world, and I'm wearing milkbone underwear." We were in the middle of what these absent folks call America.

Imagine going to a baseball game in Oklahoma City on the Fourth of July while the U.S. is enjoying one of its far-away wars. They never did get round to singing "Take Me Out to the Ball Game." Before the first inning of the Red Hawks' game against Memphis, right after a military national anthem, a guy on the PA led the crowd in a recital of the U.S. oath of allegiance. At the fourth inning they all sang "Oklahoma!" For the seventh-inning stretch it was "God Bless America!" And to start the ninth, another recital of the oath of allegiance. Imagine if it had been a foreigner who blew up that building in Oklahoma City!

The Texas experience, we decided later, was good to have had, but we were glad when it was over. It started well, with a rimrock sunset in Palo Duro State Park just outside Canyon, Texas. In addition to the starkly beautiful rock formations, we spied two deer, a dead lizard, two jackrabbits, two tarantula spiders and a long-horn bull. But from there southwestward it is mostly grim and boring landscape, widely separated low bushes staying alive on dead flat ground—and it goes on for days, even if you hurry, as anyone in their right mind would. But the Texas experience is mainly there in what its peculiar human beings do, showing up as a constant mean threat in all the "Christian" billboards, the newspapers, the unrelenting fake friendliness in the salespeople and so on. I have to admit that the little AA ballpark in Midland was a pleasant relief. Instead of the pledge of allegiance we had two big guys performing the chicken dance, and when a local player hit a home run the fans went down the aisles and shoved dollar bills through the wire. "Bring your green," said the PA, "to the screen." There were five homers in all, as the local Rockhounds dispatched the visiting Tulsa Drillers. Still, Midland bills itself as the home of George W. Bush and his wife. You can go around and photograph the houses he used to live in. Less than a year after we bypassed downtown and spent a couple of nice hours in the ballpark, Robert Creeley, the great U.S. poet, died in nearby Odessa, Texas. Some ironies hurt more than others.

Anyway, the following day, Jean just did not want to stop, so we drove well over a thousand kilometres, and bought ourselves an extra day and night in Tucson, Arizona, a town I have liked since I was first there as a young visiting poet in 1963. Before that I knew the place through my reading of hundreds of western novels. It was 104 degrees Fahrenheit, whatever that is, just the way I remembered liking it, though this time I was smart enough to buy a cheap straw hat out at the wonderful Desert Museum. We also located a terrific bead shop and started another tradition. From now on all baseball trips are also art museum trips, Mexican food trips and bead shop trips. Life on the road gets better and better.

The last ball game I had been to in Tucson was a Cactus League game between the Indians and the A's at famous little Hi Corbett Field. It held about seven thousand people, and they were all there, those neat old guys in shorts, carrying scorebooks. Commissioner Bowie Kuhn was there, and we booed him. He likely told his seatmates that we were shouting "Bowie!" Now Hi Corbett had been replaced by a new building called Electric Park, and the Pacific Coast League Tucson Toros were the Toros only on Tuesday nights; the rest of the time they were the Sidewinders, because now they were a farm team of the upstate Diamondbacks. They played to a very small and very quiet audience, and after a see-saw contest the visiting Las Vegas Area 51s prevailed 7-5.

Then off we headed for the Coast. Since my cowboy novel days I had always wanted to go to or through Yuma. What a disappointment that was! We went by on the slick Interstate, and Yuma seemed to be a hell of a lot of mobile homes. But San Diego was another story. Huge Balboa Park is green and filled with interesting buildings, such as the San Diego Art Museum. Unfortunately this latter had a lot of its paintings put away so that they could show us a big Vatican exhibition and a big "New World" (they meant USA) exhibition. And the ballpark is named after a dog food company. Don't get me started. They are really proud of their new ballpark in San Diego. It is a medium-sized town in itself, down by the U.S. Navy water and alive with smiling volunteers. We sat in the notorious short porch in left field, but the closest we got was a Larry Walker drive into a left fielder's glove up against the fence right in front of us.

This is what we had told ourselves before this journey: when you see the Pacific Ocean, turn right. That took us to San Juan Capistrano, the famous mission and a very pleasant place, but the only sign of any swallows was a white blob on a bench in the sun. Still, we were in fabled California, we told each other as we sat motionless on the I-5 in the eastern part of Los Angeles for an hour and a bit. But eventually we got to Chavez Ravine, a name that used to signify a Mexican-American neighbourhood but is now a nickname for Dodgers Stadium, which sits where the Mexican-American neighbourhood used to be. It was my first visit there, and a dream come true. I have been a Dodgers fan since I was nine, and a Red Sox Fan since I was ten. I only had to wait till I was nineteen for the Dodgers to win a World Series. I got to Fenway when I was thirty-four, but I never got to see the Dodgers at home till this night in the gloaming with fifty-three thousand strangers, most of them Mexican-Americans. Nostalgia poured over me in waves as the Dodgers failed to win despite being handed a platinum opportunity in the bottom of the ninth. There was a big smile across my face as I clung to my sweetheart and let the big crowd carry us down the hill toward the parking lot. In the bathroom of our motel in Castaic, California, I peed, as the saying goes, more or less, Dodger Blue.

At Visalia, about which my guesses at pronunciation were all wrong, it was back to good old single-A baseball, in this case the venerable California League. In Visalia, inland far enough to resemble a treed Oklahoma, the most popular radio station is a "Classic Country" purveyor titled, no foolin', KJUG. The little ballpark is called, simply, Recreation Park. The first row of seats is only twenty-eight feet back of home plate. Oh, and the nearby Visalia Library has three of my novels. How could you not like this place? Jean particularly liked the Visalia Oaks' logo, a pissed-off acorn, and their mascot, a big squirrel whose tail was always knocking someone over. Now yer talking. Hooray for single-A.

Up the valley we went, hot and dusty and sniffing for something more like home. The Pacific Coast League champs were the Sacramento River Cats, who used to be the Vancouver Canadians until the ballpark in Vancouver just got too damned small for AAA baseball. At Raley Park we sat through the eleventh game of this tour with mixed feelings, watching the Portland Beavers' pitcher take a perfect game bid into the seventh inning, at which point the River Cats managed a couple of scratch hits before losing 8-1. We were sitting in the capital of California, but in our minds we were already walking into our new house in Vancouver. A couple of times during this game I chanted "Go, Habs, Go!" and no one around me had any idea why.

The next day we got out of California, though we had to drive around a little airplane that was lying upside down on the outside lane of a bend in a mountain road. We read later that the pilot was charged with flying while under the influence. Oregon looked like a good place to be a few hours later. It was a stadium-free night, so we looked around hot, hot downtown Eugene, finally found a bar, and with one other person plus the young bartender, we watched the MLB All-Star Game home run hitting contest on television. Jean was drinking a beer called Dead Man. I stuck to Vertical Gravity. As you can tell, I sure know how to show a girl a good time.

Sitting in that air-conditioned bar on a Monday night in America, I was in love with my new life. Never before had I lived and travelled with a woman who would go to baseball games with me, keep a scorebook, wear baseball pins, manage a fantasy team, learn the infield fly rule, and say "there, there" to me as the Boston Red Sox headed for yet another late-season catastrophe. I was a retired professor, a retired ballplayer, bound for geezerdom, and here by my side was a truly loving sweetheart, and we had a house waiting for us in Vancouver. Sitting in that deserted bar in Eugene, Oregon, I said to myself, "Okay, maybe you will never again take part in a picturesque double play, but you are one lucky ex-second baseman."

We had a lot of fun at Volcano Stadium in Keizer, Oregon the next night. The Salem-Keizer Volcanoes and the Tri-City Dust Devils are in the ancient Northwest League, now a short-season loop that makes for interesting baseball because it is an instructional league, so you get to see lots of hit-and-run, sacrifices, and all that strategic stuff. We had been to lots of Northwest League games, of course, in Vancouver and Everett, and last year in Boise, but we had never been to one that started at 6:30. In a single-A park (except in Batavia on Substance-Free Night) you make friends quickly, so Jean asked one of our new friends how come games started at 6:30. "Wait till you see our bullpen," six of them said. Sure enough, we were there for four hours and then some, as the V's took a 10-6 lead into the eighth inning, and then fell apart. Pitcher after pitcher strode bravely to the mound. It was truly tragi-comic. Jean laughed until there were tears coursing down her cheeks. The ironists munched on their popcorn. On the other side of the right field fence, trucks whipped by on the I-5. This was a wonderful baseball night on the edge of a little western city no one has heard of, with a supremely funny touch: when a Salem-Keizer player pops a home run, some smoke spouts from a little wooden volcano set into the centre field fence. What more could a love-smitten baseball admirer ask for?

This was our next-to-last game for the trip. We were a mere six hundred kilometres from our new home, and we had three days to kill.

The first one was easy. I had been telling Jean for weeks about my favourite room in the U.S. I can't remember what it is called, but it is upstairs in the lovely little Portland Art Museum, and it was created by someone who had a budget and a lot of intelligence. It is about late nineteenth and early twentieth-century art in Europe, principally France. The planner decided to get one work to represent each artist, and to pick one that represented him perfectly. I love to stand in the room every few years, among Manet, Brancusi, Calder, Picasso, Renoir and so on. Just being there you can feel your whole body and brain becoming cultured.

Portland is a very intelligent city. Where else in the U.S. can you find a bookstore that is a whole block in size? But Jean also wanted to see the famed Oregon coast, so we whipped out to Yachats, little dreaming that in a few months that little ribbon of a cliff-side town would become the new home of George Stanley's brother Gerald. If you ever get a chance to go to a ball game with Gerald Stanley, grab it. He is one of the funniest baseball fans of all time, and remember, baseball fans are noted for their humour. In Yachats, Jean the mushroom fan had one of her favourite all-time mushroom dishes, and learned later that people travel long distances just to attend the Yachats Mushroom Festival. But that night I took her to my favourite room in Olympia, the capital of Washington. This is the old wooden place called the Spar. Whether you are an old-timer logging guy or a self-conscious bank manager looking for lunch, the Spar is the place to chow down, winning yourself a great combination of USAmerican plenitude and authenticity. Jean had the prime rib, the sensible woman, and I had the meat loaf. What a wonderful way to anticipate home!

Unfortunately, I totally screwed up the next day. You know by now that Jean loves glass, I mean glass as art and glass as beads and glass as windows. Our last day was supposed to comprise Tacoma's excellent

Museum of Glass by day and Seattle's Safeco Field by night, where we would wind up our schedule with a game between the Mariners and the Cleveland Indians. Well, it seems that we have another tour tradition that I haven't mentioned yet. Once in a while I have a day when the left side of my neck gets a knot the size of your fist in it, and a headache starts in my left eye and consumes my whole body, and I start to throw up, and I wish I could just be unconscious or in my mother's arms. It had happened on the first day of our baseball tryst in Chicago a few years back. It would happen again in Boston, as you may learn. And it happened in Puget Sound. I had to stay in the underground parking lot, occasionally dropping a rainbow yawn into the garbage can, while Jean explored the Museum of Glass above. Then Jean drove to Seattle, and I chundered three times into our big plastic garbage bag. I felt as if I were dying, fitfully sleeping in a crummy motel in Georgetown out near the Boeing airstrip, while just a few miles north of us, the Seattle Rainiers broke their eight-game losing streak because a rookie got his first big league home run to beat the Indians 2-1.

But the next day we parked the Volvo in front of our beautiful new house, and in my imagination I carried Jean over the threshold, and I saw the romantic look in her eyes. She was gazing at the bare walls and thinking about what colours they would be when she was done with them.

For the next six weeks, when we were not buying furniture or watching Paul Naylor build our new bookshelves, we went to Vancouver Canadians games at Nat Bailey Stadium. Jean put away her scorebook: she has a rule that she uses it only for games on the road. We settled into our new home and new city and very busy routine. Retirement can be exhausting, but fantasy baseball makes it worthwhile. Jean's team, the Silk Stockings, finished dead last in our division, and my team, the High Sox, finished third, thirteen games out. We did make a few little road trips. We hustled down to Bellingham to watch the Bells of the Pacific International League lose the playoffs to the Wenatchee Applesox. And I was lucky enough to be declared the writer-in-residence of the twenty-fifth annual Grand Forks (BC) International Baseball Tournament over the Labour Day weekend. Was there really a team from Chicago called the Gravel Kings? There was a team from Taiwan, and there were the powerful Seattle Studs.

But then we had to get through an autumn with no baseball except for the miraculous Red Sox post-season on television. Everyone knows what happened in October of 2004. The Red Sox snagged the American League wild card position, and knocked over the Anaheim Angels in the first round, but then they faced the &$!#!@*& New York Yankees in the AL championship. We Red Sox fans allowed an eye-slit of hope, but then awaited the inevitable, as the Yankees went ahead three games to none. Remember, I have been a Red Sox fan since 1946—all I wanted was one win, to avoid a sweep by those smug bastards with their Derek Jeter sneers.

The Yankees got nineteen runs in game 3. Who was I kidding? Get it over with, I prayed. Let me wait another long winter for the return of joy. It was a cold night in Boston for game 4. The Sox were sipping bourbon in the dugout, and when the game went into extra innings, they were still sipping. In the bottom of the twelfth Papi Ortiz hit a homer, and the sweep was avoided. All right, I'm satisfied, I said. Game 5 was worse. It too went into extra innings, and the whiskey was again being passed around in the Sox dugout. In the thirteenth I prepared to accept doom as Jason Varitek allowed three passed balls on Tim Wakefield knucklers, but through a haze of my own bourbon I saw the Yanks strand two runners in scoring position, and in the bottom of the fourteenth, Papi Ortiz knocked one out, and the hairy, bearded, sloppy Red Sox were still in it, sort of. Because the series was going back to Yankee Stadium.

Like any Red Sox fan, I chewed on my fingers and cursed in my mother tongue. The Red Sox won game 6 in ordinary fashion, and became the first team in history to go down 3-0 and force a seventh game. I said okay, that is an accomplishment; now we will bow our heads and offer our necks. You know what happened: Pedro Martinez came on as a relief pitcher, and the Sox just buried the pinstripers. Wow, I said. It's too bad that they have to face the beautiful and overpowering St. Louis Cardinals in the World Series, but beating the Yankees in such a fashion was the sweetest thing to happen since Muhammad Ali came back from his suspension to take the heavyweight championship back from the white politicians.

Of course, the Red Sox swept the series from the comatose Cardinals. In game 4, I was cheering for St. Louis. There was no drama here. But more important—how could I possibly continue to be a Red Sox fan now that they [have] won the World Series? Next year all kinds of people who don't know the first thing about the game will be wearing Red Sox hats and shirts. It was enough, almost, to make one a Cubs or White Sox fan. Every time I see some lout in a Red Sox shirt, I want to ask him whether he prefers Bobby Doerr to Lou Boudreau. So on October 27, 2004, the Red Sox won their first World Series in my long lifetime, and then some. Baseball was over for—eight weeks!

By the winter equinox we were in Teodoro Mariscal Stadium, on the Tropic of Cancer, watching a game between the hometown Mazatlán Venados and the visiting Guasave Algodoneros. It was my first Mexican ball game in forty years, and first ever Mexican Pacific League game. Ball game? They don't have ball games in Mexico; they have baseball fiestas! There's mariachi music going. There are two PA announcers, one female and one male, and they are always yelling. One of the Jumbotrons keeps showing a big fat woman getting up and dancing to the music. The twenty thousand fans adore her, and she keeps winning the dancing contest against all comers. Incredible varieties of food are passing by, and I rue the fact that I pigged out on *chile verde* before the game. Young women with glorious breasts parade around the stadium. There are kids clambering everywhere. The noise level is intense. And the game is slow, slow, slow. The between-innings promotions are dragged out, and the relief pitchers walk as slowly as a human being can, from the bullpen in centre, and then take a dozen warm-up pitches, walking around after each one, while someone plays a bullfight song on a trumpet. Sound effects include explosions and screaming horses. Usually I like to concentrate at a baseball game. But in Mexico it is *béisbol,* and that makes all the difference. The Algodoneros won 8-4, and the Venados fans wept and cajoled and tore their hair. But they didn't really mind. The jumbo shrimp were delicious, and there would be *béisbol mañana.* That night on the beach I think Jean could see the moon glittering in my eyes, on both the natural lens and on the artificial one.

Now came the really long drought. I mean, we didn't get to another live game till the middle of March, when we hied over to Nat Bailey Stadium and watched a few contests between the University of British Columbia Thunderbirds and their conference rivals from the south. By then we just could not take the severe Vancouver winter anymore, so we flew down to Phoenix, Arizona to catch seven spring training games in six days. We also got to the art museum, and the bead shoppes, and most important, Frank Lloyd Wright's Taliesen West. In Arizona you can take a handgun into a bar, buy booze at a gas station and smoke cigarettes in a restaurant, so it is a little scary. But it is in the desert, and I grew up in the desert, and whenever I am in Arizona I feel almost at home. There are lots of Cactus League ballparks in the area, and it is fun to attend them all, checking the differences. In Peoria there is a terrific food concourse, for example, but in Tempe the fans are a good deal more intelligent about baseball.

At spring training, people with fantasy baseball teams get to check out their lineups. Poor Jean! The last time we saw Shawn Greene he was grounding into a double play to put an end to a possible Dodger comeback. This time he was a Diamondback, but he struck out three times and grounded into a double play. We saw major league ballplayers who could not catch a pop-up or a thrown ball. On March 23 in

Phoenix Municipal Stadium, we laughed and laughed for nine innings, and even the devout A's fanatic in front of us began to denounce his team's relief pitchers. Spring training. When I ran a morning comb through my hair it scraped on the sunburnt part. That day the only hat I could find was a Los Angeles Angels at Anaheim cap, and the Oakland fans let it be known that I would be allowed to stay in the park only if I stayed on my best behaviour. In that week I savoured every jalapeño and every saguaro cactus, and every line drive in the gap, because back home the Northwest League was not going to open its season till June, and you can't drive down to Seattle for a Mariners game every week. With this sad fact in mind, Jean and I began to plan our August holiday.

Let's go to Italy on my frequent flyer points, I said. So Jean went to her laptop computer and into her famous organizing mode. And fate stepped in. Bad news. Apparently nowadays if you want to go to Europe on your points, you'd better get your application in a year ahead of time. Drat, I said. Maledizioni. We will have to go to plan B. Plan B was an auto tour of New England and the Maritimes, with the odd baseball game thrown in, eh? First we would go to Toronto, because that was where the Society for American Baseball Research was going to hold its thirty-fifth annual convention. People make fun of SABR as made up of a bunch of professor-faced arithmeticians, but when we arrived at the big hotel in Toronto, we really enjoyed being among all these old geeks in team colours and white sneakers. I have never had to read more hats and shirts in my life.

But it was not easy getting there. The day we were scheduled to fly to Toronto an Air France jet crashed off the end of the runway there, and we started a series of taxi runs to the Vancouver airport. Jean stayed on the telephone all night, trying to get seats on a plane. Finally a human voice said we could go on the 9:30 A.M. flight. Hooray. The 9:30 A.M. flight will leave at 3:30 P.M., the voice said. And it nearly did. We arrived in Toronto too late for the poetry reading I was supposed to do, and too late for the hotel room we were supposed to have. But I did take part in a panel about baseball and literature the next day, and I did drop a big hint that I would have a new baseball book ready for next year's convention in Seattle.

Our first game, in fact, was at the Toronto domed stadium that now sports the name of a cable television company. The Yankees were in town, and so was SABR and so were a lot of families that had fit Toronto into their northern travel plans. More than half the grownups and kids in the stadium were wearing Yankees duds. I heard an old-timer say "Yankee go home." But I behaved myself. The Toronto Blue Jays are not the Boston Red Sox. The visitors won the game, of course, but not the Jumbotron. In the eighth inning we looked up at the giant screen over the restaurant in centre field, and saw that the camera had focused on a middle-aged black man wearing a New York Yankees jersey. The camera went in closer, until that hated raiment was fifty metres wide. Then the man smiled broadly, and like Superman pulled his Yankees jersey apart to reveal a Boston Red Sox jersey underneath! Pardon me. World Series Champion Boston Red Sox!

A couple of days later we snaffled the last room in an old lakefront motel in Cooperstown, New York, and visited the National Baseball Hall of Fame. "Shouldn't it be the International Baseball Hall of Fame?" I enquired of the young blond short-haired man at the front door. He could not figure out what I was asking, and I didn't think I had the skill to explain it to him, so we just went on in. It was my second visit there, and nowhere near as exciting as it had been the first time I had visited. That had been during the school year, when all the little kids were back home in Ohio.

"I know Who's on first," I told Jean as we motored eastward, "and I know I Don't Know's on third, but what about centre field."

"None of Your Business," she said.

So we drove through rackely-backely picturesque curling road abandoned rusty tractor rural New York, and then we picked up two new states for me—Connecticut, which was scenic and wealthy-looking, and Rhode Island, which was not. Poor little state, I said. She didn't know the reference so she did not whack me.

Once we got to Pawtucket, we knew that we were in post-miracle Red Sox Nation. Everyone at good old refurbished McCoy Stadium was in red and blue, except for those wearing I Hate Yankee shirts and hats. The place was sold out, the prices were the lowest in AAA ball, and we felt safe. This may have been because a certain amount of pressure was off the Pawsox personnel—no longer was a hotshot prospect expected to be the savior who would bring the Boston Red Sox their first World Series victory since 1918. The visiting players were the league-leading Buffalo Bisons, and for the life of me, I can't remember who won. I guess I didn't care—I was just so glad to be sitting there wearing my brand new Pawtucket cap. In Nova Scotia this area is called the "Boston States." But these hot and humid days, the only place name we hear is "Red Sox Nation." On our second day I got one of those deathlike headaches and so on, and stayed in bed in our home on US-1 for twenty-four hours. Next day I still felt a little weak and woozy, but we did make it to the Boston Museum of Fine Arts, which did not at all resemble the memory I had of it from my visit in 1970. I could not find the Cézanne landscapes I remembered seeing there, but my goodness, it was a nice air-conditioned afternoon we had, and it was good to be able to say inside one's head, "Here I am in one of the U.S.'s great art museums again." In fact, you might say that it is my second-favourite building in Boston. Maybe later I will tell you about my favourite.

Outside Boston we did Massachusetts up fine, visiting Salem and Lynn, and the wonderful Marblehead before heading to Lowell, the old French-Canadian cloth mill town just under the New Hampshire border. I had two reasons for going there: Jack Kerouac and the Class A Lowell Spinners. A few months after Kerouac died in 1969, I went to Lowell and failed to find his grave, because there wasn't a stone on it yet. In 1970 Lowell was a sooty and gloomy mill town that had passed from industry to dereliction. No wonder the young Kerouac saw spooks in the shadows and served them up in his home-town novels. But now that Lowell has been designated some kind of historical labour park by the federal government, all the bricks are clean, and there are cute coffee shops and fashion stores. I am not scoffing—Lowell, Massachusetts is proof that the great ugly northeast can be saved from crud, and the soul can see the natural beauty that it creates, according to the famous New Englander Ralph Waldo Emerson.

We drove around, looking at Kerouac's street and church and grotto, and the big monument to Jack at the corner of Church and Bridge, and I wished that we could have been there a year ago to get a Jack Kerouac bobblehead doll. At sun-smacked Edward A. LeLacheur Park each of us got a free Paul Revere bobblehead doll. I guess we were invited to think of Paul as a catcher, looking out at the pitcher and sending his signals—one finger if by land, two fingers if by sea? It would not have helped. The invading Oneonta Tigers clobbered the Spinners in that nifty little stadium, and we pointed our rented Pontiac toward Portland, Maine.

The AA Portland Sea Dogs would be the third Red Sox farm team we'd have seen in less than a week. But it wasn't to be. Every motel on the I-90 was booked up solid. We thought we might have to sleep in the car. We saw desperate families peering through the darkness at neon. Finally we pulled into a booked-up South Portland Holiday Inn, and Jean portrayed her real loveable self, melting the heart of a desk clerk who had just come on duty. He telephoned up and down the state, and got us a room a hundred miles north, at Waterville. It meant no Sea Dogs, but it meant a bed.

We took a break from baseball and drove around the Maritimes, including Campobello Island and the Cabot Trail, catching up on Canadian news and enjoying the kilometres and the cooler weather. It wasn't long till we had to turn the car westward, and sure enough: we came to the great St. Lawrence River, and one of the main stops on that historic waterway is the city of Quebec, and what they have in that city is a Canadian-American League team called the Capitales.

Off we went to the Stade municipal de Québec, the last ballpark north of Mexico where people can still sit in their seats and smoke cigarettes—and this being Quebec, do they ever! Also, in most ballparks, you cannot buy more than two beers at a time, nor can you buy any beer after the seventh or eighth inning. At the Stade municipal I saw a guy carrying five cups of beer in the top of the ninth. All the way up the river from Rivière-du-Loup, I had been announcing that I was going to get me some ballpark poutine; but when I saw some in the lap of a teenaged lad, I decided to forego the experience. It looked worse than the nachos in Anaheim. I did break my rule about one cap per trip, though, snaffling a gorgeous Capitales cap. It is dark blue with a golden Q, and inside the Q is a baseball with a blue fleur-de-lis on it. I know that I have spoken out against cluttered logos on caps, but this time I was happy to make an exception.

So that was the end of our baseball trip. The next day we went to Montreal, where there is no professional baseball anymore, and spent a few days doing what you do in Montreal—going to restaurants. We starved ourselves all day and went to our favourite, Molivos, and ate a huge meal designed by Leo, which featured the greatest appetizer west of the Greek islands—marinated and then charcoaled octopus. I would have thought that we were in paradise, except that we had been there nine days earlier. Or at least we had been to the place on Earth closest to it.

Christians, Muslims and Jews have the Dome of the Rock. People of my faith have Fenway Park. Some months before our pilgrimage, we had decided that this trip would be planned in such a way that a visit to Fenway's green walls would be its highlight. But it appeared that we were as naïve about Fenway as we had been about air travel points. The park was sold out, we were told via the net, for the season. Even the year before, before the Sox had become the World Series champs, there had been no tickets available. People in New England even drive to Toronto or Baltimore to see their team play live … All right. We would do what other people do—drive by the park and have a look, and go to games played by New England's minor league teams. On the night of August 12, for example, we would be watching the Brockton Rox of the CanAm League. Fine. I had made it to Fenway once in my lifetime. And I had never been to Brockton. I love baseball, whatever the league. Let's go.

Then one morning, Jean woke me up by the simple method of hurling herself onto my sleeping form.

"Sad news," she said.

I steeled myself.

"We can't go to the Brockton Rox game."

"Aw, well, we can find something else to do that night."

"Because we have Boston Red Sox tickets!"

"Ha ha."

"Against the White Sox."

I immediately forgave her for the way in which she had wakened me.

Apparently she had put on her magic organizer wristbands, contacted the Boston Red Sox public relations guys, and sold them a lovely bill of goods: "An important Canadian publisher has commissioned George Bowering the writer to do a baseball book, and as it happens, George Bowering has been a Red Sox fan longer than I have been alive, and he was planning to have the book's ending take place at Fenway Park. It's my job to make sure that he gets to Fenway and attends the game against the Chicago White Sox there. I don't know what is going to happen to me if I can't make this happen."

We got to the park about three hours before game time, having a beer and banter with costumed people in a baseball bar, and hanging around Yawkey Avenue, which is a lot like the French Quarter in New

Orleans—a noisy block jammed with barbecue vendors, a guy on stilts, a brass band, dogs wearing Red Sox tee-shirts, all the souvenir stores and scalpers and jugglers and baseball Annies. If Fenway is green, everything else is red.

I kept saying, "I don't believe it. We aren't going to get those tickets at the will-call wicket, this is all a big mistake, but that's okay, it's enough to be here." But then we were in the A–M lineup at the will-call, and Jean asked me for my credit card. There clearly had been some intercession from above. Our tickets were indeed there, and they had my name printed right on them! In we went, and we walked around the shrine while batting practice and general loitering were going on. Then we took our seats, high above home plate.

The White Sox were leading the American League Central. They scored the first runs off sloppy David Wells, but I turned to Jean and told her not to worry—in a typical Fenway game the score sways back and forth and ends up 10-9. Sure enough, there ensued a parade of home runs, and six and a half hours after our arrival the Bosox prevailed 9-8. I don't know how many other dreamy old guys there were in that stadium, but I'm betting that lots of them were saying inside their heads, "Here I am at last, here I really am, I am really here," and other such profundities. Half my life ago I had been here with my pal Virgil, and you have to wager that I wouldn't be back, but what a blessing it was to be here beside my sweetheart at last. The bright lights atop their steady towers illuminated the grass and the walls and those men in funny outfits, and the dove that rested for a moment in shallow left field.

This was the home of the World Series champion Boston Red Sox, the team I had loved since I was a little country boy. When they broke the spell and won it all last year, I was not teary-eyed. I was bereft, in a way. The Red Sox had taken away my irony, and the eternal hope that goes with that kind of irony. To root year after year for a team that always finds a new way to lose is somehow beautiful in its unrequited devotion. Now that was gone, and in its place there had appeared a mixture of relaxed estrangement and entry-level bliss.

"Thank you for bringing me here, Beatrice," I said.

"It's Jean," she said.

Acknowledgments

A version of chapter 8 appeared in my book of memoirs *A Magpie Life*, Toronto, Key Porter, 2001.

A version of chapter 1 appeared in *Dooney's Cafe*, Summer 2004.

A version of chapter 6 appeared in *Open Letter*, 12/5, Spring 2005.